4|12|91

The Croatian National Movement

1966–1972

by Ante Cuvalo

EAST EUROPEAN MONOGRAPHS
DISTRIBUTED BY COLUMBIA UNIVERSITY PRESS, NEW YORK

1990

EAST EUROPEAN MONOGRAPHS, NO. CCLXXXII

To Ikica, Mime, and Andja

Copyright © 1990 by Ante Cuvalo
ISBN 0-88033-179-8
Library of Congress Catalog Card Number 89-82220

Printed in the United States of America

CONTENTS

Abbreviations iv

Introduction 1

I. Origins and Ideologies of
Modern Croatian Nationalism 5

II. Decentralizing Reforms of the Mid-1960s and
The National Question in Yugoslavia 22

III. Genesis of the Croatian National Revival:
The 1960s 46

IV. Croatian Nationalism and Yugoslavia's Economy 77

V. Cultural Nationalism 104

VI. Social Elements in the Croatian
National Movement 126

VII. Road to Karadjordjevo 158

Conclusion 187

Postscript 196

Notes 210

Bibliography 254

Index 272

ABBREVIATIONS

AVNOJ	Anti-Fascist Council for the People's Liberation of Yugoslavia
CC LCC	Central Committee of the League of Communists of Croatia
CC LCY	Central Committee of the League of Communists of Yugoslavia
CPY	Communist Party of Yugoslavia
KOS	Counter Intelligence Service (Military Secret Police)
LCY	League of Communists of Yugoslavia
SFRY	Socialist Federative Republic of Yugoslavia
UDBA	Department of State Security (State Secret Police)
ZAVNOH	Country's Anti-Fascist Council for the People's Liberation of Croatia

INTRODUCTION

Since the creation of the Kingdom of Serbs, Croats, and Slovenes in 1918 (Yugoslavia after 1929) the Croatian question has been that state's Achilles's heel. The new state was founded on a mixture of the romantic idea of South Slavism, and on the resistance against the Habsburg, Magyar, and Italian domination. But most of all it was a by-product of the post-World War I settlement in Europe. For many Croatians, there has been a constant feeling that the new state was the "result of a quirk of history"[1] and not of their own national wishes or in their best interests. In an interview in 1973, the best known Croatian writer and a life-long Marxist, late Miroslav Krleža, described the unification of the South Slavic state in the following way:

> In 1918, we got together like a flock of geese. It was necessary to draw a line from Finland to the Adriatic, in relation to the Western countries. . . . And they [in the West] put us together, but without having the slightest idea what they were doing. They united us like a flock of geese.[2]

Despite the fact that the idea of "Yugoslavism" had been nurtured most of all among the Croatians, they entered the new state with a well developed sense of their own nationhood. It was this sense of nationhood the Belgrade government, controlled by the Serbian dynasty and bureaucracy, became so eager to crush. Because of their striving for independence,

1

the Croatians came into conflict not only with the Belgrade regime but also with the idea of a Yugoslav state itself. Even those among the Croatians who were actively involved in the creation of the state, were soon disappointed. Frano Supilo, Ante Trumbić, Ivan Meštrović, all of whom were leading Croatians in the Yugoslav Committee and who worked for a South Slavic unity at one point or another had to realize the futility of their endeavor.[3] Even Svetozar Pribićević, the leading Serb politician in Croatia in the 1920s and once a fierce supporter of Yugoslav unity and Karadjordjević policies, became a staunch opponent of the Belgrade regime.

The main reason for the disaffection with the regime and the state was that the political leaders of the various nations had radically different ideas as to how the Yugoslav state should be organised. Croatian pro-Yugoslavs, as well as their Slovene partners, who had advocated the break up of the Habsburg empire, envisioned a federalist system for the new country. They were for "a single Yugoslav state organized on a federative basis."[4] Soon after the creation of the unified state, Stjepan Radić, who had not opposed the Yugoslav state in principle but who had questioned the hasty unification and its unclear conditions, directed all his political activities toward achieving a neutral Croatian republic.[5] The Croatian Peasant party, led by Radić, became the major political force in inter-war Croatia because of its social and political ideology and especially because of its struggle for national and individual rights. However, because of his political activities Radić was assassinated in Belgrade's Skupština (Parliament) in 1928, which then led to the radicalization of Croatian political life. The Cvetković-Maček Agreement (Sporazum) of 1939 finally granted Croatia a certain amount of autonomy. The agreement, however, was made with a European war about to begin. The agreement had come too late and promised too little to prevent the break up of the country. Its aftermath was a bloody war between different national groups, mainly between the Serbs and the Croatians.

The Serbs conceived the unified state from a different historical, political, and cultural perspective. Their conception included the following points: the myth of Kosovo,[6] liberation from the Turks, establishment of a national state in 1878, a national dynasty, the tradition of centralized rule closely tied with a national Orthodox church, the ideology of expansionism (as outlined by a Serbian politician Ilija Garašanin in his 1844 *Načertanje*), and the expectation that Serbia would be generously rewarded for her war efforts on the side of the Allies. The Allied victory in 1918 became an opportune time to fulfill Garašanin's grand design of creating a Greater Serbia. But because of Russia's withdrawal from the War, Serbian political leaders lost their chief protector. The "Yugoslav solution" offered in Paris was accepted by that leadership only as the second best option for Serbian national interests. During the inter-war period, the Serbian favorable political position and military strength would be used to implement many of Garašanin's ideas of Great Serbianism.[7]

During the immediate post-World War II period, the Yugoslav Communist Party, which took over the power, officially declared that the national problem in Yugoslavia had been resolved. The common war effort, the federalist organization of the state, and, most of all, the new proletarian consciousness had put an end to it. Many people in the West concurred. It was believed that one of Tito's greatest accomplishments was his solution of the national problem in post-war Yugoslavia. Some claimed that Tito, by granting a "cultural autonomy" to the nations in Yugoslavia, succeeded in bringing peace to the Balkans.[8] Others argued that "the major immediate cause of the interwar conflict—the attempt of the Serbs to exercise hegemony over the whole country—has almost certainly disappeared forever."[9] Furthermore, it was asserted that Tito, as the "symbol of national unity" was popular enough to keep all nations in Yugoslavia content.[10] Thus, to many foreign observers in the Fifties and Sixties "it seemed that the nationality problem had been permanently laid to rest."[11] However, the Croatian national movement in the late Sixties and early Seventies indicated that the national question in Yugoslavia had not been resolved. Twenty years after the revolution, Tito himself was forced to admit that the national question had been solved only "in principle" but that "material and political content needed to be added."[12]

* * * * *

No monograph or historical work has thus far been published on the Croatian national movement in the late Sixties and early Seventies. A number of articles and books which touch upon the issue of Croatian nationalism have been written in the West since 1972. But these generally deal with Yugoslavia's political, social, economic, or national problems in general. The only work dealing with the mass movement in Croatia per se is

Dennison I. Rusinow's four part Field Report published between June and September 1972.[13] Most of the published material on the subject has been written by political and social scientists. As a result, the authors' primary concern has been the immediate political and social effects of the Croatian national movement upon the country as a whole. A common feature of these works is their evaluation of the Croatian national movement from the perspective of the East-West relations. The unity and stability of Yugoslavia is presumed to be *sine qua non* for the *status quo* of the geopolitical balance in Europe, and thus any "excessive decentralization"[14] has been valued as negative. Even those who considered the movement as liberal and humanistic, conclude that the leaders of the movement went too far in their demands, thus threatening the stability of the country.[15] This approach has brought most political observers in the West very close to the official Yugoslav view concerning the events in Croatia, without, however, condoning the means by which the Party implemented its policy in the post-1971 period. Thus, the mass movement in Croatia has been seen by most of these scholars in a negative light and has been judged as "dangerous romantic nationalism."[16]

In Yugoslavia itself, only two books (by the same author) and a small number of articles have been published on the subject.[17] These works basically reflect the official Party line in the post-1971 period.

In this work, I am approaching the subject from a different perspective. I will try to look at the movement itself, at its causes, its development, its nature, and its goals. I will also examine the roles of the Party, of the intellectuals, of the students as well as of other national elements. The main purpose of this study is, therefore, to understand how the national forces in Croatia from 1966 to 1972 viewed themselves and their nation at that time, and what their vision of Croatia's future was. The main sources I used were written by participants in the movement during that period: a few sources are from the post-1971 era and mostly published in the West.[18] I hope that this approach will shed some new light on the latest national revival among the Croatians and give some new insight into the national question in Yugoslavia as a whole.

CHAPTER I

ORIGINS AND IDEOLOGIES OF
MODERN CROATIAN NATIONALISM

Historical Memory

The beginnings of the Croatian national revival and integration which took place in the nineteenth century did not start in a vacuum. These processes were a reflection of both national and historical experiences as well as of the political and cultural situation in Croatia and Europe at the time.

Croatians settled on the eastern shores of the Adriatic Sea in the middle of the seventh century. They were soon recognized as the new rulers of their present homeland. Being positioned between Byzantium and the Frankish kingdom, they, however, had to acknowledge the sovereignty of their eastern and western neighbors for some time. During the reign of Knez (Prince) Branimir (879-892), Croatia gained its full independence, but it was Tomislav (910-928) who created a united and strong Croatian medieval kingdom. It stretched from the Drava and Mura rivers in the North to the Adriatic Sea in the South and from the Raša river in the West to the Drina river in the East.

The Croatian medieval kingdom was ruled by native rulers until 1091. After the short rule of king Stjepan Trpimir (1089-1091), there was a power vacuum in the state, and a major struggle for the throne began. This struggle lasted twelve years. One of the contesting parties for the throne was led by Helen, widow of King Zvonimir (1076-1089) and daughter of the Hungarian King Bela I. She claimed the throne for her brother Ladislaus, because the last two kings, Zvonimir and Stjepan Trpimir, died without leaving a successor.[1] Croatia, however, had always been an elective kingdom, and the opposing, "national," party elected Petar Svačić as the new king. As a result, a war was started between the two factions as well as with Hungary, which lasted until 1102. The problem was resolved with a compromise. The Hungarian king Koloman, who succeeded Ladislaus, made an agreement with the Croatians, known as *Pacta Conventa,* by which he and his successors were to respect Croatian rights and privileges. In return, the Hungarian kings would be recognized as kings of Croatia. This personal union under the crown of St. Stephen marked the end of full Croatian independence. A similar union between the Croatian nobility and the Habsburgs was made in 1527, as a consequence of the Turkish victory at Mohacs (1526), which marked the end of full Hungarian independence. The union with the Habsburg crown lasted until the break up of the Habsburg empire in 1918.

As a result of its geographical position and the decline of its power, Croatia has always been an easy prey to foreign pressures and invasions. For centuries she was surrounded by stronger neighbors: Hungary in the north, Venice in the south-west, the Ottoman Turks in the east, and the Habsburgs in the north-west. After the Turkish invasions in the fifteenth century, it lost most of its territory either to the Christian or to the Islamic neighbors. In the beginning of the nineteenth century, what legally remained as the Kingdom of Croatia was just a fragment of the original kingdom. Most of its parts had been parcelled out and either occupied or administered by the neighboring powers.[2]

Throughout the troublesome centuries of the personal union with the Hungarian and Habsburg crowns (1102-1918), and despite the occupation of most of her territories, Croatia, however, preserved the nucleus of its statehood. The existence of the Croatian kingdom, legally, and even in practice, never fully ceased. It had safeguarded its separate political, legal, and administrative institutions. But the most important historical feature for modern Croatian nationalism was that the idea of Croatian individuality and self-consciousness was preserved through the centuries.

The main guardian of the historical rights, and at the same time of the idea of Croatian nationhood, was the native nobility. Though getting weaker with every decade, this tiny layer of the population succeeded in preserving the nucleus of Croatianism until the nineteenth century, when the young intellectuals, mostly of common origin, turned this historic memory into a national movement. The leaders of the Croatian national revival, in the 1830s and 1840s, added a new dimension, that of national rights, to the old Croatian *Jura municipalia* (Municipal Rights).[3] They envisioned a new Croatian nation built on new and modern liberal political concepts.[4] Thus, in the middle of the last century, the leaders of the Croatian national movement combined the Croatian historical experiences and rights with contemporary political thinking and needs. These two dimensions, past and present, have played an important part in Croatian nationalism, from the time of its revival until today.

Beside the preservation of the idea of political identity, the consciousness of a cultural uniqueness had been kept alive as well. The most obvious example of this is the use and maintenance of the glagolitic (glagoljica)[5] script, in the Middle Ages, and of vernacular language in Croatian literature and church liturgy. In its religious allegiance, caught between Rome and Constantinople, Croatia sided with Rome. It, however, resisted the Latinization by zealously guarding the vernacular in its church liturgy.[6] Although Latin became the language of high culture in Croatia and in most of its churches, the vernacular remained in use among the common people as well as among the native higher and educated class. It was precisely for this reason, the use of both languages by the Church and by the native higher classes, that Croatia was able to integrate the ideas and movements of Western Europe into its native culture. This dualism, the strong desire to preserve self-identity and, at the same time, the striving to be up to date with the mainstream of Western Civilization, has been a major characteristic of Croatian cultural history.

Humanism and Renaissance especially have made a strong mark on modern Croatian cultural and national life. In many ways, it set a stage for the national revival of the nineteenth century. In addition to the revival of classicism and the interest in humanism, shared by all the followers of the movement, Croatian humanists, both those in the country and those wandering throughout Europe, drew from the riches of the native medieval literature. Most of all, however, they shared a common concern for their homeland. Apart from being interested in universalism and antiquity, Croatian humanists also focused their attention on their particular political and cultural situation. The Ottomans were at the peak of their power.

Most of the Croatian lands were already in the hands of the Turks or threatened by them. Another enemy and threat to the national interests and culture was Venice. Witnessing the destruction of their homeland, the Croatian humanists were speaking about their "desolated Croatia,"[7] their "scattered homeland" (rasuta bašćina).[8] Some of them even participated in battles or others wrote poems and prayers against the Turks.[9] The theme of the threatened homeland and a cry for survival contributed to the sense of national identity. Similarly, the national survival was an essential part of the Croatian national movement, in the early nineteenth century, and it remained an intrinsic part of the Croatian national consciousness until the present time.

The Croatian humanists were writing both in Latin and, as they called it, in the "Croatian language."[10] It is clear from their writings that there had been a feeling of "belonging to the Croatian nation" (Nationis Croatae).[11] They, however, also introduced two new concepts into Croatian national life: the Illyrian name and Slavic reciprocity. The Illyrians were people who lived on the eastern shores of the Adriatic in the pre-Roman time. The humanists wrongly concluded that the Croatians, as well as other Slavs, were descendants of the ancient Illyrians. Thus they resurrected this ancient name, which they used simultaneously for Croatians as well as a collective name for all of the South Slavs. The name was later revived by Napoleon and his Illyrian provinces (1809-1813) and by the Croatian national revivalists, shortly after the fall of Napoleon.

After the fifteenth century, when threats came from all sides and help from nowhere, some Croatian writers began to dream that help might come from other Slavic nations. At first, all their hopes were focused on Poland, the strongest Slavic country at that time,[12] and later on Russia.[13] Besides the immediate political need for the support of other Slavs, there was a real up-surge of Slavic pride among the Croatians, in the sixteenth and seventeenth centuries, especially in historical writings. After the rediscovery of ancient Greece and Rome, intellectuals began to look at their own past. It was very much a legendary historiography in which desired, and even expected, results were very much predetermined. Thus, a confusing history was created in which Slavism, Illyrism, and Croatianism were intertwined in a single myth. As a result, from the seventeenth century on, the Illyrian or Slavic dimensions were strongly felt in the Croatian national historiography and remained an integral component of

Croatian nationalism in modern history. Consequently, the dicotomy between Croatianism and Slavism (Illyrism and Yugoslavism) will be an ever present tension in the Croatian national political and cultural development.

Beginnings of Modern Croatian Nationalism

The development of modern Croatian nationalism began in the 1830s. The moving spirit of the national revival were young intellectuals and students, helped by the growing native middle class and by some members of a withering native nobility. They came under the influence of the wider European movements of Liberalism, Romanticism, and Nationalism, as well as of a growing Pan-Slavism. The true foundations of the early Croatian nationalism were, however, of domestic origin. The revivalists sought their arguments in the Croatian national, political, and cultural history. Their goal was to bring about the emotional charge necessary for developing national pride and to translate that pride into a political power.[14] No less important, however, was the political situation Croatians found themselves in, at the middle of the nineteenth century. Pressures of Austrain centralism and Budapest's policy of Magyarization stimulated the growth of Croatian nationalism and also contributed to its wider Slavic orientation.

The initial phase of the Croatian national revival of the nineteenth century is better known as the Illyrian movement. From its beginning, the movement had two dimensions: Croatian and Slavic. The first one stood for national autonomy and for the integration of all Croatian lands. The Slavic dimension of the Illyrian movement was primarily the result of Croatia's weak political and economic position in the empire as well as an outcome of Croatian humanism and the contemporary Pan-Slavism. The movement was based on the (false) conclusion that all Slavs are a single nation and should, therefore, strive for unity and mutual assistance. The Croatian Pan-Slavists, on the other hand, the same as their humanist predecessors, never imagined or advocated a unified state of all the Slavs. Their Slavism was of cultural and "brotherly hand" nature.[15] In order to make the Illyrian movement more attractive and acceptable to other South Slavs, the Croatian national revivalists were willing to compromise in some aspects of their cultural heritage, but they believed that each

Southern Slavic national group should retain its proper name and identity. In 1842, a Croatian Illyrian activist wrote in this sense:

> The Croatian, Serbian, and Slovene names are genetic in southwestern Slavia, as the names of the three main branches of the southwestern Slavic people. But we know that a brother does not tolerate his brother's overlordship, and experience teaches us that a Croat will never accept a Serbian or Slovene name, a Serb will never accept a Croatian or Slovene name, and neither will a Slovene accept a Croatian or Serbian name.[15]

Thus, the Illyrian name was chosen to be the common surname for the three national groups. This is why Ljudevit Gaj, the leading figure of the movement, was able to write a popular and vivacious reveile *Još Hrvatska ni propala* (Croatia has not fallen yet) and at the same time dream of (South) Slavic unity.

The real scope of the movement, however, remained much narrower than its members had expected. The response of the Serbians, Slovenes, and Bulgarians to the Croatian initiatives was limited and often even negative. First, neither Slovenia nor Serbia, or Bulgaria felt threatened by the young and aggressive Hungarian national movement of the late eighteenth and early nineteenth centuries. The Croatians, however, did feel that this movement was a major peril to their national existence and, thus, could not be ignored. Second, Serbs and Bulgarians were more interested in immediate political goals and in the building of their own nation than in unclear and uncertain romantic Illyrian ideals. Thus, the South Slavic nations had no common enemies or common goals as a possible unifying factor. Each nation was looking at the contemporary political situation from its own perspective. Some Serbs even interpreted the movement as a cover-up for the efforts of the Roman Catholic Church to destroy not just their Orthodox Church but also the Serbian national identity.[16] They even went a step further and claimed that the population in Bosnia, Hercegovina, Montenegro, and most of Croatia was Serbian.[17] Slovenes, too, looked at the Illyrian movement with suspicion and perceived it as a threat to their newly discovered national identity. Thus, the Illyrian movement was limited to the Croatians and, in reality, it was the Croatian national awakening under the Illyrian name.

A Struggle for Survival

One of the major characteristics of Croatian nationalism has been its defensive nature. It began in an era of intensive political struggle with the Hungarians, and it continued to be one of the major means for self-preservation until the present time. During the absolutistic rule of Joseph II (1780-1790), the weakened Croatian nobility joined their Magyar counterparts in the struggle for preserving their common rights and their autonomy against the policies of centralization and Germanization. Because of this common effort and as a protection from a possible recurrence of Habsburg absolutism, the Croatians surrendered a major part of their independence to the Hungarians, in 1790. The Croatian Sabor (Diet), thus, relinquished major decision making powers, including all legislative rights, to the Hungarian-Croatian Joint Diet. Although the Croatian delegates to this government body had a special position, they still remained weak junior partners to the Hungarians.

During the same period, in the late eighteenth century, the Hungarian national revival was taking place, in the course of which Magyar was made the official language for all the lands under the crown of St. Stephen. The fact that the majority of the population in the kingdom was not Hungarian did not influence this decision. As a result, the language issue became the testing ground between the Hungarians and the Croatians. Although Latin had been retained for the time being as the administrative language, in 1827, the Croatian Sabor was pressured to make Magyar a required school subject in Croatia. This was a major blow to the budding Croatian national pride and a clear sign of the weakening political autonomy of the country. In return, the young Croatian intellectuals began to fight back, and it was in such a heated atmosphere between the Croatians and the Hungarians that the Croatian national revival began. Some members of the native nobility, the middle class, and young intellectuals began to unify their forces in order to revive the national pride and to create a new political and national force which would be able to withstand outside pressure.

The most important immediate goal of the young Croatian movement was to resist the aggression of Hungarian nationalism and prevent Hungary from expanding its boundaries from the Carpathian Mountains to the Adriatic Sea. The Croatian revivalists knew that in order to be able to withstand such a pressure, it was necessary to end the old administrative and political divisions in their country, which had been brought upon the land by the foreign powers. They had to stand as a united and rejuvenated nation to all foreign aggressions.

In order to unify the nation, the most important thing needed was a unified Croatian literary language; the decision was made in favor of the most prevalent *štokavian* dialect.[18] By the middle of the century, Croatian had replaced Latin and had become fully the official administrative and political language. Just as before the Hungarian language served as a means of Magyarizing non Magyar lands, Croatian was now to serve unifying purposes, as well as being a defensive weapon against any foreign cultural aggression. One should keep in mind, however, that the Croatian national revival had not just been a struggle for the old rights, or just a language revival. Neither was it only of defensive nature. There were a number of other factors, social, cultural, and psychological, for example, which helped to lay the foundation of modern Croatian nationalism.

As a major result of the national revival, in the middle of the nineteenth century, the first political parties were organized in Croatia. The Croatian-Hungarian party, known as "Magyarons" (Magyarophiles), was organized in 1841. At the same time, the Nationalists gathered in the Illyrian party, and they were the victors in the 1842 elections. Soon, however, the nationalists were accused of subversive activities by the Magyarons. Furthermore, Turkish authorities complained to Vienna about the spread of Croatian nationalist ideas from Zagreb into Bosnia and Hercegovina. As a result, the Illyrian party and the Illyrian name were banned in 1843, only a year after their victory. At the same time, Illyrism and its Pan-Slavistic dimension lost all significance. There were no positive responses from any other South Slavic nations to the Illyrian ideas, and there was also no common agreement on the meaning of Pan-Slavism among the Slavs. Thus, the Illyrian party became the National party, and the Illyrian movement came to be known under its proper name, Croatian national awakening.

National Ideologies

According to a Croatian historian, there have been "five complete ideological systems" in the process of Croatian national integration: "Illyrism; Yugoslavism; the ideology of the Party of Right (in its original form); the ideology of the peasant movement led by the Radić brothers; and the ideology of social democracy."[19] If looked from another point of view, however, one may see two basic trends in Croatian nationalism from its revival in the early nineteenth century until today. There was the vision of a wider, South Slavic (including Bulgaria), unity within which Croatians and others would preserve their identity and have full autonomy. The other major ideological stream stood for a distinct Croatian national development and an independent state, as the only guarantee of national consolidation, existence, and prosperity.

Already the Illyrian movement contained both of these elements. Its leaders were caught in a dicotomy between Croatianism and (South) Slavism, which, they hoped, could be harmonized. Clearly, the idea of Illyrism was based on historical and political myths. The preconception that the Slavs, and more specifically the South Slavs, were a single nation which spoke the same language was clearly a myth. Just as false was the preconception that they had similar national and political interests and that they had a special role to play in the future of European society. The idea of a possible South Slavic cultural and even political integration, however, continued even after the Illyrian movement was dead. The vague ideal of Slavic reciprocity held by the Croatian humanists and the ideals of Illyrism were turned into an ideology which came to be known as Yugoslavism.

A Croatian Catholic bishop of Djakovo, Josip Juraj Strossmayer (1815-1905) became the best known promoter and a symbol of Yugoslavism. To him and his National (Liberal) Party, Yugoslavism meant first of all a building of a common South Slavic culture, a 'spiritual community.'[20] Strossmayer, best known for his cultural efforts, was a liberal intellectual and a great philantropist. He organized many cultural institutions and supported numerous intellectuals, in order to foster South Slavic unity.

The political side of Strossmayer's Yugoslavism was, however, dampened from a number of sides. To Vienna and Budapest, his political contacts with other South Slavs outside the Monarchy, namely the Serbians, were treasonous. The Serbian government was in touch with Strossmayer, but their aims were not the same. The Serbs were after specific political and territorial gains. At the same time, they were suspicious of Strossmayer and his Catholicism, although he was known as one of the most liberal and ecumenical bishops in the Catholic church at the time. Another factor that weakened Strossmayer's political influence was the growing opposition to Yugoslavism in Croatia.

Strossmayer's political Yugoslavism was mainly in the line of Austro-Slavism. His immediate goal was the reorganization of the Monarchy, in which the South Slavs would have full autonomy. But the question of a unification of all the South Slavs, those within and outside the Habsburg Monarchy, was envisioned as a possibility in the future. Since he and his followers were conscious of the historical, cultural, and religious differences among the South Slavs, they foresaw a possible unity only when each group would retain its separate identity. Still, it seems that the advocates of Yugoslavism were not certain themselves what should be the final political result of their ideology. Strossmayer's contacts with the Serbian government did not have a smooth ride either. He and his National Party were basically used by the Serbs as a bargaining chip in their dealings with Vienna, the Hungarians, and even with the Ottomans.

Since Strossmayer had a feeling of a personal Christian mission, he dreamt of a Christian, in this case Catholic and Orthodox unity, and he wished to contribute to it personally. Thus, one may say that for Strossmayer Croatian national interests were seen in the light of his much wider goals. South Slavic solidarity, cultural and perhaps political unity, were looked upon as important steps in the process of building a bridge between the two Christian traditions, between the East and the West.

Another type of Yugoslavism developed at the beginning of this century. Its promoters were found among various student groups who rejected both the Croatian and Serbian historical state rights as well as the cultural differences among the South Slavs. They did, however, consider Serbian political tradition and culture as the firm base of their national ideology. As such, they stood more for Serbianization of the non-Serbs than for "Yugoslavization" of all the South Slavs. This type of nationalism led some young Croatian students in the immediate pre-World War I period to advocate a unitaristic Yugoslav state, even under Serbian militarism. Their models were unified Germany and Italy. But it seems they did not realize that the political, cultural, and psychological situation among the South Slavs was completely different from that in Germany or Italy. While, for example, the German identity and its spiritual unity existed much earlier than its political unification, in the case of the South Slavs the unification was brought from above. It had never had a solid psychological, cultural, or political foundation which would assure its success. The ideology of Yugoslavism, unitaristic or federalistic, has never found mass support among the Croatians. It did, however, have an unproportionately important impact on Croatian politics. Intellectual circles, which supported Yugoslavism, played an active role in the creation of the Kingdom of Serbs, Croats, and Slovenes, established in 1918. But, among the Croatians, Yugoslavism lost most of its appeal after the creation of a united South Slavic state. Its romantic dimension was crushed by a harsh political reality in the inter-war period. It was revived, however, once more in the post-Second World War era, in the context of the solidarity of the working class and Communist internationalism. But then, too, was discredited and abandoned in a relatively short period of time.

The major characteristic of the second stream of modern Croatian nationalism was the advocacy of a fully independent Croatian state. This integral Croatian national ideology was just the opposite to Illyrism and Yugoslavism. The founder of this ideology and of the Party of Right[21] was Ante Starčević (1823-1896), known among the Croatians as *Otac domovine*—the Father of the Homeland.

Starčević's political thinking was based on the modern notions of Liberalism and on the ideals of the French Revolution. He believed that the right to rule did not come from above (God) but from below (People), and, like the French Revolutionaries, thought that the word "people" meant a specific ethnic group (nation). All of this provided him with the notion that Croatians, like any other nation, have the right to determine their own national fate, that they have the right to an independent Croatian state.

Another important source of Starčević's arguments were the old Croatian historical state rights, which had been preserved through the centuries. By using both the modern and the historical arguments, he finally challenged the Habsburg right to rule in Croatia. Since Croatians freely entered into a personal union with the Hungarians (1102) and the Habsburgs (1527), he said, this was a contract of a sovereign people and their ruler. If the ruler breached the contract, as the Habsburgs had been doing ever since 1527, Croatians and other peoples had the right to terminate their relations with him.

In the wake of the 1848 revolutions, Francis Joseph had introduced an absolutistic rule, in order to suppress all centrifugal and revolutionary forces in the empire and to create a centralized state. In the face of the Habsburg oppression, Starčević defiantly raised the issue of the Croatian historic and natural rights. The Habsburgs, according to him, were no longer legitimate rulers in Croatia. The contract had been broken, and the people had the right and duty to start a new phase in their history. The unification of Italy and Germany made Starčević and other Croatians even more aware of their political peril, and it was further proof of the Habsburgs' disregard of their political and national rights. Starčević did not think that the Habsburgs and their empire might reform. For him „despotisms do not improve; instead they should be destroyed."[22] Thus the only way to go was to work toward an independent Croatian state.

Starčević was strongly opposed to any type of South Slavic unity, primarily because of the growing Serbian nationalism and its political and territorial aspirations.[23] Also he believed that the Croatian national well-being could be guaranteed only in a Croatian state and not in unity with Belgrade, Vienna, or Budapest.[24] According to him, the time had come for all the nations to develop freely their own talents and by doing so, to contribute to the unity and progress of the whole world.

Starčević's ideology had a much greater influence on the psychology of Croatian nationalism than the idea of Yugoslavism, because it was better focused, well defined and uncompromising. Furthermore, it proposed more certain political and national categories. Yugoslavism was new and without historical precedence. The old Croatian kingdom, the historic rights, the common historic and cultural memory were ideas not only essential to Starčević's political program but also ideas all the Croatians could identity with. The followers of Yugoslavisms, on the other hand, were constantly in conflict with the already developed Croatian identity. Even the ideology of Illyrism and Yugoslavism as its modified successor was based on the fundamental Croatian identity. Thus, Yugoslavism was more an extension of the political conditions of that time and of uncertain desires than a national identity.

Strossmayer, the promoter of Yugoslavism, and his followers were elitists, and they mostly gathered around higher cultural and church institutions. His party, and Yugoslavism as such, always remained on the periphery of the Croatian masses. Starčević, on the other hand, came from a village, and he struck the nerve of the Croatian national feeling primarily among the lower middle class but also among people living in the country. His teaching truly penetrated the Croatian national and political life. Consequently, in the second half of the last century, his party became the strongest party and his ideology became a major pillar of Croatian nationalism.

Although Starčević did advocate democratic changes in Croatian politics, for example, universal manhood suffrage, he was not a social reformer. Still his party was closer to the common people than that of Strossmayer. Starčević was against any political and cultural categories which were being built from "above." He saw the people, the Croatian nation, and its free will as the foundation for the future progress. So far, the masses and the peasants had been outside of the political process and were neglected and uneducated. Starčević, however, believed that it was the mission of his party to gather lower middle class intellectuals, and in turn they would educate the masses and bring them into the political arena. One can say that Starčević was a spokesman for all those who were outside of the political life in Croatia, at the time. That is one of the reasons why his teachings had such a positive response among all elements of Croatian society.

Both ideologies, Strossmayer's as well as Starčević's, stressed the role of the intelligentsia in the national integration. For Strossmayer, however, the major role of Croatian scholars, at that time, was to bridge the difference between the South Slavs[25] and to provide a proof for an already chartered ideological course. Starčević, on the other hand, considered it one of his main missions to awake the national consciousness of the Croatian intelligentsia which would in turn educate the whole nation and bring the Croatian people culturally and politically up to date.

Starčević and his party of Right also added a new dimension to Croatian nationalism. He separated religion and nationality. Thus, he was the first major public figure in Croatia, and most probably one of the few educated men in Europe, who sincerely considered Islam and Christianity as equals. At the time when the Young Ottomans in the Turkish empire were promoting a return to the original Islamic spirit and the Ottoman identity, based on the imperial greatness and Islam, Starčević stressed that the Muslims in Bosnia and Hercegovina had nothing to do with the Turks nationally, but that they were the purest descendants of the medieval Croatian nobility. As a result, a number of Muslim intellectuals became followers of Starčević's ideology and they propagated the Croatian national idea among the Muslims in Bosnia and Hercegovina.[26] The Party of Right had also a good name among the Orthodox in Croatia. At the same time, there was even the idea to establish a Croatian Orthodox church.[27]

At the beginning of this century, however, the Party of Right underwent a number of changes and divisions. Some of Starčević's successors deviated from the original ideology[28] and the popularity of the party declined. The political uncertainties and the war experiences contributed to the birth of a new national force and a new kind of unity.

Croatian Peasant Party

At the beginning of this century, the Croatian Peasant Party played a unique role in the process of Croatian national integration and Croatian politics. It began in 1904 as a small party and in only two decades it represented the entire Croatian nation. In the few years after 1918, its energetic and capable leadership succeeded to mobilize and politicize even the last village in Croatia.

The Croatian Peasant Party was founded (1904) by two brothers, Antun (1868-1919) and Stjepan (1871-1928) Radić. They were well educated men of a poor peasant background. While the older brother, Antun, contributed greatly to the ideology of the party, Stjepan was its moving spirit. With his inexhaustible energy and charismatic leadership, he woke "the sleeping giant"—the peasants—and made them aware of their national and political rights. He taught them the principles of peaceful and democratic political participation and, thus, made them the major political and national force in Croatia. His program was simultaneously national and social, with national freedom, social justice, and harmony as the desired goals.

Radić's teaching was based on four major principles: Croatian statehood, Slavism, people (peasant) democracy, and political liberalism of the Western European tradition.[29] Freedom and statehood of the Croatian nation remained a primary goal. Like Starčević, Radić made use of the Croatian historical and natural rights, when arguing for the full sovereignty of his nation.[30] In the pre-1918 period, he advocated a unification of the fragmented Croatian lands, and then he called for a full national statehood within a Danubian federation.[31] At the time of the break up of the Habsburg monarchy, Radić did not reject the possibility of a unification of the

South Slavs. He, however, strongly opposed the small number of Croatian politicians in the newly organized National Council who were eager to help create a unified state, but who totally disregarded the consequences. Thus, before and after World War I, Radić's position that every nation should be formed independently and freely remained unchanged. Moreover, he put much emphasis on the principle of self-determination. Only free nations could create a "common [Danubian or South Slavic] federation of their own free will, and on equal terms."[32] It was because of this principle that he objected to the haste and the way in which the Kingdom of Serbs, Croats, and Slovenes was put together.

Radić's Slavism, however, was not of exclusivist or communal nature like Russian Slavophilism. His program was a combination of Western liberalism and native institutions and culture. His ultimate goal was the harmony of individual freedoms, social, and political life. The basis for such freedom and harmony Radić found in the notion of the traditional Croatian *dom*, which means not only a house, but a family, security, warmth, love, happiness, freedom, and sharing. What the *dom* was for the individual, the state was for a nation. Thus, he believed that there should not only be a national and social harmony in Croatia, based on peasant democracy, but that there should be peace and harmony among all the nations.

It was after the creation of the common South Slavic state that Radić's party achieved its prominence. For the first time, peasants gained the right to vote and Radić was the one who articulated their desires. He soon became the tribune of the Croatian nation, and as such he used all the peaceful means at his disposal to achieve personal and national rights for the Croatians. For him the ultimate political goal was a neutral Croatian peasant republic.[33] First, he used a policy of abstinence and non-recognition of the legitimacy of the existing state, which was ruled by the Serbian dynasty and bureaucracy as if it were their expanded state. Then Radić turned to the Western powers for understanding and help, but he was rejected. He even turned to Soviet Russia for assistance, but, as he stated, the Soviets 'did not want allies, only servants.'[34] After exhausting all other peaceful means, he accepted the political reality and, in 1925, began to work through the existing system, always hoping that sooner or later he would be able to achieve the desired goals.[35] His life and work, however, were cut short by an assassin's bullet, in Belgrade *Skupština*

(Parliament), in 1928. Stjepan Radić was mortally wounded, two of his Croatian colleagues were killed, and two others wounded during the same tragic event. This marked an even greater oppression in the country and was the beginning of a radicalization of Croatian nationalism. In the decade before the Second World War, there were three main political streams in Croatian nationalism: the Peasant Party, the *Ustaša* revolutionary movement, and the Communist Party. The Peasant Party continued with oppositionist tactics. In 1939, the Party leadership made an agreement with the Belgrade government by which Croatia achieved greater autonomy. But this did not satisfy either Croatians or Serbians. While the Croatians thought they received too little, the Serbians believed they gave too much.

Soon after the 1928 shooting in the *Skupština* and the introduction of dictatorship in the country, a revolutionary Croatian organization was established under the name of *Ustaša* (a rebel). It strove for full independence of Croatia and used all available means to destroy Yugoslavia. As a result, it found a natural alliance with other European revisionists of the time and, in 1941, with the help of the Central powers, it established a Croatian state.

The primary goal of the Yugoslav Communist Party was to achieve a dictatorship of the proletariat, but they could not ignore the national problem in the country either. Finally, after several shifts, the party accepted federalism as the basis for South Slavic unity, which it implemented in theory after it took power in 1945.

Both, Yugoslavism and pure Croatianism played major roles in the development of Croatian consciousness and in its national integration. Despite their differences, both currents stood for the unification of a politically divided Croatia, for a reaffirmation of the Croatian statehood in one form or another.[36] Those who followed Strossmayer's tradition tended to stress the Slavic or South Slavic dimension of the Croatian national integration. Those who followed Starčević's line of thinking stressed the purity of Croatian nationalism. Radić, in a sense, combined the two national streams. He was a strong advocate of Croatian statehood and of the principles of self-determination, but at the same time he was willing, under certain conditions, to accept a South Slavic political framework. His participation in Belgrade politics from 1925 to 1928 was, in his thinking, pure necessity and not a change of his national and political goals. The harsh reality in the newly organized South Slavic state, especially after the shots were fired in the *Skupština*, however, made him doubt even the possibility of South Slavic unity.[37]

It is ironic and at the same time tragic that, at the moment when the Croatian national integration entered the phase of its most popular revival under the leadership of Stjepan Radić, it was deprived of its natural course of development. The new state and its regime tried to crush all political opposition and Croatian national aspirations. Thus, Yugoslavia became a new arena for the same old Croatian struggle for self-preservation and self-determination.

CHAPTER II

DECENTRALIZING REFORMS OF THE MID-1960s AND THE NATIONAL QUESTION IN YUGOSLAVIA

On the national question in Yugoslavia, President Josip Broz Tito, at the Eighth Congress of the League of Communists of Yugoslavia (LCY) in December 1964, declared:

> I think that the Eighth Congress must pay full attention to intranational relations. Not because the national question represents a problem which is not in principle solved. No, that is not the issue. For us Communists, the solution of the national question has been an integral part of the political line which was already definitely decided before the War. . . .
>
> There are persons, however, and even Communists . . . who think that nationalities in our socialist development have outlived themselves and should wither away. They confuse the unity of the people with the liquidation of nations and establishment of something new, artificial, that is the [creation] of a single, Yugoslav nation, which is tantamount to assimilation and bureaucratic centralism, to unitarism and hegemony. The Yugoslav socialist integration is a new type of social community in which all nations find common interests.[1]

The Eighth Congress was the turning point in post-war Yugoslavia on the question of national relations within the country, and also a turn about in the history of the Communist Party of Yugoslavia.[2] Ever since the end of the World War II, the official policy of the Party had been to force not only social and economic equalization in the country but also cultural and national unitarism, in order to create a new, "Yugoslav," national identity. The culmination of this policy took place during the Seventh Congress of the LCY, in 1958. There it was declared that a "socialist, Yugoslav consciousness" was the basis of the unity of Yugoslavia.[3] But as late as 1963 many in the Party, including Tito, were still openly in support of cultural and economic "Yugoslavism." In December of 1962, Tito complained that intellectuals in some republics were creating obstacles to the "establishment of Yugoslavia as a unitary economic area."[4] Three months later he stated on the issue of Yugoslav socialist consciousness:

> If we want to create a socialist culture, we must also have a common program. It must be Yugoslav. Not every republic and every nationality can create its own socialist culture. . . . We must strive to mitigate contrasts which always exist within us and in such a way as to create in our country a unique socialist culture, which only by the fact of being Yugoslavian will be the property of all our nationalities.[5]

Tito still hoped that the new generation might accept the new identity, which had been actively promoted by the Party in the postwar period.

On the other side, however, even among Party leaders, especially in Croatia and Slovenia, there was a feeling that their republics were economically exploited in the name of "brotherhood and unity." Besides the Croatian and Slovenian economic grievances, cultural unitarism was passively and actively resented by all non-Serbian nations and ethnic groups, even by those groups who benefited financially from centralist policies. The belief was that with "bureaucratic centralist tendencies" the remnants of the great-Serbian nationalism were being implemented under the disguise of "Yugoslavism."[6] The change of mood even among the Party leadership was expressed by Edvard Kardelj, the leading Party man from Slovenia and chief ideologue of Titoism. In his speech at the Eighth Congress Kardelj said:

We Communists did not forget, and we must not forget in the future either, that economic matters are actually of detrimental importance for intra-national relations. The starting point of intra-national economic relations is certainly the economic independence of every nation. This guarantees independence of work and profit from the fruit of one's own labor. In other words, this creates a material basis for the development of one's own culture and civilization.[7]

The above words are very different in tone and context from Kardelj's previously held views on this subject:

Everything that is reactionary, ideologically backward, or momentarily disoriented in our society is expressed in nationalist manifestations.

...Nationalism, in our condition, is one of those reactionary ideological factors which draws [people] backwards, closes socialist perspectives, obstructs the formation of socialist consciousness, and cripples that practical socialist creative activity which does not act from today to tomorrow but ensures lasting results for an entirely determined historical period.[8]

From the time of the Seventh Congress of the LCY, in 1958, until the next one in 1964, an important shift took place among the Party leaders, especially among those from the northern republics, Slovenia and Croatia. This shift affected most of all the attitudes of these politicians toward the relationship of the individual republics to the federation and to intra-national relations. The movement for national (republican) economic autonomy based on the principle of self-management was in the making, but a quest to bridge the economic gap between the regions was not abandoned. However, there was a growing pressure from the more developed republics—whose money was invested in the southern regions—upon the party leadership to look for better and more efficient ways to help the less developed areas. They opposed simply transferring money from one area to another through the central fund because this fund was controlled solely by the federal government. They pointed out that such a method of "equalization" did not work and that the bureaucratic forces controlling the central funds were too closely connected with Serbian national interests. Two major groups emerged in the Party in the early 1960s. One group had Slovenes and Croats as its major force. It advocated the decentralization of federal powers, called for economic independence of federal units, and wanted to introduce a market economy. The other group was centered in Belgrade and was mainly supported by the Serbs and Montenegrins. The major goal of this group was to defend centralism and centralized economic policies. The reformers, group one, gradually gained ground and controlled the outcome of the Eighth Congress. But a strong opposition to the reforming liberals still remained in the Party and the federal administration. The conservatives had lost a political battle, but they were still running the central government and the country.

The leading man of the forces opposing the reform movement was Vice-President Aleksandar Ranković, who, among other things, controlled the secret police and who was the most powerful man in the country, next to Tito. The liberals finally came into control after the Fourth Plenum of the Central Committee, in July 1966, when Ranković was stripped of his functions. But even after that historic event, which some considered the "climax in the struggle over the future course of Yugoslavia's economic development,"[9] most of the intra-national issues remained only partially solved. In the early Sixties, however, economic problems as well as other major intra-national questions were slowly brought to the open. Especially after the fall of Ranković a major change was in the offing.

CPY and the National Question

In order to better understand the Croatian national movement in the 1960s and Yugoslav policies on the national question in general, it is necessary to look at the position of the Communist Party of Yugoslavia (CPY) regarding this important issue. This specific issue has haunted this multi-national state ever since its creation, in 1918, because right from its beginnings this country had been composed of diverse peoples, cultures, religions, and languages.

From 1919, when the CPY was established,[10] to 1924 the Party advocated the creation of a "Yugoslav Soviet Republic." Centralism, national, and state unitarism were strong points of its program during this period. The existing national problems, especially between Serbs and Croatians, were seen as a reflection of the economic struggle between the two national bourgeoisies. But because of a strong manifestation of nationalism in the non-Serbian parts of the country, as expressed through the support of the opposition bourgeois parties in the 1923 elections, the Party was forced to take a second look at its stand on the national question.[11] Already at the Second Conference of the CPY, held in Vienna in May 1923, the belief that all South Slavs are a single nation was rejected. But it was still upheld that a Yugoslav nationality was in the making. The Third Conference of the CPY, which took place in Belgrade in December 1923, supported the principle of self-determination and of the struggle against Serbian bourgeoisie. The "right" wing of the Party, led by Sima Marković, a leading Serbian Marxist, however, continued to argue that the national problem was only a constitutional question and nothing more. The "left" wing proclaimed that the struggle of both the oppressed nations and the working class in Yugoslavia had common goals. Therefore, the national question had to be part of the Party's program. Because of the internal situation and under the directives of the Comintern, the CPY advocated, from 1924-1935, the policy of self-determination and even separation of Croatia, Slovenia, and Macedonia from Yugoslavia.[12] In 1935 the Party once more became a fervent advocate of Yugoslav unity. Now the idea of federalism, however, was to become the future solution of the national problem in the country. It was decided to establish national Communist parties in Slovenia, Croatia, and Macedonia in order to show the non-Serbs in Yugoslavia that the Party was not only concerned about international and class struggle, but also about national problems. Another reason was "to create a party leadership from the ranks of the oppressed peoples, diminish the influence of the bourgeois national movement and fight their pro-fascist separatist alternative."[13]

The victory of the National Socialists in Germany caused the Comintern to change its policy toward Yugoslavia. The Soviet controlled Comintern began to consider Yugoslavia as a buffer zone against Germany, and the CPY had to follow directives obediently.[14] In 1937, a major reorganization of the Party took place: The Slovene and Croatian Communist parties were established. Former General Secretary of the CPY Milan Gorkić (Josip Čižinski) became a victim of the Stalin purges, and

Tito was sent back to Yugoslavia from the Soviet Union as the new head of the Party. Also the headquarters of the Party moved from Belgrade to Zagreb. Despite its federalization, the Party, however, became more and more "bolshevik" and centralist in character, as Tito's words at the Fifth Party Congress (1948) clearly indicate:

> The purge of our Party from different foreign elements began in 1937. The impossible situation which lasted a long number of years in the Communist Party of Yugoslavia ended toward the end of 1937. The last remnants of factional and clanish elements, whose destructive work prevented the development and bolshevization of the CPY for 15 years, were removed during 1937 and 1938. The leadership [of the Party] headed by Gorkić was removed, except for one member (Tito) who received this order from the CI (Communist International): to form a new leadership in the country and carry out a full purge of the Party.[15]

But even after the party discipline was affirmed, many of the old differences in the Party ranks remained, as shall be seen later in this chapter.

During the Second World War, in order to get the support of the different nations living in what was old Yugoslavia, the Party strongly stressed that the new state would be a federation of free and sovereign peoples. They guaranteed that national differences, historical aspirations, and even individual statehoods would be assured. Full equality was promised in contrast to the inter-war policies of oppression of some national groups and in contrast to the open Serbian hegemony in Royalist Yugoslavia. This policy became one of the cornerstones in the second meeting of the Anti-Fascist Council of National Liberation of Yugoslavia (AVNOJ). In this meeting, which took place in Jajce, in November 1943, the foundations of the new country were laid. After its victory in 1945, the Party, however, introduced policies of a strong centralism and unitarism. "The new state was federal in theory, the political system was clearly centralized and dictatorial in practice."[16] But this time the policies were being implemented by the Communists rather than by a dictator king. Only in the late 1950s and early 1960s, federalism began to be implemented; however, not to the satisfaction of those regions of the country that felt economically exploited or culturally oppressed by the centralized Party and federal government.

Apart from the official stance of the Party on the national question, there were from the beginning two main lines of thinking on this important issue within the socialist movements of the South Slavs. Those two were mainly determined by national experience, by tradition, and by interest. The Croatian and Slovene social democrats had been a part of Austrian Social Democracy. Moreover, Croatians preserved, throughout the centuries, their traditional parlamentarism (Sabor). Such republics as Dubrovnik and Poljica, and independent towns contributed to the idea of national participatory government. Thus, this first group had a strong democratic tradition and stood for national and political pluralism. On the other hand, the Serbian social democrats, whose Byzantine cultural background of Caesaropapism was reinforced by their education in Russia, were much closer to the Soviet Communists and the Bolshevik line of thinking. They considered themselves to be true Communist revolutionaries and internationalists in contrast to those who came from the "newly united regions" (Croatia and Slovenia). These attitudes can be clearly distinguished from reports sent by the Party leaders to the Comintern, during the first few years after the unification.

> From the time of the establishment of Yugoslavia, our Serbian Social-Democratic Party found itself facing numerous problems. Firt of all, as the strongest (Social-Democratic Party] it had to unite all other old Social-Democratic Parties [in the country] . . . . But this work was much aggravated because of the inheritance from former Austria; beside feudalism and clericalism, we received even socialist-patriotism.[17]

The report further states that the Social-Democratic parties of Croatia and Slovenia with "their separatist inclinations and leanings" were hindering the unification of the Party.[18] Meanwhile, the mission of unification, supposedly, "was undertaken by the Serbian social-democratic workers' party, [which] because of its revolutionary tradition and organizational capabilities was able to accomplish this task much easier."[19] As a result, Sima Marković, a leading Serb in the Party, tried to prove to the delegates of the Third Congress of the Comintern (1921) that 'the Communist party of Yugoslavia was [only] a successor of the Serbian socialist party."[20] On the one hand, there was the stress on the merits, on the capabilities and the strength of the Serbian workers' party, while, on the other hand, socialist parties from the "newly acquired regions" were accused of being under nationalistic and bourgeois influences, and even of being particulary "uncultivated and uneducated."[21]

Already from its beginning, the united Communist Party of Yugoslavia felt the Serbian dominance, even though the parties from the former Austro-Hungarian empire were larger. The more dominant role of the Serbian Communists can be seen from the following table which indicates the numerical strength of the Party according to regions, number of organizations, and representatives at the Second Party Congress held on June 20-25, 1920, in the town of Vukovar:

TABLE 1

National and regional representation at the Second Congress of the CPY

	Membership	Number of Delegates	Number of Organizations
Croatia	15,500	91	74
Dalmatia	2,092	3	9
Serbia and Macedonia	14,931	134	67
Slovenia	11,990	21	26
Vojvodina	8,921	55	16
Bosnia and Montenegro	7,424	37	26
Central Forums	—	33	—

Source: Jozo Ivičević, "Odrednice unitarističkoga nacionalnog programa I i II kongresa KPJ," *Hrvatski znanstveni zbornik*, Vol. I, 1971, p. 177.

The discrepancy between membership and number of delegates at the Congress from the former Habsburg empire is striking. Even though the opposition of the non-Serbian members to the bolshevization of the party was strong, the Congress promulgated a strongly centralized program.[22]

In retrospect, one can easily trace two continuous tendencies among the Communists of Yugoslavia, throughout the history of their Party. Generally speaking, among Slovene and Croatian Communists there was always a strong line of support for decentralizing policies, stemming from their cultural inheritance and national interests. Because of this, they have been often accused of separatism and nationalism by the Serbian dominated Party, since the top Party echelons tend to advocate the policies of centralism, in the name of internationalism and revolutionism. Croatians, however, saw these ideological claims as euphemism for Serbian domination. As we shall see later, during the period of the Croatian national reawakening in the 1960s and early 1970s, the general tendencies of the republican parties would follow their traditional paths; decentralizing forces with more pluralistic and national tendencies of the Croatian leadership would clash with the Belgrade advocates of "democratic centralism" and firm hand policy.

The Yugoslav Road to Socialism

Communist Yugoslavia has undergone a number of important political and economic changes in its forty year history. The innovations in these two important spheres have had multiple effects on the country as a whole and on the lives of its citizens; they affected Yugoslavia's foreign policy, the national relations within the country, the standard of living, and the country's social and demographic mobility.

Generally speaking, the evolution of the Yugoslav system can be divided into four different periods: the immediate post-war period until 1952, known as "administrative socialism"; a transitional period from 1952 to 1965; an era of Reform implementation from 1966 until 1972, followed by a return to the Party's democratic centralism coupled with further decentralization.

During the immediate postwar years, the CPY was one of the most faithful regimes to Stalin. Even after the expulsion of Yugoslavia from the Cominform in 1948, the country's political, economic, and social policies remained within the limits of the Stalinist socialist model. These Moscow-like policies were officially inaugurated by the 1946 Constitution, which had been modeled after the Soviet Constitution of 1936.

The main characteristic of "administrative socialism" was Party control over every aspect of life in the country. Even though Yugoslavia had been recognized as a federated state, it was controlled by a strongly centralized Communist party which showed no concern for the proclaimed national and republican rights. "The Yugoslav State was federal on paper, but highly centralized in practice."[23] The government was indistinguishable from the Party. Economic development, cultural expression, social experience, and the lives of ordinary citizens were subject to the Party's firm control.

The Party was hierarchically organized, which meant that the leadership passed down directives and orders which the lower ranks of the Party had to carry out, regardless of the practicability or profitability of the orders. There was very little room for intra-Party democracy and definitely none for those outside the Party. The country was firmly under a "centralist global social system." It resembled an "unfissured monolith. . . divided into sectors or subsystems and founded on all-inclusive-State-ownership monopoly over means of production, what ends they served, and at whose behest."[24] At the top of the power structure was Tito himself. His functions in the Party and in the government clearly indicate the nature of the entire system. During the period in question, he was "Premier of Yugoslavia, Secretary General of the Communist Party and chief of its Politburo, President of the People's Front, Marshal of Yugoslavia, Minister of National Defense, Commander-in-Chief of the army, a deputy in the Assembly, and a member of the Presidium. His top lieutenants also were officials in the party, the government and the People's Front."[25]

The locus of this centralized power system was Belgrade, the capital of the First Yugoslavia and of the republic of Serbia. Both of these facts, the centralized power and the place where it was dispensed, became a strong reminder of the pre-war Karadjordjević regime and its dictatorial policies.

"Prior to 1948, the Yugoslav Communists saw themselves as the best and most faithful interpreters of Marxism-Leninism-Stalinism."[26] However, only very few, if any, of the post-1948 Yugoslav scholars would admit that "administrative socialism" was a zealous imitation of the Soviet system, adapted to the local needs and conditions. Those who were in favor of the regime stressed that the country needed a strong centralized political power because it had to be rebuilt, industrialized, and put on the road of economic development. The class enemy had to be destroyed, the new state defended, revolution saved, and the country's unity preserved.

The expulsion of Yugoslavia from the Cominform and the break with Stalin did not result in an immediate rejection of Stalinist Communism. For example, in the field of agriculture, in which Yugoslavia had so far followed the Soviet example in a limited way, a radical change took place.

A rapid collectivization was introduced, not so much for economic but for political and ideological reasons. This reform was an important step in the socialization of the village[27] and a proof to the Soviets and other Communists that Yugoslavia was ideologically on firm ground. Some historians even think this move is an indication that the CPY was looking for a return to the Soviet fold.[28]

Despite Yugoslavia's attempts to prove its allegiance to the Stalinist type of Communism, the Soviets were critical of Yugoslavia's agricultural policy. They accused the Yugoslav leadership of "pursuing an incorrect policy in the countryside by ignoring the class differentiation in the countryside and by regarding the individual peasantry as a single entity, contrary to the Marxist-Leninist doctrine . . . ."[29] Indeed, some of the government's attempts toward an increased socialization and collectivization failed, so that the country was forced to moderate its communist goals. The stubborn resistance of the country's peasants to collectivization and the complete economic failure of the program, forced the Party to abandon collectivization in 1953 and to return the land to the peasants. A ten hectare limit, however, was put on land holdings. The earlier collectivization and imposition of forced labor on those peasants who resisted it, as well as the later limits on land holdings, alienated the peasantry from the regime. As a result, agricultural production declined, and Yugoslavia had not moved any closer to the Soviets. Nor did this help Yugoslavia's image in the eyes of the West, which was eager to see a split in the Communist bloc. Another negative effect of the policy of collectivization was that it became yet another proof of national inequality in the country, because it had been much more vigorously enforced in Croatian than in Serbian regions.[30]

Even though the regime apologists maintain that the period of "administrative socialism" was the *conditio sine quo non* for the Yugoslav situation, at that time, there were quite a number of negative consequences connected with this period, consequences which affected both the country and its people. For example, individual and group initiative was stifled. The Party membership and the obedience to its doctrines was rewarded while talent and self-initiative were hindered. Most of the higher positions, not only in the Party but also in the economy, education, and culture were given to the most loyal elements of the regime and not to the ones best qualified for the job. Also, enterprises were not only state owned but completely controlled by state administration; sales, prices, costs, and profits were determined by the central government. One of the most important weapons of the federal government was the central investment fund. Through its policy of "equalization" it built numerous "political factories." Local or republican pride, or paying back personal favors, rather than economic feasibility, determined whether a factory was built or not.

This kind of federal policy had a negative impact on the more economically advanced republics, Slovenia and Croatia, because they were footing the bill for projects about which they had very little or nothing to say. When their grievances came into the open, in the early 1960s, it was clear that these two republics felt exploited by the Serbian controlled central government.

Such centralistic policies which were in direct contrast to the proclaimed federalism easily translated into national antagonism. Thus, economic policies of the central government, along with other oppressive measures, were one of the main causes for the Croatian and Slovenian demand for a "federalization of the federation."[31] The economic grievances were also one of the major elements that united the liberal wing of the Party in Croatia and the Croatian nationalists, as will be discussed in later chapters.

As a result of the break with the Soviet Union, in 1948, the leadership of the CPY found itself in a traumatic position. It had been rejected by the man and the Party that had been idolized as the only official interpreters of Marxism and Leninism in the world. Once the Party realized that there was no return to the mother party, the leaders of the CPY had no choice but to look for an ideological explanation of the Soviet attacks on them and to search for an alternative way to build socialism. The Party ideologists Milovan Djilas, Edvard Kardelj, and to some extent Boris Kidrič, came upon the idea of a "free association of producers," better known as self-management. It was to be the alternative to Soviet bureaucratic centralism. Its philosophical explanation was based on the Marxist theory of the withering away of the state. Highlighting this aspect of Marxism also became a useful tool for anti-Soviet propaganda. The CPY attacked the role of the State in the USSR, because it was a deviation from Marxism. At the same time, the Party pointed out that self-management was ideologically closer to Marx and his theory of the withering of the state. It assured mass participation in state affairs and was, therefore, a better road to Communism.

The Yugoslav officials and ideologists claim, however, that the "anti-dogmatism" of the CPY did not start as the result of their expulsion from the Cominform. According to them, the antidogmatism had been present in the Party before and during the war, and it was the gradual process of "crystalization" which turned the Party into an "independent antidogmatic force."[32] True, there had been Croatian revisionism as early as the 1930s. But as far as the leadership of the CPY was concerned, the evidence clearly pointed out that self-management and Yugoslav "anti-dogmatism" were the results of the break with Stalin and the CPY's desire to differentiate itself from the Soviet system and find its own way out of the country's ideological and economic crisis.

What is important for us here is the fact that with the introduction of the idea of self-management, the process of decentralization was set in motion, although the "CPY never for a moment gave up ultimate control over the political, social, economic and even cultural developments in Yugoslavia, it only changed the methods of control to suit the new conditions."[33] In solving the economic, political, and social problems, the Party could not turn back. It had to put into practice, at least to a certain extent, what it was proclaiming as its policy.

Even though the principles of self-management and decentralization were hailed publicly by the entire Party leadership, there was a deep division within the Party over the implementation of those principles, especially when it came to decentralizing the economy. On the one hand, there were the conservatives, mostly from Serbia and Montenegro, who opposed the changes and stood for a strong central government, for a monolithic Party and a planned economy. On the other hand, there were the liberals, mostly from Slovenia and Croatia, who advocated a stronger role for the republics in decision making, a less important role for the Party in non-political fields of life, and a full implementation of self-management. At the Eighth Congress of the LCY (1964), the "liberals" had the majority and dominated the Congress, but the full victory had not yet been won. Only in July 1966, after Vice-President Ranković and his closest allies were exposed as opponents of Reform and as a threat to Tito's regime itself, the liberals became the leading force in the Party and in the country. But soon the liberals would face a variety of challenges from the still powerful centrists and the growing nationalism.

The Fall of Aleksandar Rankovic

The Fourth Plenum of the Central Committee of the LCY, held on the island of Brioni on July 1, 1966, was the climax of the on-going struggle between the liberals and conservatives within the Party. This conflict had especially intensified after the Eighth Congress of the LCY (1964) and after the inauguration of the Reform in July 1965. One could even say that this struggle was a logical result of the introduction of self-management. As one Marxist scholar put it, sooner or later the forces that advocated "decrease of self-management for the benefit of the authority of the state, and those that believed in the dwindling of the state authority for the benefit of self-management"[34] had to face each other. Miko Tripalo, a young Party leader from Croatia, explained:

> [The main question at the Fourth Plenum of the LCY was], shall we continue developing self-management as a political system to the end and draw from it radical consequences (not only in regard to the economy but also in the organization of enterprises, in the role of the League of Communists, in intranational relations, etc.) or shall we remain on [the line] of etatism or at most of dwarfed self-management?[35]

Conservative forces not only opposed but also obstructed reforms which the Party as a whole had inaugurated. Soon, they found themselves on a direct collision course with the reformers, who gained the Party majority by the time of the Eighth Congress, but who did not have full control over the Party's functional mechanism. Until the Brioni meeting, the political power was held by the conservatives and their leader Aleksandar Ranković, Vice-President of Yugoslavia since 1963, organizational secretary of the Party and head of the Yugoslav secret police since the war. There were three main sources of Ranković's power and of his conservative cohorts: his absolute control of the police apparatus, his jurisdiction to appoint Party personnel, and his strong backing from the organization of war veterans. These three elements were united into a single force by Serbian nationalism, because all three of these organizations were dominated by the Serbs.[36]

On February 25, 1966, only a few months before the Brioni Plenum, Tito warned at the Central Committee meeting:

> One of the chief obstacles [to the Reform] lays within circles of the League of Communists. . . . This is not the case everywhere, but there are individual Communists who are for the reform in word, but remain passive in deed or even act counter to its intentions. . . . There is no room in the League of Communists for those who do not carry out its decisions. Let them get out.[37]

Despite such strong words of warning, Tito, at this time, did not name any obstructionists. Only a few months later, however, at the Fourth Plenum, he finally took the side of the reformists and identified Ranković as the leader of that faction which had been hampering decentralization process in the country. Finally, the well guarded image of the Party unity was broken and the conservative power center was ruptured.

The ouster of Aleksandar Ranković—who was believed to be Tito's heir apparent—together with his top aides was a major victory for the reform leaders. Tito assessed the July meeting saying that "perhaps never until now in our Party, in our League of Communists, has a single meeting or decision made such an impact as the Fourth Plenum did."[38] Others considered the ouster of Ranković to be the most important event in the country since the break with Stalin in 1948.[39] It affected numerous aspects of life in Yugoslavia, such as economic reforms, federalism, intraparty balance, republican and national relations, and freedom of expression.

One should, however, keep in mind that there had been no disagreement between the two factions on the Party's leading role in society or on its political power. The disagreement was about the question of how the monopoly of power should be implemented. Ranković and his group were for a highly centralized and hierarchical power structure, naturally, under his personal control. The liberals, on the other hand, opposed bureaucratic centralism and advocated a sharing of responsibilities through the system of self-management; but they thought it necessary for the Party to remain the only political power in the country. After the Ranković affair, the Party stressed even more its own importance "as the ideological-political force," because without it, the country and the system might be in danger.[40]

The dichotomy of self-management and power monopoly in the Party was going to remain one of the weak points of the liberals. On the one hand they fostered principles of self-management, and, on the other, continued to be self-appointed representatives of the working class. This meant that only the Party still had the right to decide what the lives of the citizens should be like. This inherent contradiction was one of the reasons why many liberals of the Ranković era, in a few years only, became neoconservatives.

The immediate cause for Ranković's fall was the discovery that the secret police under his orders had "engaged in a large-scale operation of eavesdropping and checking on individuals and institutions."[41] They had even included the offices and residences of numerous leading Communists as well as Tito's offices and bedroom.[42]

The documents from the Fourth Plenum, however, show that the real cause of Ranković's downfall was his political ambition. Tito identified the underlying issue of the crisis when he stated in his remarks "what is involved here is . . . a factional struggle, a struggle for power."[43] Although there had not been an immediate danger of Ranković's take over, evidence strongly suggests that he was preparing the way for his ascendancy.[44]

In its report to the Fourth Plenum, the investigating commission stated on the issue of power build up: "Many even serious and sensitive problems are being settled through personal contacts and authority, and not by normal, legally established channels."[45] Ranković and his circle used the secret police apparatus, which "was almost the exclusive monopoly of individuals,"[46] to organize their own network of political power. Thus, they were accused of abusing "the organs of State security in order to establish control over the entire society, from the enterprises up to the highest ranks."[47] Tito compared the situation to Stalinist times because "people had started whispering, and distrust toward each other was gaining ground from top to bottom [of the Party]."[48]

In 1962, "Tito [had] put himself unequivocally on the side of Ranković" and the conservatives.[49] Beside the fact that Tito, at the time, was still in love with "Yugoslavism" and suspicious of "republicanism," his support of Ranković was reinforced by the on going rapprochement with the Soviet Union. The relations between the USSR and Yugoslavia were strained because of the Soviet intervention in Hungary in 1956; but the split between China and the Soviets presented itself as a good occasion for Tito to get closer to Moscow. Certainly, Ranković's party line and his Serbian heritage were more acceptable to the Soviets than that of the liberals from the Western republics. At the Fourth Plenum, however, Ranković was accused of going further than being useful to Tito in his dealing with the Soviets. Milutin Baltić stated that Ranković had been creating "a policy different from that of the League of Communists on both the internal and international plan."[50] In other words, Ranković was getting close to the Soviets on his own. He was supposed to have had close contacts with the Soviet intelligence and their ambassador in Belgrade. Moreover, Brezhnev had personally intervened on his behalf after his ouster in 1966.[51]

Apart from his control of the secret policy and Party personnel, Ranković also had almost complete power over the Secretariat of Foreign Affairs, through which he controlled the appointments of ambassadors. This also helped him to establish personal contacts with foreign countries.[52] If Ranković had succeeded in coming to power, policies of centralism and etatism would have been reaffirmed once more, while, on the international level, it would have meant "abandonment of the policies of nonalignment."[53] Even though Ranković's methods and his line of political thinking were known, especially to those at the top of the Party, his opponents were not able to challenge him or his policies, as long as he had Tito's support. Only when Ranković overplayed his hand and touched Tito's authority, did he meet the end of his political life.

Why would Ranković and his supporters capitulate so easily? Allegedly, they "had the entire Party" in their hands[54] and wielded great authority. One possible explanation is that Tito really had absolute authority, which the Ranković people had to recognize and surrender to. "There is only one historic personality [in Yugoslavia], and that is comrade Tito," it was proclaimed at the Fourth Plenum.[55] Thus Ranković and his lieutenants, like so many others, became victims of their own myth making.

Implications of the Brioni Plenum

The fall of Ranković affected political life in Yugoslavia in several ways: It demystified many relations and questions in the LC and "took off the aureole of its false unity."[56] It had an impact on implementation of economic reforms and altered the "alignment of forces on which the entire system rested."[57] But most of all it profoundly affected the intra-national relations in this multi-national state. In spite of the Commission report, Tito and other participants at the Brioni Plenum tried to avoid discussing the effects of the Ranković affair on national emotions, Serbian and non-Serbian. Yet, there were concerns at the highest level about its impact on the masses because the whole atmosphere around this affair had aroused sensitive national feelings.[58] For example, the "July Plenum in Brioni was originally scheduled to be held in Belgrade, the capital of Serbia as well as of the Yugoslav federation,"[59] but it was abruptly moved to Croatia, where Tito felt safer. Also, it was the military counter-espionage service (KOS) which uncovered microphones in Tito's private quarters, the most damaging accusation to Ranković. But it happened that both, the most instrumental man from KOS in this affair, Ivan Mišković, as well as the minister of national defence, Ivan Gošnjak, were Croats, while UDBA was overwhelmingly Serbian dominated.[60]

The liberalism and conservatism in the Party had strong national connotations. The major liberal forces came from Slovenia, Croatia, and, to a certain extent, from Macedonia, while most of the conservatives were of Serbian and Montenegrin background. Although the Brioni events were "tied directly to the problem of regional economic competition,"[61] Croatian and Slovenian Party leaders were regarded as economic nationalists, even though they discussed the problem in class rather than national terms. Despite all their use of Marxist terminology the national element in matters of economic relations could not be covered up. A Croat sociologist and a loyal Titoist wrote in this sense:

> The unitaristic and hegemonistic forces were more and more linking themselves with the remnants of greater Serbian chauvinism, and by doing so they were encouraging similar remnants of narrow minded nationalism, revanchism and hegemonism among all other nations and nationalities.[62]

That the national question went beyond economic relations can be seen in the Macedonian case. Because the republic was one of the material beneficiaries of centralist policies, it would be hard to consider Macedonian nationalism as economic in nature. The republic, however, was strongly in favor of republicanism because the Macedonians, too, felt the pressure of traditional Serbian expansionist intrusions.[63]

On the national implications of the Brioni Plenum, Tito himself remarked at the end of the meeting:

> When approaching such a major problem as the one this Plenary Meeting has been dealing with, it was not easy to reach the decision to tackle it, for nobody could know for certain, what the impact on our internal life and development would be, how our people would feel about it.[64]

Clearly, Tito was uncertain about the reaction of different nations, especially of how the Serbs would react to the fall of the man who was considered the protector of Serbian interests at the top of the Party hierarchy. That is why Tito had asked Serbs to speak at the Plenum against Ranković and his actions, while Croats and Slovenes were relatively silent.

Tito's decision not to undertake any legal action against Ranković or other UDBA officials[65] and the fact that there were no purges in the Party, also had intra-national implications. Probably, he was afraid of a Serbian reaction if the accused officials were tried or purged from the Party. But to the Croatians and other dissatisfied national groups in the country this decision was yet another indication that inequality was there to stay, and that Croatian nationalism was treated as more dangerous than Serbian.[66] One observer comparing the fall of Ranković and the crisis in Croatia in 1971 concluded:

> The purge of Vice President Ranković in 1966 has been retrospectively viewed as a victory for non-Serbian nations, particularly the Albanians and the Croats; yet it has never been labelled a 'nationalist crisis.' On the other hand, the Croatian students who protested federal regulations governing the distribution of foreign currency during their strike in November 1971—an attempt at political participation—were assumed to be nationalists from the start.[67]

This is one of the reasons why Croatian party leaders in the post-Ranković era have stressed that unitarism is nothing more than greater Serbian

nationalism and a primary cause for the rise of other nationalisms. Moreover, it is even more dangerous than the centrifugal nationalisms of other
nations, specifically Croatian, because unitarism has a well organized basis
and an infrastructure in the federal government.[68]

But it should be kept in mind, that the fall of Ranković did not mean
the same thing to all Croatians. To the old unitarists it was a big blow. To
the liberals it was a victory, especially for the decentralizing reforms,
which were supposed to help eliminate economic, social, and national
problems. It was also proof to them that the Party was healthy enough
to purge itself, while continuing its revolutionary role. At the same time,
to many other Croatians, not only to the traditional nationalists but also
to a large number of the intelligentsia on the Left, the exposure of Ranković was the direct proof that the new Yugoslavia was not much different
from the old one as far as national equality and personal freedom were
concerned. They differed only in ideology. These groups saw greater-
Serbian nationalism as the essential ingredient of the issues dividing the
country. One of the best known Croatian contemporary intellectuals, a
long time Marxist, Ivan Supek, characterized Ranković's forces in the
following way:

> All these various instruments would not have been enough if he
> [Ranković] had not also made use of an old source of strength—
> greater Serbian nationalism. The promoters of his empire were
> mainly Serbian nationalists, most often wrapped in unitaristic and
> red radical slogans. His main strategy was to strengthen the central
> administration and powers of the townships, and to diminish the
> independence of individual republics—for the most part the old
> Serbian royalits politics in new circumstances.[69]

For this and similar reasons, a major goal of the Croatian national movement, in the early 1970s, was the national statehood and sovereignty in a
confederated Yugoslavia. In fact, this became one of the hottest debated
subjects of the proposed constitutional amendments in 1971. Whether
this could have been the first step to complete independence remains open.
The leaders of the national movement did argue that unity could and
should be preserved only as long as it served the interests of all nations in
the country. Therefore, the road to independence or some other combination of alliances was left open.

The reaction to the Brioni Plenum in Serbia was not as jubilant as in other parts of the country. On the contrary, it was one of dismay and disappointment. The news of Ranković's fall came "as a blow to the Serbs"[70] because he was considered the defender of their interests and the future number one man in the country. "Ranković was a great personality and well liked," was the opinion of a man on a Belgrade street, a day after the Plenum, and his attitude toward the situation was "wait and see."[71]

The change in policy also frustrated a large part of the federal bureaucracy. As a Serbian leading Party man, Milentije Popović put it mildly, "bureaucratic nationalism became a kind of fashion in the *Čaršija* [Belgrade]."[72] The Plenum decisions were seen as anti-Serbian in nature and the fall of Ranković's group was regarded as "a serious defeat and degradation for Yugoslavia's most numerous nationality [the Serbs]."[73] Even after Ranković went into political oblivion, he still remained a national symbol to the Serbs, but a reminder to non-Serbs of Serbian hegemonism. To the Serbs he was a defender of Serbian national goals. The fact that a huge crowd had attended Ranković's funeral, on August 22, 1983, and turned it into a political demonstration indicated that he had remained a powerful image in Serbia until the end of his life.[74]

In order to ease Serbian fears, all government and Party posts held by the removed officials were filled by Serbs.[75] This, as well as the leniency toward the accused officials was seen by many in Croatia as a change of form and not substance in intra-national relations in Yugoslavia. In this sense, a man in Zagreb said in his reaction to the Brioni events: "What is the difference. His [Ranković's] place will be taken by another Serb."[76] Another indication that relations had essentially stayed the same is the fact that, although out of power, the former UDBA officials continued to have good connections in the federal bureaucracy. For example, one of the leading UDBA men in the Ranković era, Radomir Lukić, "became the most prosperous private lawyer in Belgrade, and probably in the whole of Yugoslavia," because with the help of "old friends" in high places he was able to win "the most complicated cases."[77] Others ended up opening private restaurants or were "transferred to large trading corporations in Belgrade."[78] Interestingly enough, these corporations and Belgrade banks became the main targets of Croatian and Slovene complaints after the fall of Ranković, because they were the major blocks to decentralization.

UDBA Abuses

One of the most vivid causes of intra-national antipathy was the UDBA, which changed its name in 1966 to State Security Service, but continued to be known as UDBA. It had been under Serbian control from its beginnings, and as such brought to memory many police practices of inter-war Yugoslavia. For example, in the UDBA of the Ranković era Croats represented only 5 percent of its personnel, while they represented 25 percent of the country's population.[79] Anyone who was not considered loyal to the regime or to the state was harassed or persecuted in one way or another. The persecutions were felt especially strong by the Albanians in Kosovo and the Croatians. The commission investigating UDBA absues in Croatia, for example, reported that police files were kept on some 1,300,000 citizens of the republic of Croatia.[80] Its population in the early Sixties was just a little over four million. This meant, if children and old people were excluded, most of the working population was under police surveillance and considered "suspects" of anti-state activities. The number did not include the Croats outside the republic, who were traditionally considered to be even more "unreliable" than those in the republic. No wonder then that "there was elation in Zagreb"[81] after the July 1966 events. Nerkez Smailagić, a Croatian scholar and a member of the Party, wrote a few years later:

> In Croatia it [Fourth Plenum] was saluted as a defeat of conservative bureaucratism and as liberation from the nightmare of the police system. The Front of Croatian national emancipation was aware that this was a case of resistance to Great-Serbian police unitarism and not a political struggle against the Serbian people. . . . The bureaucratic-unitaristic front is not made up only of those oriented to Great-Serbianism from Serbia, but in their pretentions they were equally supported by the conservative forces from the other republics too. It has been cautioned, therefore, that unitarism is an all-Yugoslav phenomenon, but Great-Serbian hegemonism is the political essence of its ideology.[82]

Most people had known about UDBA tactics and abuses, but they were surprised that the Party came out into the open with the abuses of an organization that was once praised as the "sword of the revolution."[83]

As far as the secret police (UDBA) was concerned, it would be naive to believe that the Party leadership, including Tito, had not been fully aware of its methods and abuses of power. In most instances, they were even in agreement with its practices. Only when Ranković and his forces became a threat to thier own party line and to their positions, did they separate themselves from that organization of terror. As early as 1948 Mika Špiljak, one of the leading Party officials from Croatia, indicated in his criticism of UDBA that the nature of this organization had not been a secret. Špiljak said:

> The UDBA is pretty unhealthy. They [the UDBA officials] think that their rights are above the other Communists in the organization [Party], that they have privileged rights above other people, and that they carry the heaviest share of the work, etc. Lately, they are boasting that they are special communists, above all others.[54]

At the Fourth Plenum, Tito clearly stated that "various anomalies"—the misuse of the secret police apparatus was supposedly among them—had been discussed by the Party leadership at an earlier time already but nothing had been done. A top level meeting concerning the secret police powers took place in Split, in March 1962. What exactly went on at that gathering is still veiled in mystery and rumor. One thing is certain, a major clash took place between the reformists and Ranković's forces. The session had been secretly taped on Ranković's orders, so that it could later be used in the power struggle.[55] But most probably, the participants in the 1962 session were not free enough even to try to establish the "source" of the "anomalies," though the crimes of the secret police and the "source" of the Reform opposition was a public secret. For example, Kardelj, Tito's right hand man, had known for a long period of time that his house telephone was being "bugged," but he thought that it had been ordered by Tito.[56] This simply proves that the illegal work of the secret police was an accepted practice by the regime as a whole, and that its work must have been known to the Party leadership. Nobody questioned it because there were issues, which as Vladimir Bakarić said, "nobody was allowed to discuss" in the pre-Fourth Plenum period.[57]

It is certainly possible that the liberals, by publically exposing the major crimes of UDBA, wished to get greater public support in their struggle with the conservative forces in order to keep them on the defensive. This also might indicate that the liberals were not sure about their strength in the Party, and enlisting public support might have been helpful to their cause.

While some political, economic, and social changes did take place after the Brioni Plenum, it is also true that many of the old problems remained basically unresolved. The old centralist forces: army, war veterans, police, federal and banking bureaucracy remained intact and they continued to resist decentralization. Belgrade remained the political and economic power center. Financial control shifted from the central government to Belgrade banks; bureaucracy continued to be one of the main tools of the central government, and the police apparatus remained "omnipresent and omnipotent."[88] In Croatia, the UDBA's forces were even strengthened by new members of Serbian nationality.[89] The following statistics, published in 1970, show the national composition of the leading personnel in the SUP (formerly UDBA), which indicated that this important organization continued to be controlled by the Serbs, a fact which had not been helpful in intra-national relations. The percentages were:[90]

Serbs	61	Montenegrins	9
Croats	16	Yugoslavs	1
Slovenes	9	Others	4

Even in Zagreb, the capital of Croatia, there were 56.5 Serbs and 40.8 percent Croatians on the city police force in 1971.[91] Thus, as one foreign observer concluded, the fall of Ranković "was more a victory in appearance than in substance."[92]

The struggle against centralism and unitarism continued, however, with some important differences. Issues were discussed more openly, and the debate spilled over from the Party ranks into cultural institutions and even engaged the general public. These changes facilitated a national rebirth among the Croats, slowly growing into a national movement which culminated at the end of 1971.

CHAPTER III

GENESIS OF THE CROATIAN NATIONAL REVIVAL: THE 1960s

The relative absence of intra-national conflicts in the immediate post-war period in Yugoslavia was more the result of official unitarist policies and police suppression—which none dared oppose—than the solution of pre-war ethnic conflicts, as shown by the accusations against Ranković and his men. Also some leading Marxists in Croatia and other republics believed that, as an outcome of the socialist revolution, the national question as well as the nations themselves would "wither away." Nationalism as the product of a bourgeois world order would disappear, and class solidarity would become the foundation of the new society and country. A well known Croatian Marxist intellectual, Petar Šegedin, who believed in such a bright future, confessed:

> During the long post-war period . . . led by the elan of building [socialism] and by engaging in revolutionary changes, we did not pay special attention to national problems, believing that industrialization would solve all such old conservative problems. The factory would solve everything—it was said! It became evident, however, that the factory was not able to solve [even] its own problems. It also became clear that actually the factory and its construction had been and still were used in the interest of those forces which we thought would be prevented by that same factory.[1]

Socialism and Yugoslavism became the myths of the day. By the belief that "socialist patriotism" would eradicate the old problems and bring forth a new nation and harmonious society was false. Nationalism was quite alive under the surface and had been pushed aside rather than resolved. That is why the Eighth Congress (1964) of the LCY was forced to deal with the national question openly, and why the old unresolved problems dating back to the inter-war period surfaced once again.

There were three major social elements which played an important role in the Croatian national revival: the intellectuals, the students, and the liberal party leaders. Initially, in the late 1950s and early 1960s, there was no cohesion among these groups, but with time they became more and more a unified force which mushroomed into a mass movement, in the early 1970s.

The Early Stage of Student Nationalist Activities

In Croatia, like in many other European nations, there has been the long tradition that intellectuals and students play leading roles in national and revolutionary movements. The Croatian University in Zagreb had for a long time been a hot-bed of Croatian nationalists who fought against Hungarian and Austrian dominance during the Habsburg rule, prior to World War I, and resisted the Serbian oppression in inter-war Yugoslavia. At the same time, however, the university was also a stronghold of the Communist Party. But even for some of those on the Left, the national question was a part of their revolutionary class struggle. This becames obvious when we look at the pre-World War II history of the CPY and when we study the Communist publications of that time in Croatia.

As in the past, the first tremors to be felt on the Croatian national question in Tito's Yugoslavia came from the students A number of Croatian nationalist student groups as well as various individuals were tried and sentenced to long prison terms, during the 1950s and early 1960s, allegedly because of their work against the "people and the state." Some of the trials were held in secret, while some of the better known student nationalist groups were tried in 1954, at the end of 1956, April of 1957, September 1959, July, 1964, late 1965, and early 1966.[2] The main center of student nationalist activities was Zagreb, the Croatian capital, but similar trials were also taking place in other Croatian cities. However, those nationalist activities were not just limited to university students, but they found followers among the nation's high school students as well.[3]

The first open protest of the Croatian younger generation came on May 11, 1959, when about two thousand students took to the streets. The demonstration started at the university cafeteria in Zagreb and quickly spread to the streets, where there was a clash with city police and UDBA agents. As a result of this incident, some students were expelled from the university, a number of them were tried and jailed, and one girl was killed.[4]

This sign of discontent, coming from the generation raised in the spirit of socialism and Yugoslavism, "seriously embarrassed the Yugoslav leadership."[5] The regime blamed the "class enemy," a term which includes everybody whom the regime considers to be disloyal, for misleading the students. The pretext for the demonstrations was lack of food. Most importantly, though, the student turmoil pointed to a number of deeper issues, namely, economic, ideological, and social problems, and, in one way or another, all of these issues were tied to the intra-national relations. It was not an accident that thousands of young Croatians were escaping to the West, that most of the political trials were taking place in Croatia, and that the first student strike in the country took place in Zagreb. These and other indicators were a clear expression of Croatian national dissatisfaction and of a quest for a change.

Ideologically, the student movement in the 1950s and early 1960s was not only nationalist but also anti-Communist in nature. These two aspects were very much intertwined. Many believed that Communism was the chief enemy of their personal and national freedom. There was also the misconception that the West was very much concerned with the fate of the peoples in Eastern Europe. They accepted the anti-Communist pronouncements of the West as a true reflection of sincere political efforts. This anti-Communism did not only reflect a desire for freedom, but it also was proof of being on the "right side," which, as the popular belief was, would win sooner or later. To the members of these student groups Communism, just like the Serbian hegemony, came from the East, and the two often seemed to reinforce each other.

The regime, on the other hand, considered all those who expressed or even entertained thoughts of a nationalist nature to be remnants of the

(pre-war) Ustaša movement (and its regime during the war), and it accused
them of having contacts with the Croatian emigres and other "dark forces"
in the world.⁶ Any expression of Croatianism, even by a Communist, had
been always "identified with Ustashism, most of all to deny it all humanity."⁷

Because of the general suppression of any national manifestation and
of any open discussion of intra-national problems, the regime actually
contributed to the process of reconciliation among Croatian nationalists
and Communists. Primarily the intellectuals in the Party "were slowly
beginning to believe that the Croatian struggle [in the Partisan war] had
been swindled."⁸ This transformation began to take place in the middle
of the 1960s. The ideological divisions between those inside and outside
the Party were beginning to blur. Concerns for their nation's future
began to bring different groups closer, which meant the beginnings of a
"Croatian revolutionary-national emancipatory front."⁹ Some of the
old Croatian "Yugoslavs" and long time Communists, together with the
younger generation of Party members, began to raise their voices on behalf of their people. The old anti-Communism of the nationalists, on the
other hand, subsided. Marxists began to admit openly that the national
problem had not been solved by the revolution.

While the ideological differences among Croatians were narrowing, the
gap between the liberals and conservatives in the top leadership of the
LCY was widening, thus reflecting the basic national tendencies among
the Party leaders. This was the period when the Croatian national movement began to enter into a new phase. One of the main characteristics of
this phase is that it began to work through the existing system, emphasizing the most liberal side of its proclaimed political principles.

Party Liberals and Nationalism

During the period after Tito's break with Stalin, the old national antag-
onisms continued to simmer. At the same time, a number of other factors
were undermining Belgrade's centralism and were catalyzing the slow rise
of a national feeling even among the Communist elites. One of these factors
was self-management. Its introduction was a useful ideological means of
resisting a monolithic and dogmatic Soviet-style Communism. This ideological innovation and the break with Stalin served as an example for the

nations within Yugoslavia. These factors provided them with a legitimacy in their own quest for national individuality. One Slovene scholar observed that, on one hand, Yugoslavia, advocated an international toleration of every state and its specific needs and desires, while internally it forcefully implemented centralist policies without taking into account the needs and desires of the individual peoples within its own borders.[10] Thus, "Yugoslavism" as a cloak for unitarism was slowly rejected and national differences were officially recognized in 1964. The Party liberals, especially those from Croatia, Slovenia, and Macedonia, played an important role in this shift of emphasis.

Vladimir Bakarić, Tito's closest ally in the republic and a life-long anti-nationalist, was among the first Party functionaries in Croatia to speak openly about certain issues touching upon delicate national relations. In an interview with the editor of a leading Belgrade weekly, *Nedeljne informativne novine* (NIN), published on March 8, 1964,[11] he criticized the "old way of approaching things," acknowledged that there was the lack of a "cohesive element" among the federal units, and said that "in theory we have all rejected [the views of Pero Živković][12] but not in all practical questions . . . ." Thus, he implied that national relations had remained the same as they had been in the Old Yugoslavia. Bakarić also identified some of the underlying issues raised by the Croatians: a massive emigration to the West, unemployment, lack of economic power to create jobs, low wages, and stagnation of agriculture. He even suggested that all of the republics should have a say in the area of foreign relations, because each republic is affected differently by Belgrade's foreign policy decisions.

This interview indicates that there was a deep dissatisfaction in Croatia and in some other republics with federal policies—Slovenia, for example. The Party leadership in Croatia was feeling public pressure from below and within the Party. On this subject, Bakarić stated:

> In the matter of politics . . . the problem of the old approach to problems in Croatia, for example, is evident in a number of things. People are blaming us, here [at the republic] and are saying: You are never insisting on Croatianism, you are not concerned about the development of the Croatian nation—all for the sake of creating some kind of new thing, which very often resembles the image of Pero Živković.[13]

In a major speech on September 17, 1964, Bakarić again identified economy and nationalism as the two major problems in the country, while blaming the "old system" for most of the problems:

> The old system is desintegrating . . . no one can tolerate it any longer. The old system, in the first place . . . the centralist system of planning, has caused and is causing in its prolonged existence a whole series of dead end situations.[14]

He also spoke strongly against "republicanism" and said that newer and better ways had to be found for resolving regional differences. The "old system" was requiring the northern republics to carry a disproportionate burden in the development of other regions:

> If we want the old differences in Yugoslavia to remain, then it is the end of socialism and of Yugoslavia; it is our end too . . . . Accordingly, we have to know that our relative participation in Yugoslav production has to change . . . . We have to find the ways and means, so that our community, a socialist community, will reduce the differences without hurting anyone and will work for our mutual benefit.[15]

Because of the central economic policies a new type of nationalism was emerging which

> was no longer the work of the reaction, that is of the Ustashe or Maček's followers [former Croatian Peasant Party members] but of our nationalism. It actually grows as the result of the disintegration of the old economic system and demoralization of a certain number of people in the process of that disintegration . . . . [16]

One could argue with Bakarić about whether the economic problems and decentralization had indeed caused nationalism or whether Serbian nationalism had played an important role in Belgrade's centralist policies and thus caused the economic problems. Most likely, the growing nationalism had been a result not only of economic grievances but of a number of unsettled questions that had led to a growing gap among national groups. The process of "disintegration" was not, as Bakarić claimed, a major cause of nationalism. It merely provided a way for it to surface. As can be seen from Ranković's case, national inequality had strong influences on the decision making process even though it was not discussed openly till the Eighth Congress (1964), or more precisely until the fall of Ranković (1966). It is certain, however, given Bakarić's comments, that there was growing pressure from Croatians on republican leaders to speak for their national rights and interests. The pressure was coming not only from outside the Party, but from within; most of all from some Croatian Marxist intellectuals and former Tito's partisans.[17]

Bakarić was expressing his views a few months before the Eighth Congress of the LCY which was to be held in December of 1964. In those pre-congress months, Party liberals were putting public pressure on conservatives and sending a clear message to the top leadership that the "old system" of centralism, bureaucratism, and hegemonism, had to be changed in order to keep rising nationalists under control. Otherwise, nationalism might become a threat to the Party and unity of the state.

To Bakarić the unity of Yugoslavia was not based on some old idea of Slavic unity, but on the "social progress" of all members in the federation.[18] The "progress," however, was being stifled, according to him, in some republics, namely Slovenia and Croatia, for the sake of the progress of others. Consequently, the liberals from the northern republics demanded that the policies of self-management, decentralization, and democratization be implemented and that the old partisan guard should be replaced by a younger and better qualified personnel on all leadership levels.[19]

Thus, these "liberal" demands for decentralization and change were not an expression of "nationalism" but a response to the growing economic and national problems in the northern republics. The liberals believed with Tito that the national problem had been basically resolved; but they also believed that economic centralism and its supporters prevented the implementation of Party policies and was causing economic and national problems. The major obstacle to the advancement of "socialist progress" was bridging the gap between the proclaimed policies and their implementation. They believed that once centralism was broken and self-management implemented, nationalism would fall into its proper place.[20] The process of disintegration of nations would continue while class consciousness would be gaining strength which would then lead to the desired socialist society. This is one of the reasons why the Eighth Congress and the fall of Ranković were greeted as a victory of the liberals and considered a final blow to Belgrade centralism and bureaucratism. Centralist practices, however, would continue to haunt Yugoslavia even after the fall of Ranković, but in different ways and forms.

Although Bakarić was the first high ranking Party official who publicly attacked the Belgrade's economic centralism, he never belonged to the "nationally minded" Croatian Marxists. His remarks were the result of intra-Party struggle and of the pressures within the republic. Thus, Bakarić and the main stream Party liberals cannot be considered as the ushers of the Croatian national movement. They contributed to it, unintentionally though, by providing a more open political atmosphere in the country, which accelerated the growth of nationalism. The prime movers of the national revival were the Croatian intellectuals. For them, Croatian national struggle had been always a part of the revolution and, after their revolutionary idealism, they came to accept the fact that the nations were there to stay much longer than many had thought. Finally, in the late Sixties, a number of younger Party liberals joined the intellectuals and they too began to advocate openly the Croatian national emancipation as part of the revolutionary process.[21] At the same time, Bakarić and a number of former liberals joined the conservatives in condemning Croatian Party leadership, students, and intellectuals for demanding the full implementation of proclaimed federalism and self-management.

National Revival Among Croatian Intellectuals

On the issue of national cultures in Yugoslavia, Tito declared at the Eighth Congress (1964) of the LCY:

> The development of a common Yugoslav culture can be understood only as a free and multisided blossoming of national cultures of all our nations and nationalities.[22]

He acknowledged the fact that every nation in the country had its "national individuality in cultural creativity."[23] Diversity was strengthening and not endangering intra-national relations. He also condemned those who thought of themselves as above national cultures and who advocated "Yugoslavism" as superior to all other national identities in the country.[24]

This official acceptance of the cultural particularity of each national group was a major shift from the policy of Yugoslav cultural integralism which had been inaugurated immediately after the war and had peaked in the late Fifties. As noted above,[25] even in the early Sixties Tito was still on the side of Party conservatives, supporting economic and cultural integration. He also believed that public discussions about national cultures, which began to creep up, were "poisoning" the youth, and that there was too much freedom of expression.

> . . . We were of the opinion that nobody will get hurt if we let everybody speak and write what they want. But we have gone too far in this regard . . . we will not allow anybody to write nonsense. . . . We will not allow the rift, national antagonism and chauvinism, to spread, [that is] what's happening . . . in our education and other areas of social life. . . .[26]

On another occasion he said about the rise of nationalism in the spheres of culture:

> We have permitted that anything can be written in our papers. Look at different magazines and articles, and you will see their destructive influences. They are even poisoning our youth. Man simply gets sick seeing how chauvinism is beginning to take root even among our youth.[27]

But nationalist and liberal forces were strong enough to prevent full implementation of integralism. Realizing that there was too much opposition to "Yugoslavism" and that its enforcement was creating reaction, the Eighth Congress of the LCY acknowledged the right of every nation to preserve its own identity.

The opening salvo against "socialist realism" in culture was made by Miroslav Krleža, a long-time Marxist and leading spirit of pre-war "revisionism" in Croatia. Socialist realism, according to which art, as everyting else, should be at the service of the revolution, was introduced along with bolshevization of the CPY after Tito's return from the USSR in 1937. In his speech at the Third Congress of the Union of Writers of Yugoslavia, held in Ljubljana on October 5, 1952, Krleža openly stood against the submission of the arts to the revolution and instead advocated a synthesis of the two. Later (1979), he stated that the speech was not a true expression of his thinking, but that it was the "product of a compromise."[28]

Even though Krleža's speech dealt with ideology and artistic expression and had no apparent connection with national cultures in the country, it was a sign that traditional national cultures could no longer be ignored. Writers as well as artists in general began to turn slowly to their cultural traditions for identity and inspiration. On one hand, the link with the past was re-established; on the other hand, the resistance against official cultural "Yugoslavism" gained strength among all those who felt that the "new culture" meant slow cultural Serbification. Tito publicly complained that some "people are reverting to their own [national] history, they are starting to dig into it, and are forgetting about the future development of our socialist community as a whole."[29]

The first major public discussion on the subject of cultural integralism and autonomy took place in 1961 between a Slovene writer, Dušan Pirjevec, and a Serbian novelist, Dobrica Ćosić. Ćosić had been a well known Serbian nationalist and a strong advocate of cultural integralism and was a man who enjoyed the "personal confidence of Tito"[30] and Ranković. As might be expected, Ćosić argued that particularism had to be overcome and that a new socialist unity had to be built. Pirjevec, on the other hand, defended the need for cultural autonomy and accused Ćosić that his kind of cultural integralism carried with it Serbian centralism.[31]

There was a relatively long silence on the national question among the Croatian intellectuals. The major reason for this silence was the fact that the group had shrunk considerably in number during and after World War II. Intellectuals who were anti-Communists and those who did not support the revolution either left for the West, were killed, or were jailed in the after-war period. The remaining anti-Communist intellectuals had to keep a low profile, because the regime considered them a reactionary element in society. Thus, this group of intellectuals could not play a significant role in post-war Croatia.

The Croatian Left intelligentsia had always been divided in their views on Croatian nationalism and party centralism. While one group stood for national and social struggle and opposed the bolshevization of the Party, the other group saw everything in the light of the proletariat's pursuit of victory. A large number of Croatian Left intellectuals lost their lives during the war because they were considered a subversive element against the existing Croatian state. Strangely enough, most of the intellectuals killed during the war came from the more liberal and nationally minded wing of the Party.[32] Those who did survive, however, continued to work quietly for national rights and for autonomy within the Yugoslav socialist framework. Those intellectuals who supported the bolshevization of the Party, on the other hand, were victorious and idealized the revolution for quite some time. Acknowledging some faults in the system, they believed, however, that war and revolution were the final solution not only to class exploitation but also to the Croatian national question in general. Abuses were usually justified as being unavoidable during such an important phase in the country's socialist development. But soon a number of Marxists, some even from this second group, began to take a closer look at the reality they lived in and realized that the reality was quite different from the official proclamations and ideals they had fought for. Many of the old pre-war problems had remained, only in a different form. Finally, in the mid-Sixties, a change took place among the Croatian Left intellectuals. Now, the liberal forces were reinforced by the younger generation who tended to be highly critical of the Party's dogmatism and its unitarist policies. As a result, the liberal Left wing became the major intellectual force from which the Croatian spring of the late 1960s was born.

It seems that the discussion of the Croatian national question among the Left intellectuals began within small private circles. There was a growing feeling that the Croatian nation was being "seriously threatened: biologically, economically, politically, [and] culturally . . . . And about those feelings, the members of the League of Communists talked only in private conversations."[33] But many Left intellectuals faced the ideological dilemma of defining the role of a Left intellectual in the nation. How could they bridge the dichotomy between Communist internationalism and revolutionism and the life threatening issues that their own nation was facing. This dilemma was expressed in 1965 by one of the leading Croatian Marxist intellectuals:

> . . . Today, in the bare praxis of reality, doesn't it often mean to make a small craftsman in the administration out of the Left intellectual . . . . If we have liquidated the classes, what is this we live in? Society! But society is a concept too abstract. Naturally, by

itself, [the concept of] nation comes up and is followed right away
[by the question] : what nation? The nation that one belongs to. I
said naturally, because the classes can be liquidated (at least formally) within two or three generations, but the nation lives and will
live for a long time yet to come in the consciousness of people,
because that psychological fiction has living roots in life: language,
customs, history, etc. The nation is richer with myths than any
class, and, more so, classes most often put on national myths. That's
why it is natural that in a society which has eliminated classes
'nation' appears, with all its inventory of values. But how did we
as socialists prepare ourselves for this [process]? Not at all! . . .[34]

The conclusion is clear. The Left intellectual is a part of his people, and
if it happens that he is part of a small nation, his responsibility for the fate
of his people is even greater, whether he wants that responsibility or not.

No matter how the Left intellectual tries to put his feelings of belonging to his people as a nation, into the second or third category
[of his values], at the moment when the threat or disintegration of
his people becomes a reality, the problem of [his] responsibility
will appear with more immediate and stronger force.[35]

The Sixties were years of transition among the Croatian Left intellectuals: for many, there was a shift from earlier internationalism to a
more concrete concern with their own nation. Also, there was the growing feeling that Croatia's future as a nation was in danger. It was then
when the liberal Left stepped forward to undertake the responsibility of
defending Croatian interests in Yugoslavia and of achieving as much as
possible autonomy within the existing state and system. This autonomy,
they claimed, had already been won during World War II; but it had never
been put into practice.

130th Anniversary of the Croatian National Revival (1966)

The first occasion after the war which brought together various Croatian
national elements was the celebration of the 130th anniversary of the
Croatian National Revival. (A more familiar name for the Croatian National

Renaissance of the 19th century is Illyrian Movement.) The commemoration took place in Zagreb, on March 29-31, 1966. Sponsors for this event were the major Croatian cultural institutions: Matica hrvatska, the oldest cultural society in Croatia (established in 1842), the Yugoslav Academy of Arts and Sciences, the Croatian National Theater, the Croatian University in Zagreb, the Writers Association of Croatia, the National and University Libraries, and the Historical Society of Croatia among others. There were a number of significant indications at this celebration that a new national revival was in the making. The decision to celebrate the 130th anniversary of the movement was unusual in itself. Very seldom, if ever, were such occasions celebrated, and the list of participants and guests show how important the event was politically. For example, the Croatian Communist leaders actively participated in the celebration. Also, for the first time after the war, the leadership of the Catholic church in Croatia was invited to a government sponsored function and the response was positive. Invitations were also sent to a number of Croatian intellectuals abroad who had fled the country when the Communists took over.[36] Thus, the gathering signified a new quest for the rediscovery of the national past. Moreover, it warned various elements of the Croatian nation that time had come to work for national reconciliation and unity.

The speeches and addresses delivered during the celebration were at least as significant as the organizational conception of the event. One could notice a shift among the intellectuals to an increasing nationalist point of view. For example, Miroslav Krleža, who made the opening address, pointed out that the Illyrian movement had been only a Croatian "experiment" and, therefore, was truly a Croatian national Renaissance. While the "uncurable dreamers, the Illyrians, turned into Yugoslav romantics, liberals, uncompromising preachers of national unity,"[37] Krleža said, the others, primarily the Serbs and Bulgarians, were only interested in looking for their political advantages and in expansion and were using their language as a political instrument.[38]

It is significant that Krleža, as an old Marxist and pro-Yugoslav, agreed to be the main speaker in the celebration of national history. He was one of the more vocal Croatian Marxists for whom such commemorations were only stumbling blocks to human progress. In his younger days he wrote that all "traditions, and Renaissances, and academies . . . all that was a sick phenomenon."[39] But more important than the change of his view on the past is the fact that he was pointing out that the South Slavs had had two conceptions of "national unity": one "incurably romantic," Illyrism and Yugoslavism, and the other utilitarian–expansionist and hegemonistic. What Krleža implied is that these two elements were still present in the unified state.

The celebration is sometimes referred to as a "turning point" in the political and cultural life of post-war Croatia.[40] Possibly, this is an overstatement, but the event was definitely a significant indication that Croatian intellectuals were taking a second look at a Yugoslav political and cultural reality in which they had sacrificed too much for the sake of "brotherhood and unity."

The jubilee ended with two rather cautious messages to the public: one to the Croatians indicating a desire for national unity, and the other to the central government and the Party suggesting that the time had come for more autonomy of the individual nations in the federation.

In order to fully understand the importance of the event, however, it needs to be looked at in the wider context of the struggle between the liberals and the conservatives at that time. Although the fall of Ranković came only three months later, the celebration itself could not have been possible without the ongoing differentiation process within the Party. And most probably, the Croatian Party liberals were supporting such an event precisely because of the struggle at the top, primarily in order to put more pressure on their opponents, and not because of their Croatian patriotism. There are indications that in the eyes of the CC LC of Croatia some of the intellectuals had gone too far in their presentations at the celebration. But no one from the Party voiced complaints about the opinions expressed during the event. Only when the intellectuals went a step further and demanded constitutional changes regarding the 1954 Croatian and Serbian language agreement, the Party reacted.[41]

Declaration on the Croatian Language

As a result of the victory of the liberals at the Fourth Plenum at Brioni in July 1966, an important step was made in the process of liberalization. Since the government had openly admitted that some nations and nationalities were treated differently from the others and because people were given more freedom of expression, nationalism finally had a chance to surface. Even high ranking Party officials such as Miko Tripalo argued against the conservatives that democratization did not cause nationalism, but that it "only made it possible for the existing problems and contradictions to appear in a clearer form at the surface of political life."[42]

Despite the attempts of leading "liberals" to keep discussions about intra-national problems wrapped in Marxist phraseology and under their control, other national forces in Croatia actually began to talk more in national instead of class terms. They pointed out that certain issues, especially those between the Serbs and Croats, had to be discussed openly and that without their resolution true equality and socialism was not possible. Direct political questions, however, were still untouchable, especially those of intra-national nature. For example, Mihajlo Mihajlov's attempts (1966) to establish an opposition paper and to organize an opposition party, was a struggle on a purely ideological level. It had very little to do with the national question directly, except that he was essentially an advocate of integral Yugoslavism.[43]

The first open manifestation of nationalism by Croatian intellectuals was in the field of language. The "Declaration Concerning the Name and Position of the Croatian Literary Language" was signed in Zagreb on March 16, 1967, and was published a day later in *Telegram,* Zagreb's cultural weekly.[44] It was endorsed by nineteen Croatian cultural institutions, by literary and learned societies, as well as by 130 leading intellectuals, and more than 70 of them were members of the League of Communists.[45] According to the Declaration, the Novi Sad Agreement (1954), which combined the Croatian and Serbian languages into Serbo-Croatian or Croato-Serbian, and the Constitutional provisions concerning the languages were too fuzzy in their formulations. It also pointed out that Serbian was favored as the "state language," while Croatian "[was] disregarded and it [was] being reduced to the status of a local dialect." The signers of the document proposed Constitutional changes which would guarantee the equality of "the four literary languages: Slovene, Croatian, Serbian, and Macedonian," as well as of the minority languages.[46]

Two days after the publication of the Declaration came a reaction from the Serbian Writers Association, a document entitled "Proposal for Consideration." The signers of the Proposal basically accepted the Croatian suggestions; but at the same time they went further and demanded full linguistic and cultural independence for the Serbs in other republics, especially in Croatia. The goal was to bring the Serbs under the Belgrade tutelage.

The Communist leadership declared that the real goal of the Declaration was not the equality of the languages, but "to show in a twisted light the intra-national relations in our country" and that it was "a political diversion" against the state. The signers of the Declaration were accused of nationalism, chauvinism, and "political blindness." They were said to be only interested in "their own political goals" and were thus working against the revolution. Moreover, the Communist leadership accused the signers of being involved with the "foreign services" and of "stabbing [the Party] in the back."[47] But despite all these condemnations, the Party leadership in Croatia acknowledged the fact that certain cultural problems did indeed exist. At the Seventh Plenum (April 19-20, 1967), Miko Tripalo, Secretary of the EC CC LC of Croatia and a harsh judge of the Declaration stated:

> It is certain that the Declaration cannot be looked at as an isolated act. The nationalist climate and dissatisfaction is in question. This climate has been slowly gaining strength, especially in the field of culture. Certain bases for this, even though without justification, are found in the unsuccessful resolution of numerous questions in areas outside economy, especially in the area of culture.[48]

Both documents, the Croatian Declaration and Serbian Proposal, and their signers were put into one category and were condemned by the Party as negative nationalistic deviations which had to be destroyed. They "were two fingers of the same hand which had to be cut off together, because they [were] threatening the foundations of our society, for which the best sons of our people gave their lives."[49] There were calls for stiff punishments. A "liberal" newsman in Belgrade told a *New York Times* correspondent regarding the Declaration:

> It is even better that a few persons be killed than that thousands die in the kind of war that would occur here if there were even an effort to split Yugoslavia according to national lines.[50]

But, at least on the surface, the severity of the punishment did not correspond to the sharpness of verbal attacks on the Declaration and those who stood behind it. This does not mean that the signers of the Declaration did not undergo personal and professional hardships because of their action. Some were removed from their professional positions, those who were Party members were reprimanded and as many as ten were expelled from the Party.[51] Also, the best known individual among the signers, Miroslav Krleža, resigned from the Central Committee of the LC of Croatia.[52] But no one was put on trial or jailed because of the Declaration.

There might have been another dimension, however, to the Declaration story which was not so apparent. Although Tito declared that the Party did not have any foreknowledge about the Declaration, there are indications that some high Party officials in Croatia and the secret police knew that the Declaration was being prepared.[53] The Party did not stop its publication because it wanted to use the Declaration for its own balancing act: Ranković's fall in the summer of 1966 had to be counterbalanced half a year later with a hit on, what the Party called, the nationalist "hot spots" in Croatia. The "hot spots" were the Matica hrvatska, the Association of writers of Croatia, the Institute of History of the Workers' Movement in Croatia, and the Matica iseljenika Hrvatske (the republican institution for contacts with the Croatian emigrants). It was not by accident that the worst attacks were made on the two institutions which had nothing to do with language itself, the Institute and the Matica iseljenika. The head of the Institute, Dr. Franjo Tudjman, a former partisan general and an historian, was expelled from the Party and lost his teaching position at the Political Faculty of the Croatian University in Zagreb. He and his followers were removed from the institute. At the same time, another partisan general and head of the Matica iseljenika, Većeslav Holjevac, came under special Party attack. Both of these were the leading figures of the "nationally conscious" wing of the Party in Croatia. Holjevac was well known for his opposition to Belgrade's unitaristic policies. As a high official of the republican Party and former mayor of Zagreb, he had tried to protect Croatian interests as much as he could. He was also the author of the controversial book *Hrvati izvan domovine* (The Croatians Outside Their Homeland) which was published the same year Holjevac fell from grace. Tudjman, a historian, had been a particular problem to the regime. In his research he had pointed out that the real cause for the break up of the First Yugoslavia was the Serbian hegemonism, and he also indicated that the national policies in the Second Yugoslavia did not correspond to the goals and promises agreed upon during the partisan war. Gradually, the Institute had become a major, and possibly the only, critic of the official version of the Party history (1963), and this created a bitter polemic within the Party.[54]

In this respect, the Declaration had a negative effect in Croatia; some of the leading intellectuals were silenced and pushed out of the Party. But on the whole, it had a major positive impact in the development of the Croatian national movement. The demands of the Declaration were not as important as its implications and the reactions to it. The document was supported by a large number of top Croatian Communist intellectuals and it was published outside the Party framework. Obviously, the supporters of the Declaration thought that the Party in Croatia was not able or willing to achieve full cultural equality for the Croatians in the federation. Thus, they were looking for alternative channels to raise this question. Despite the vehement attacks of the Party, none of the signers withdrew his support for the document. In fact, the Party's assaults may have even strengthened the opinion that, at the present moment, equality was unattainable. The assumption that once Ranković was gone, even major issues could be discussed openly was obviously wrong. The Party still held firmly to the monopoly of power and would not allow any outside initiatives, especially in touchy areas as the national question. Clearly, there had been no major change in the system.

As far as the language issue was concerned, it remained on the national stage even after the storm about the Declaration has passed, it only "remained off the front pages" for a while.[55] Only three years later Croatian intellectuals looked at the Declaration as a weak but positive document that had played an important role in the process of Croatian national revival.

Today [1970], when there should not be any taboo themes if they are of public interest, we can with clear conscience say that the Declaration, with all that it did not say and with its vagueness, as a final result brought positive fruits. At the time when manifesting even Croatian nationality was being hindered, the Declaration was the first to point out the fact that the Croatian language had been manipulated as with a language of a nation which is under [foreign] domination.[56]

The Novi Sad Agreement was formally revoked by the Croats in 1971,[57] but after the purges of 1972 the act was denounced by the new policy makers. The Declaration had a profound impact on the future development of the Croatian national movement. It was the first time since the war that the Croatian national question was put to the public for discussion. It was also a united action of the Croatian Communist and non-communist intellectuals on behalf of their nation. With this act the Left intellectuals had stepped to the forefront of a new national movement that had already been in the making, and, only a few years later, some of the Party leaders who had condemned them, for example, Tripalo, joined in with even more radical demands.

The Case of Hrvatski Knjizevni List
(Croatian Literary Gazette)

Almost exactly a year after the signing of the Declaration on language, an independent Croatian literary monthly began to be published in Zagreb, *Hrvatski književni list* (HKL). The paper, a kind of sensation from the start, was the first fully independent paper in the country since World War II. Readers of the paper fell neatly into two camps: they either praised it or condemned it. Both sides, however, agreed that the paper, even in its short existence (April 1968–October 1969), had an important impact on the development of the Croatian national movement. It also made a significant contribution to the events which led to a relatively open discussion about the unresolved economic, cultural and even political relations of Croatia to the federation.

The publisher of the paper was the Association of Independent Writers— TIN, an organization founded in 1968 upon the unification of three smaller groups of artists: the independent group of writers—TIN, the Society of Worker writers, and a small circle of writers who were in the process of froming an independent group but decided instead to join the TIN group.[58] The name TIN was taken in honor of a Croatian poet, Tin Ujević (1891- 1955), who was well known for his bohemian life style and sharp criticism of everything that restrained freedom of the human spirit. The paper declared: "This is why we follow Tin. The colors of our flag are the magnitude of the Word, and power of the Letter; true Love, and freedom of Truth."[59]

A number of characteristics distinguish this group of writers and their paper from other literary circles in Croatia at the time. This was the first independent paper in the country, published without any institutional or government support. It was also the first to be identified as Croatian in name itself. In its first issue the publishers stated:

> The title of our paper clearly defines its [Croatian] identity and its initiators, but we explicitly emphasize that its pages are wide open to all.[60]

And a number of writers from other republics and nationalities did contribute to it during its short existence. The paper also stressed its closeness to the common people, and it opened its pages to literary talents who were not acceptable to the cultural establishment. It criticized older literary papers and their writers for being in "an ivory tower" and away from the cultural needs of the people. Because of their snobbery, Croatian culture had been losing ground and its tradition.

> We ask who are the guilty ones? The immediate creators of such a cultural climate are sailing today on the Adriatic. They are buying baroque furniture or are immersing themselves in cabalistic texts; to them everything is boring, about disappointments we will not even talk.[61]

The editors of the new paper believed that the existing literary publications in Croatia were ignoring national heritage and local talent, while showing off their cosmopolitanism, by paying too much attention to foreign writers and literary trends. In their program they announced:

> We, in contrast to some other attempts, are starting in another direction—the opposite way—from the national toward the international.[62]

It was also stressed that their goal was to raise the cultural level of the Croatian people, not by rejecting the nation's heritage but by building on old foundations.

> Culturally inferior people are not able to cooperate on an equal basis with other peoples. Its relation will remain inferior! That is why we firmly stand in the defense of traditions and consider its affirmation our main goal.[63]

Socialism was accepted by these young writers, but they praised a different kind of socialism than the one they lived in.

> Socialism is on our hearts, the real one, the inspired human life in socialism, full of beauty and justice; the one which our forefathers wanted for us, life free of insinuations by its enemies! We are for truth and victory of true self-management, where we will truly govern with our voice in our realm. We are not for social reform in word only, we are for the reform of human relations . . . . [64]

The HKL attempted to close the existing gap between different social, regional, ideological and even ethnic gaps in Croatia. The members of the board ranged from the best known Croatian composer of this century, Jakov Gotavac, to worker and peasant writers. They resided in different places in the republic and came from various religious and ideological backgrounds: Catholic, Orthodox, Muslim, Marxist, and non-Marxist.

The paper covered a variety of subjects which other cultural literature or school text books had ignored since the war. It provided an opportunity for the younger generation of Croatians to discover their national heritage. But beside unveiling the past, the paper slowly began to deal with current problems. A number of touchy issues were brought to the public's attention: a massive Croatian emigration, the economy, division of "surplus of labor," etatism, resolutions of the Ninth Party Congress of the LCY, and the World War II victims among others.[65] The problem of language was mentioned in one way or another in most of its nineteen issues. Actually, what broke the camel's back in the eyes of the regime, as far as the paper was concerned, was an article published in November 1969 on the use of language in the Yugoslav armed forces by Jaka Avši], a retired army brigadier general from Slovenia.[66] That was the pretext for banning the paper.

The board of Republican Fund for Advancement of Cultural Activities refused to grant any financial aid to the paper, though all other cultural publications in the country were subsidized. In its explanation for refusal the board denounced the "conceptual and esthetical orientation of the paper,"[67] but without giving any specific objections to the paper's content. The publishers made public and legal appeals in response to the verdict, but all their efforts were in vain. It was clear that the Party stood behind all decisions.

The paper, however, proved that it could exist on its own. In its nineteen months of existence, its circulation tripled, from 12 to 35 thousand copies, which was "far more than all other literary journals combined in Yugoslavia."[68] Even Party officials publicly acknowledged that "the circulation of the HKL was growing and that phenomenon should be examined."[69]

HKL was discussed at a number of Party meetings including those of the Central Committee of the LC of Croatia. The paper was unanimously condemned at all of them. At one such meeting it was declared that "some papers and magazines" in Croatia, "especially the HLK," insist

on a re-evaluation of the recent Croatian cultural and political past. *Hrvatski književni list,* from issue to issue, publishes treatises from cultural history in which it is trying to correct the judgments of the Communist Party of Yugoslavia about some important persons from the political life in Croatia till the unification [of Yugoslavia] and in the inter-war period. On the other side, in *Hrvatski književni list, Kolo, Kritika,* [the last two were literary magazines published by Matica hrvatska] and also in some other magazines there is not a word about the activities of Marxist intelligentsia in the inter-war period . . . .[70]

Although the official reaction to the appearance of HKL was one of condemnation, Party leadership did not ban the paper immediately or confront the publishers with trials and jail. This was a major departure from traditional dealings with "nationalist elements." The bulk of public confrontation with the paper was "delegated" to those who were "paid to write,"[71] to the Zagreb Committee of the LC, and to other groups under Party control. Their duty was to discredit the paper on intellectual, esthetic and ideological levels. One of their chief accusations was that the paper dealt only with ghosts from the past and not with present needs and problems. But once the paper began to discuss contemporary problems, especially economic ones, it was attacked for meddling in political issues."[72]

The strongest attacks on the paper, as well as on the alleged rise of nationalism, came from Miloš Žanko, vice-president of the Yugoslav Federal Assembly at the time, a Party "conservative" from Croatia. His vehement onslaught, however, came without the blessing of the republican Party leadership. He wrote a series of articles in the Party organ *Borba* immediately before the Third Plenum of the CC LC of Croatia (February 21, 1969). It was obvious that he was not only condemning the alleged rise of nationalism but also putting pressure on the Central Committee in Croatia to change its liberal policy. Eventually, these articles and another series (November 17-21, 1969) would cost him his political career.[73]

Even though the Central Committee condemned the paper, and the Zagreb League of Communists in July 1969 declared that the paper "has formulated ideas and a political program directly opposed to the policies of the League of Communists,"[74] its publication continued. The Party's new method of dealing with the situation was expressed by an official when at a Zagreb May 1969 meeting on "socio-political questions" that the Party must face "certain problems" and influence them "not by decrees, but more often by contacts, arguments, and confrontations."[75] Because of these tactics the paper and its supporters experienced constant "confrontations" which were blatant harassment. For example, the post office sometimes "failed" to deliver the paper, and teachers would caution students not to read it.[76] *Borba* announced that workers in various print shops in Croatia refused to print the paper because of its anti-socialist ideological content, and for that reason, *Borba* alleged, its printing site was changed four times, ultimately moving to Ljubljana, capital of Slovenia. HKL, however, maintained that it had excellent relations with workers but was required to change printers in Croatia for financial reasons and strikes in printing plants. The paper also accused "police and administrative" officials of putting pressure on the printers in order to prevent its publication.[77] But when the paper ceased publishing in October 1969, it was alleged that workers in the name of self-management refused to print it. Hence Savka Dapčević-Kučar, president of the Central Committee LC of Croatia, boasted at the Tenth session of the CC LC of Croatia (1970) that the paper "died without being [officially] banned." This confirmed the belief among "liberals" that the new Party tactics worked.[78] But in 1974 one high Party official in Croatia openly stated that the paper had been practically "banned."[79]

The *Hrvatski Književni list* had a significant impact on the development of the Croatian national movement in the 1960s. In a sense, it tested the waters before the movement got into higher gear after the Fourth Plenum of the CC LC of Croatia in January 1970. It is interesting to note that the paper did not attract open support among most of the best known names in contemporary literary life in Croatia, as the Party leadership was proud to point out.[80] But neither did they come out against it. There are several possible explanations why the Croatian cultural establishment as a whole did not lend its name to the HKL. As explained earlier, the paper separated itself from the establishment from its beginning. After the affair with the Declaration, the leading intellectuals and institutions possibly held back in order to see what would happen to the new paper and the individuals associated with it, individuals who were younger in age and less known. But even more importantly, HKL, while accepting socialism as its ideal, was very critical of socialism as implemented in Croatia. At the same time, mainstream Croatian intellectuals and the liberal wing of the Party came closer and began to work from the same platform. For this reason, the president of the CC LC of Croatia was able to report to the Tenth Plenum that

> . . . not only from the time of the so called Declaration until now [nationalist] matters were not getting worse, but on the contrary, the communications and contacts of the Central Committee LC of Croatia and the LC with the cultural and intellectual workers have increased. This has taken place not because of some departure of the Central Committee from the principles of its political platform, on the contrary, [this has taken place] because this platform has been accepted by an ever increasing number of people.[81]

It seems, the Party moved closer to the liberal intellectuals and as a result, a common platform was formulated at the Tenth Plenum. But soon after the Plenum rift began to occur between the intellectuals and some liberals, as well as among the Party liberals themselves, over the interpretation and implementation of that platform. To one liberal wing of the Party, intellectuals were going too far and thus perceived as a threat to them and to the system as a whole.

Without minimizing the significance of the HKL and its influences on the Croatian public in general, one should keep in mind that, long before its appearance, the more established Marxist intellectuals had been trying to bring out Croatian grievances through the existing institutions. A major difference between the HKL and the other intellectual circles was that the HKL was oriented toward the general public, while other Croatian journals were of a more scientific nature and, therefore, of a much more limited scope. Writers like the late Miroslav Krleža, the best known Croatian writer of this century, Petar Šegedin, Marijan Matković, Ivo Frangeš and the historians Franjo Tudjman and even Vaso Bogdanov, a Serb from Voivodina living in Croatia, were, among others, well known names among the Left intellectuals who contributed to the Croatian national revival in the late Sixties. Periodicals like *Forum,* started by Krleža (1962) and published by the Academy of Arts and Sciences in Zagreb, *Putevi revolucije,* published by the Institute for the History of Workers Movement in Croatia, under Tudjman's leadership, and a cultural weekly, *Telegram,* published numerous artices touching the Croatian question. Many of the articles dealt with the problems and injustices of the past, mostly from the inter-war period, but by doing so, they were pointing to similar unsolved questions in the post-1945 era. Intellectual circles like these were putting pressure on the republican leadership to discuss the question of national rights and (in)equality. Their activities had already been felt at the Party's VIII Congress (1964), which reopened the touchy nationality question.

In the late Sixties, new cultural periodicals appeared dealing with economic, cultural, and historiographical problems. But these periodicals had a firmer ground to stand on than independent papers like the HKL. Their publishers were organizations like Matica hrvatska and the Writers Association of Croatia, and their contributors were leading professors at the Croatian university in Zagreb and other intellectuals, many of them active members of the Party. In May 1969, a major Belgrade paper wrote about the situation among the Croatian intellectuals:

The literary periodicals abound, more than ever in the post-war period, with political and economic treatises, which speaks not only about a major interest of the writers for political and economic affairs in our country, but also about a desire to have an important influence on those affairs. Of these efforts in Croatia, especially noticeable are the editorial boards of [journals] *Kolo, Kritika, Dometi, Dubrovnik,* and definitely, *Hrvatski književni list.*[82]

In the late Sixties, Matica hrvatska, an old cultural institution with a well established national tradition, gathered different intellectual circles and generations and became, once again, the leading force of the Croatian national revival.

All of these shifts and changes did not go unnoticed by the Party. One official stated:

Major attention should not be paid to [HKL], even though it is very aggressive at this moment. . . . A serious notice must be directed toward the ideological battle against major bearers of the nationalist and chauvinist phenomena which are coming to surface in *Kritika, Kolo* [publications of Matica] and some other journals.[83]

One semi-official interpretation of the events in Croatia in the late 1960s is that there was a planned coordination between various nationalist groups in the republic. In that "conspiracy" *Hrvatski književni list* served as a diversion while other forces, namely those around Matica hrvatska, were better organized.

It can be stated that *Hrvatski književni list* for a certain period of time did really attract the attention of the public and the League of Communists, while [at the same time] Matica hrvatska, that is its central office in Zagreb, and the governing board of the Writers Association of Croatia did not draw any serious attention upon themselves. But, exactly in those institutions and precisely at that time, the nationalistic orientation was being formed and was getting wider and was expressed more fully than at the time of the Declaration (1967).[84]

The major significance of the new Croatian publications was that they served as a catalyst in the differentiation process within the Party. On the one hand, it was Žanko and the conservatives who led the attacks on the HKL and on the growth of the national movement in general. On the other, there were the liberals, including Bakarić, who were relatively silent on the issue at this time. The "liberals" regarded unitarism a greater threat to the country and to the system than an open discussion of national history and intra-national relations. The head-on confrontation between the two factions came during the Tenth Plenum, when the liberals won the battle over the conservatives. At this meeting, as at many before and after, the national question was the decisive issue over which the Party leadership would split.

Tenth Session of the CC LC of Croatia

From the Fourth Plenum of the CC LCY, in July 1966, until the Tenth Session of the CC LC of Croatia, held January 15-17, 1970, the process of decentralization had been progressing steadily. The Chamber of Nationalities in the Federal Assembly, which met for the first time in December 1966, began to play an increasingly stronger role in the federal government. By 1971 it became the most important component of the Assembly.[85] The Ninth Congress of the LCY (March 11-15, 1969) formalized the already achieved powers of the republics and of the devolution of the federation.[86] It also strengthened further the path of decentralization by making some important institutional changes. The number of Presidium memberships was raised from 34 to 45. Its members were to be elected by the republican Parties and not selected by the center as in the past. This was one of the reasons why the Congresses of the individual republics were to be held before a joint congress of the League of Communists of Yugoslavia. Each republic had six delegates, each province three, and the Army three seats in the Presidium.[87] The presidents of the republican Central Committees of the LC became ex officio members of the Presidium. The fifteen member Executive Bureau was elected by the Presidium among its own members. The Party members were given more freedom to disagree with official decisions, but not to work against accepted policies. The republican parties had more autonomy in their respective republics and autonomous provinces, while nationality problems could be discussed more openly. The Ninth Congress, one could say, was the final result of the process which had started after the fall of Ranković in 1966. A high ranking Party official from Serbia claimed that the Congress was a victory "of the democratic and anti-bureaucratic [Party] line" which had been introduced after the Fourth Plenum in 1966.[88] Not everything, however, went smoothly during this period. There had been ideological and national clashes, as well as major international pressures. The conservatives did not totally disappear from the political scene after Ranković's fall. They were still an influential group at all levels of the Party and government hierarchy. Their main concern was the alleged growth of centrifugal forces in the country, not only of nationalism but of federalism and decentralization in general.[89]

A group of younger Marxist intellectuals who gathered around the Zagreb journal *Praxis* called for a return to the original Marx and advocated "criticism of everything that exists."[90] They clashed with official Yugoslav Marxism and were directly attacked by Tito. The journal was temporarily suspended shortly after the fall of Ranković in 1966.[91] There was also student unrest in June 1968 in Belgrade and other universities. Students called for the introduction of "true Marxism" and for a clean up in the existing bureaucratic system. These phenomena, though coming from the socialists, were considered destructive because they did not suggest to solve the country's problems through "existing self-managing and political institutions."[92]

Also, clashes between republican economic interests were increasingly surfacing for public discussions. The Slovene road affair is a good example of the on going intra-republican conflicts. There had been an agreement between the World Bank and Yugoslavia, in 1969, to get a loan for road construction in Slovenia, Croatia, and Macedonia. But, in July 1969, the Federal Executive Council decided not to give the allocated share to Slovenia. Because of strong anti-federal reaction in Slovenia, the decision, however, was rescinded. Still, the whole affair had initiated strong accusations of republican egoism.[93]

Even at the Ninth Congress itself the economic interests and "alienation of the surplus of labor" was an important issue. Most of the suggestions for solving economic problems that came from Croatia had not been accepted. The main reason for the rejection was that money should be kept and controlled by those who earned it. Thus, Croatian observers of the Congress concluded that centralized economic means would continue to be, more or less, used to transfer surplus of labor from some republics into others, but in a new way and under a new pretext.[94]

On the international level, beside the usual balancing act between the East and West, the invasion of Czechoslovakia by the Warsaw Pact forces in August 1968 had pushed the Party to look for the people's support. One way of getting this support was by giving a little more room for individual and national expression. Franjo Tudjman, a Croat historian and former Tito general, concluded:

> The Soviet occupation of Czechoslovakia . . . and reconfirmation of the Yalta agreement concerning Yugoslavia meant an external threat to its sovereignty. Thus, the aim was to settle internal affairs and satisfy national-federalistic aspirations in order to strengthen the position externally.[95]

The Soviet actions in 1968 had also been used by the regime to prove that if federalization would go too far, the Soviets might move in to save socialism in Yugoslavia. Thus, it was better to have Yugoslav centralism than Soviet occupation. This was one of the main reasons why, in 1971, the regime as well as other forces which saw the Croatian national movement as a threat to the *status quo* tried to connect the Croatian Party leadership with the Soviets.[96] For internal as well as external reasons, the Soviet threat to Yugoslavia was blown out of proportion whenever needed, even though there had been no clear signs that the Soviets intended to march into the country.

Unlike in other republics, the two Party factions in Croatia, were on a collision course not only over the process of federalization but most of all over the issue of Croatian nationalism. The conservatives considered the alleged growth of nationalism the greatest threat to Party and country. The liberals believed that, even though there had been some excesses in this area, the nationalist forces were weak and disoriented, and unitarism was a real danger. The showdown between the two forces came at the Tenth Plenum of the CC LC of Croatia (January 1970).

The immediate reason for the Plenum was a second series of articles written by Miloš Žanko and published in *Borba* (November 17-21, 1969), in which Žanko vehemently attacked alleged Croatian nationalism in all its manifestations. The articles were alarming and implicitly accussed the Croatian Party leadership of allowing nationalist forces to arise. In her main address at the Plenum, Dr. Savka Dapčević-Kučar, president of the CC LC of Croatia, indicated what was involved in Žanko's attacks:

> What is really hidden behind his [attack], having in mind that a comrade at a very high political function is in question? Fears spread among some not well-informed people, among some old partisans cadres, among some people in Serb communities [in Croatia], where horrors of the recent past are still very much alive. Such description of matters could create an impression that nationalism is flaring up in Croatia and that the leadership is permitting it. This could have extremely negative consequences.[97]

As far as nationalism was concerned, the president and the Plenum as a whole took a middle of the road position. Both nationalism and unitarism were condemned as two sides of the same coin.

> While [unitarists] deny altogether the need for national equality, [nationalists] approach the national question from bourgeois positions. Neither do they look at it nor do [they] try to solve it within the context of socialist relations in our country. Also they do not understand its relationship to class.[98]

The liberals, however, concluded that

> Communists, as the avantgarde of the working class, are an intrinsic part of their people, so they cannot be freed from the feeling of belonging to their nation.[99]

The speakers at the Plenum also noted that Croatian nationalism had been judged differently than other nationalisms in the country.

> [The unitarists] panic in fear just from the use of the word Croat, Croatian, Croatian language or the like . . . .

. . . There are people even today who are perturbed when the Croatian name is mentioned, when the 'Lijepa naša' (Croatian national
anthem) is played . . . when renovation of the Croatian national
theatre is being discussed etc.[100]

To the liberals there was "no nationalism which could be more pleasant or
less dangerous." Both kinds of nationalism, separatism and unitarism, were
dangerous, but at the current time, unitarism was a larger threat than
separatism.[101] They also believed that the solution to national problems
was not to be found in administrative measures but in solving those problems which had given rise to national grievances. The reforms of the 1960s
and their implementation were the true answer to intra-national problems.
Moreover, the Party as the avantgarde of the working class and as an integral part of the nation had been and had to continue to be the only institution to guide the implementation of those reforms.

As a result of the Tenth Plenum, Žanko was stripped of his government
posts and even his closest friends, ideological sympathizers, and followers
openly condemned him. But most importantly, the Plenum was at least a
temporary defeat of unitarism in Croatia.[102] Apart from condemning
unitarism, the session legitimized in the eyes of the Croatian people
demands for economic changes and national equality. Furthermore, the
Plenum was considered a "turning point in the history of the Croatian
party" because its leadership began to take on a more national coloring
than in the past.[103] From then until December 1971 even the unitarists
had to pay lip service to the spirit of the Tenth Plenum. The young leaders
at the top began to come even closer to the point of view of the Croatian
intellectuals, while some others from the liberal camp joined conservative
forces in a relatively short period of time. With Tito's help the Croatian
leadership was toppled and the democratic process was stopped in December 1971.

CHAPTER IV

CROATIAN NATIONALISM AND
YUGOSLAVIA'S ECONOMY

It has frequently been assumed that the main causes of national antagonism in Yugoslavia, and therefore the main obstacles to its unity, have been religious and cultural prejudices among its peoples, especially among the Croatians and Serbs.[1] But what often seemed an extreme dedication among the Croatians to the national past has been a defensive mechanism in the struggle for national self-preservation. National enmity has more often been the result of political, cultural, and economic inequalities rather than of some primordial hatred or mere romantic nationalism. Apart from the historical heterogeneity among the nations in Yugoslavia, there are certain unresolved issues which have been causing national grievances, especially among the Croats, ever since the establishment of the South Slavic state. For example, the question of the economic exploitation of Croatia was an important part of the Croatian national movement in the Sixties and early Seventies. This does not mean, however, that the primary cause of nationalism is economic. Economic issues played a major role in pointing out the national inequality in the country, but the roots of Croatian nationalism lie much deeper, that is, in national history and in a desire to assert itself in the modern world. Economic issues also helped to draw a large number of the Party members in Croatia into a debate of intra-national relations, which brought them closer to the nationally conscious Croatian Marxists and the more traditional nationalists.

The National Question and
Yugoslav Economic Policy Since 1918

Before various regions in the newly organized South Slav state (1918) became a single political and economic unit, there existed important economic diversities among them. For example, they had different economic structures, levels of development, sizes of markets, and diverse economic experiences in general. The former lands of Austria-Hungary—Slovenia, Croatia, Bosnia and Hercegovina, and the Vojvodina—had been among the least developed parts of the former empire. In 1918, however, they became the most developed regions of the new state; but the size of their market and their chances for economic growth diminished considerably. After having been part of a large empire, they ended up in a relatively small state. On the other hand, for the eastern parts of the state, especially for the former Kingdom of Serbia, economic opportunities grew and the size of the market increased. In addition, Serbia came out of the Great War on the victors' side, while the former Habsburg regions had fought on the losing one. Because of all the political and economic changes, and because of certain psychological effects of those changes, the new state was seen in a diverse light by the different nations within it. The late Rudolf Bićanić, a well known Croatian economist, summarized the results of the changes as follows:

> Self-congratulations on one side and disappointment on the other were to be at the root of many tensions in the future between those [Serbs] who considered it their sacred mission to consolidate their war gains and build up a self-contained (autarchic) Nation State, and those [Slovenes and Croatians] who felt more or less clearly that the development of the country's economy required larger markets and a wider extension of economic forces than the Yugoslav frontiers permitted. The former developed a sense of economic xenophobia, originating in an inferiority complex about underdevelopment and insecurity caused by fear of foreign competition. The later considered themselves able to meet foreign competition on an equal footing in specialized fields of production, as had been the case before 1914, and they favored an open economy which would trade with foreign countries on a wide scale. This struggle between

two conceptions continued through the inter-war period and even after the socialist revolution.[2]

Even though Croatia and Slovenia were economically and culturally more advanced, they shared very little political power in the new state. This was especially true for Croatia whose major political leaders refused to accept the centralized type of government and the inferior role in the state. The Croatian Peasant Party, which became the major political force in the Croatian national movement of the 1920s, remained in opposition to the regime almost for the entire inter-war period. All political and military powers, for example, were held by the central government located in Belgrade and thus were controlled by the Serbs. For example, in 1938 there were 165 active generals in Yugoslavia. Only two were Croats and two Slovenes, while 161 were Serbs.[3] Similar nationality proportions were reflected in the major government ministries and administration.[4] These powers were then used not only for political oppression but also for economic exploitation of the "newly acquired territories." As a result of such economic and political policies, the national problems in inter-war Yugoslavia rose steadily until they reached a bloody climax in the breakup of the country, in 1941.

The first Yugoslavia was an overwhelmingly agricultural land. For example, in 1941 over 86 percent of the population lived in villages and only 13.9 percent in towns.[5] After Serbia had gained its autonomy, in 1815, its ruling class engaged more in trade than in industrial development.[6] On the other hand, when the South Slav Kingdom came into being, most of the industry was located in former parts of Austria-Hungary. In 1918, former Habsburg regions had 1,733 industrial plants with 125,263 workers and Serbia, Montenegro, and Macedonia had only 328 plants with 30,255 workers.[7]

Croatia was the strongest economic unit at the time, not only in industry but also in banking, export, import, and other fields.[8] For example, in 1925, when her share in the population was around 27 percent, her participation in industry was 33, agriculture 28, cattle breeding 30, forestry 38, crafts 30, trade 27, and banking 49 percent.[9] However, right after the unification, Belgrade's government introduced economic policies which were not necessarily good for the country as a whole, and especially not for the regions of the former Habsburg empire. The main goal of the ruling oligarchy became to improve Serbia's economic status and to make Belgrade not only the center of the political life but also of financial power. Behind all this was the Serbian ruling clique, known as *čaršija*, which strived for improving its own financial positions.[10] The following economic policies are the direct proof of this kind of political behavior: an unfair exchange of the former Austro-Hungarian crown for the Serbian dinar, inequitable taxation laws, investment policies, public works, foreign debt repayments, banking, and state monopolies,[11] to mention only a few. The state became the "biggest capitalist . . . employing more than 400,000 people, excluding the military apparatus. . . . All of that was in the hands of the ruling Great Serbian bureaucracy headed by the king and his royal camarilla."[12] The Royal government controlled much of the country's wealth and resources.

> [It] possessed coal and iron ore mines, forests and the largest agricultural estates; enjoyed a monopoly in retail trade of tobacco, salt, matches and kerosene; and was the largest wholesale trader, transporter, importer and exporter, banker, building entrepreneur and real estate owner.[13]

As to the effects of this kind of economic policies on the national question in the country, Bićanić concludes:

> Redistribution of national income by political power was the main function of the state in Jugoslavia between 1918 and 1939; in it, therefore, the various nations could never achieve equal political rights.[14]

To all the complaints of non-Serbian nationalities the most popular government response was that all these economic measures were needed for the well-being and the preservation of the state. Thus, every economic complaint was considered as anti-state in nature and was treated as a political crime.

After 1945, the reunified state under Communist rule was supposed to be rebuilt on radically new social, political, and economic bases. One of the main preconditions for the Party's successful war effort was its promise to rectify the injustices of the Karadjordjević regime. As a result of this promise and of the Party's federalist program, Tito was able to reunite the country, in which he established six republics and two autonomous provinces.

All of the governmental powers, however, were once again centralized in Belgrade and were dominated by a Serbian bureaucracy. This is one of the reasons why the complaints of non-Serbian peoples, especially of the Croatians during the inter-war and post-war periods, were so similar. In 1968, a well known Croatian economist and Party member, Šime Djodan, stated about the role of the federal government in post-war Yugoslavia:

> In the centralized economic model, which was organized on the principle of total monopoly of both political power and ownership, the primary role of organizing the expanded reproduction was given to the state, that is to the central state or federation. The republic was perceived, on the one hand, as a national form without substance, and on the other hand, as a local organ of the central power. In reality, the republic was the executive local organ of the federation and, because of this, federalism has only been a formality.[15]

The causes of nationalism are similar in both the pre- and post-World War II Yugoslav states. As far as the Croatian national movement is concerned, however, there were two new elements in the 1960s. First, the economic policies of the central government became a major divisive element between Party liberals and conservatives, and it functioned as a major demarcation line between different national groups in the country. Second, primarily the Croatian but also the Slovene Communist leadership began to raise openly the question of economic exploitation. By doing this, they precipitated a public debate on national relations, which "became a central problem, first economic and then political."[16]

A young Croatian publicist, the late Bruno Bušić, wrote about the link between national and economic questions:

> We all know that national equality is not based on formal equality under the law. It rests most of all on the independent economic capabilities of each nation. Only in this way a nation can create the material basis for its own development and become a part of the international division of labor.[17]

A leading Croatian political commentator gave an even firmer opinion on this problem: "All major sources of today's intra-national sensitivity can be found in the new type of bureaucratic accumulation of economic power."[18] Although with changes in Yugoslav Communism came a change in economic policies. According to Bićanić, there were three major periods in the economic policies in Yugoslavia: "the centralized model of planning (1947-51), the decentralized model (1952-64) and the polycentric model, after 1965."[19] Most of the economists in Yugoslavia, even the most liberal ones, admitted that, in the immediate post-war period, while the country was being rebuilt and an economic infrastructure was being developed there was a need for a centralized economy. This economic program, however, had an important negative side effect. Its initial successes

> created an illusion about the omnipotence of a strong central state machinery. The longer this system lasted, the stronger became the self-assurance of the bureaucracy about its own infallibility and indispensability.[20]

Thus, the centralist bureaucracy

> resisted reduction of the economic rule of the center and the placement of the center under the supervision of all nations within SFRY. The central bureaucracy was privileged economically and politically. Its members belonged mostly to the largest nation [in the country]. During the Ranković era, unitarist ideology was created as a means of protecting the [bureaucratic] interests and the expansion of the nation it belonged to. Every social reform has been interpreted by the bureaucracy as an attack on its own nation. The bureaucracy, however, forgot that its own [Serbian] nation has long been—in all aspects—transgressing the rights and interests of the other nations [in the country].[21]

The persistent centralist economic policies became one of the major Croatian complaints in the 1960s. The Party liberals had brought the issue to the surface hoping to resolve growing economic as well as national problems, but ultimately it became a major rallying point for a national movement.

Major Economic Grievances

While certain external signs of traditional nationalism, flag waving and singing of patriotic songs, were present among Croatians in their national revival in the 1960s and early 1970s, it should be kept in mind that one of the main causes for the national grievances was economic problems which helped to open the door to the national movement. In a similar way, the Croatian students went on a strike in November 1971 because of unresolved economic issues between the republics and the federation. This was the final act of the "Croatian Spring" which precipitated the downfall of the Party's liberal leadership in the republic and brought about wide ranging purges and imprisonments of Croatian students and intellectuals. Finally, then, the economic issues became a convenient channel through which deeper national grievances were expressed.

An indication of overwhelming economic concerns is the strong consensus among different social elements in Croatia that their nation, regardless of its relative progress, had been a loser in the Yugoslav state. Unresolved economic problems, in their eyes, had an important effect on all other aspects of national life. There was also a sense of urgency to resolve these and other intra-national issues without any delay. It was believed that if federal policies continued as in the past, the future existence of the Croatian nation itself was at stake.

The major Croatian economic complaints were: collection and distribution of federal funds—especially the government's investment policy, concentration of financial power in Belgrade banks and exporting companies, and federal policies on foreign currency exchange.

Ever since the war, the more developed republics were carrying a disproportionate economic burden in the federation. This resulted in an unjustifiable siphoning off of wealth from Croatia and Slovenia into the less developed republics, namely, Bosnia and Hercegovina, Montenegro, Macedonia and Serbia. The following table, for example, gives some indication of the republican contributions to and receipts from the federal budget in the pre-reform period:

TABLE 2

Contributions to and Receipts from the Federal Budget in Percentages:

Republic	Contributions	Receipts
B. and H.	13.91%	3.8%
Montenegro	1.34	2.39
Croatia	31.11	18.89
Slovenia	20.11	7.18
Macedonia	4.28	3.02
Serbia	29.17	68.13

Source: *Statistički bilten Narodne banke FNRJ* Vol. 4, No. 2, 1963, pp. 26, 79 as in Šime Djodan, "Gdje dr. Stipe Šuvar 'pronalazi' nacionalizam, a gdje ga ne vidi," *Kolo* Vol. 7, No. 7, 1969, p. 706.

Despite the Reform in 1965 and its policies of decentralization, the money that continued to flow from Croatia into the federal center was disproportionate to her population and her economic strength. The amount of collections even increased, and all that had changed during the Reform was the methods. For example in 1964, before the Reform, 58.01 percent of the republic's collected revenues went to the federation. In 1968, the percentage was 59.9%; in 1969, 60.83%; and in 1970 it reached 63 percent.[22] The situation was openly compared to the unfavorable Croatian economic relations of Croatia with Hungary in the pre-World War I period. At that time, under the Croatian-Hungarian Agreement of 1868, Croatia had to pay 56 percent of the money collected on her territory for common state expenses.[23] According to one Croatian economist, more than eight percent of the Croatian national product was taken by the central government, which was more than above the republic's share for paying the expenses of the federal administration and armed forces, and nothing was given in return.[24] These financial obligations were seen as pure exploitation of the republic and as an unacceptable extension of past discriminatory intranational relations.

During the post-World War II period, tremendous amounts of money were spent for developing the "underdeveloped" republics and regions. Many of these projects, however, were undertaken not because of their profitability and even not to ensure the economic growth of these areas, but for political expediency and local patriotism. Soon these projects came to be known as "political factories." Most of these enterprises, even though not returning any profits, continued to operate with subsidies from the federal government.[25] Croatians, as well as Slovenes, began to complain that their money had been unwisely invested, and they saw no reason why they should continue to pay for someone else's mistakes while their own economies were shrinking. While most of the new investments had been going to less developed regions, the money left for the Croatian economy was not enough to modernize the old factories so that they could keep a reasonable pace with the modern standards of production.[26] During the period from 1956 to 1970, the federal investment fund was distributed to the republics in the following percentages:

TABLE 3
Federal Investments 1956-1968 in percentages

B. and H.	13.72%
Montenegro	7.85
Croatia	18.02
Macedonia	10.82
Slovenia	6.11
Serbia	43.48

Source: The same as Table 2, p. 707.

The investment distribution during the reform period (1965-1970), when the republics were supposed to be gaining their autonomy, was as follows:

TABLE 4
Federal Investments 1965-1970 in percentages:

B. and H.	14.1
Montenegro	6.8
Croatia	16.5
Macedonia	11.4
Slovenia	6.6
Serbia	46.6

Source: *Ekonomska politika Jugoslavije* (Zagreb: Školska knjiga, 1970), p. 122.

The above tables indicate that, even during the decentralizing years, the money invested in Croatia actually decreased by almost two percent, which was contrary to the proposed reform principles. Although the factories and means of production in the western republics generally were older than the newly built plants in the east, their production was higher. For example, in order to earn one dinar in the mid-1960s, it was necessary to invest the following amounts in the different republics and provinces:

TABLE 5
Amount Invested for Every Dinar Earned According to Republics and Provinces in the Mid-1960s:

B. and H.	4.84 dinars
Montenegro	13.09
Croatia	1.46
Macedonia	7.62
Slovenia	1.96
Serbia proper	3.62
Vojvodina	3.14
Kosovo	9.34

Source: *Osnovni indikatori ostvarenja društvenog plana razvoja Jugoslavije od 1966. do 1970. godine i razvojnih mogućnosti od 1971. do 1975. godine.* (Belgrade: Savezni zavod za plan, 1970) as cited in Šime Djodan, "Aktuelni gospodarski položaj Zagreba," *Kritika* Vol. 3, No. 13, 1970, p. 494.

This was yet another reason why the Croatians demanded a change in federal economic policy. They claimed that the money earned by them should be invested first of all in their own aging industry where it would bring optimum profits. They opposed investments that were based on political favoritism[27] or that helped the centrally planned and controlled economic equalization of the country.

The Financial Barons

As part of the major economic reforms and decentralization, in the early 1960s, former federally controlled funds were transferred to three major Belgrade banks with a symbolic interest of one percent.[28] In theory, the Bank and Credit Law of 1965 was an important change in the banking system. It was supposed to free the banks and investment funds from the control of the political apparatus and to base the financial institutions on the principles of self-management.[29] At that time, the Croatian party leadership had high hopes that finally the problem of centrally controlled funds would be resolved. They soon realized, however, that the banks which inherited the federal funds became a major problem in national relations, because the federally privileged banks were basically under the control of the same bureaucracy that previously dominated federal funds.[30] A few years after the Bank Law was passed, a Croatian publicist explained:

> Bureaucracy constantly keeps changing its forms, but it preserves its mentality. In order to narrow down and prevent its activity, it is necessary right now, without any delay, to decentralize the existing financial centers and their responsibilities.[31]

After the changes in 1965, the bureaucracy had even more freedom to do what it pleased in financial matters because much could be justified by the principle of self-management.

The number of banks diminished from 112, in 1966, to 25, in 1972.[32] The former federal banks, which remained in the capital, had absorbed a number of smaller banks across the country, while other banks had no choice but to assume a local character. The concentration of financial capital in the central banks was simply overwhelming since the central banks controlled "54.2 percent of the total Yugoslav capital."[33] Also, because their headquarters were in Belgrade, they functioned at the same time as banks of the republics of Serbia and as clearing houses of the federal government.[34]

A similar financial and national problem arose with large and privileged import-export enterprises located in Belgrade. These companies, working on their own or as partners with the central banks, were making large profits, however, not by their own working but by exploiting others.[35]

These two kinds of Belgrade financial barons, the central banks and the giant export-import enterprises, became the major targets of the Croatian national movement in the late Sixties and early Seventies. With the transfer of federal financial control to the central banks came also a transfer of investment powers. In this way, the banks and the federally privileged import-export houses, became a major determining factor in regional economic growth. To the Croatians and other non-Serbs this meant that former federal centralism was not simply "decentralized" into a small number of power centers within the same old framework. Instead of one federal bureaucracy in the past there were now two more: financial and business. All three were controlled by one national group located in the same city. In any multi-national state, but especially in Yugoslavia with its antagonistic national relations in the past, this had to intensify the national question.

The following statistical data were some of the arguments brought to public attention by Croatian economists to indicate the basic trends in the policies of the former federal banks. For example, in 1966, Croatian banks received 18.8 and, in 1968, 16.3 percent of the total credits of the National Bank, while Serbian banks received 51.7 and 58.6 percent for the same years.[36] The investment figures also point out that those institutions were inclined to invest first of all in those regions where they were located and in those industries where they were able to make the best returns. The economic needs of a specific republic, most of all Croatia, were not considered as particularly important. As a result, from 1966 to 1970, 40.1 percent of the total investments of these banks were in Serbia.[37] And if viewed from a wider regional aspect, the eastern part of the country, Macedonia, Serbia and Montenegro, received a disproporationately large share of investments in relation to the distributions made to the whole federation.

Croatian economists and leading politicians began demanding a dismantling of those financial centers which had started their fortune with someone else's money and which continued to be protected by the federal government. These financial centers were exploiting the working class all across the country, especially in the northern republics, with their unscrupulous policies. The Croatian economists were also demanding a revision of the traditional belief that the western part of the country was "developed" and the eastern "underdeveloped," and, because of this belief, the money had to flow from the west to the east. They pointed out that the eastern republics had controlled the investments and also had the newer means of production. But the reasons why they were not catching up with the western republics must lay somewhere else. For example, in 1969, the credit and productivity potential of each republic was as follows:

TABLE 6
Credit and Productivity Potentials According to the Republics
in percentages (1969)

Republic	Credit Potential	Productivity Potential
Bosnia and Hercegovina	7.8%	11.7
Montenegro	2.4	1.8
Croatia	17.7	27.2
Macedonia	9.0	5.0
Slovenia	12.8	17.5
Serbia	50.3	36.8

Source: A. Žuvela, *Analiza privrednih izmjena u kreditnoj politici i poslovanju banaka* (Zagreb: Privredna komora Hrvatske, 1970) as cited in Šime Djodan, "The Evolution of the Economic System of Yugoslavia and the Economic Position of Croatia." *Journal of Croatian Studies* Vol. 13, 1972, p. 82.

The table shows quite clearly that the western half of the country (Slovenia, Croatia, and Bosnia and Hercegovina) had much larger productivity potential (56.4) than its share of credits (38.3). On the other hand, the eastern part (Serbia, Macedonia and Montenegro) had larger credit potential (61.7) while its productive capabilities were lower (43.6).[39] There is no doubt that the financial power was with the eastern and not with the western part of the country,[40] as it was often thought, and that there was a large discrepancy between productivity and credit potential in the various republics.

Because of these rather partial financial policies of the central financial institutions, Hrvoje Šošić, a leading Croatian economist concluded:

Because of the creation of financial power centers primarily within the frames of former federal banks and import-export houses outside the Croatian territory, the economic development of the republic depends primarily on the will of those financial despots who can cut off their investments at any moment and in any area they please. In this way, they can bring whole regions to the verge of ruin . . . .[41]

Comparing the centralized economic policies in Ranković's era with the central banks' dealings during the time of decentralization, Šošić concluded that economic Reform merely substituted "bank factories" for "political factories."[42]

Croatia had been the main supplier of hard currency for the whole country. Tourism, industrial exports, shipping and remittance of money from workers in the West were the three major sources of foreign income. Thus, the republic contributed 50 percent of all foreign currency entering the SFRY. Only a small percentage, however, remained in its own banks and enterprises. While Belgrade banks controlled 81.3 percent of the entire amount of hard currency in the country, banks in Zagreb had to be content with only 9.7 percent.[43] The central banks controlled all of the money market in Yugoslavia. They regulated credits and investments, charged high interest rates, and made large profits on the differences between the real and official exchange rates of the dollar and other foreign currencies. The members of the Croatian national movement in the late Sixties and early Seventies felt that this left the banks in their republic powerless and at the mercy of federal financial policy. Thus, they unanimously demanded that the federal financial institutions be "nationalized for the second time."[44]

The financial centers were especially interested in making investments in fast growing tourism, the so-called "white industry." This was a way of getting the much needed Western currency. Most of the tourist industry, however, was located in Croatia because of its long Adriatic sea coast. Even the Yugoslav Agricultural Bank (Poljobanka) was more eager to invest in tourism than agriculture, for which it was designated.[45] Clearly, the bank's primary goal was to gain entry where foreign money was being made and not the development of agriculture.

The conditions under which credits and investments were being granted by the central banks and by the import-export enterprises were considered even more damaging to the Croatian economy than investment inequality itself. At first glance the interest rates seemed relatively low. The investors, however, were getting a number of additional benefits from state and local governments, and secret agreements were made with the tourist enterprises themselves. This way, the creditors were making enormous profits.[46] A foreign observer concluded that "the terms of credit granted to [the Croatian enterprises] were so harsh and the premium payable on foreign exchange so high, that the banks and re-exporters were exploiting the Croatian economy."[47] Practically, many tourist businesses had to turn over most of the profits, especially their foreign currency to the investors. In this sense, a Croatian economist described the practices of the federal banks and exporters as "the most shameless and unrestricted robbery."[48] A leading Party man in Croatia agreed with this judgment, saying that tourism in Croatia had been pushed into a position of "working exclusively for the interests of central hard currency funds and its own creditors."[49]

Only the central banks and re-export enterprises were permitted to handle hard currency since the dinar was not convertible. Thus, most of the hard currency from the whole country had to pass through the financial institutions in Belgrade. In this way the banks were able to accumulate and control large amounts of financial capital which was earned by other enterprises and in other republics. This was the main and fastest way of transferring financial wealth from Croatia to the federal center.

Another problem was that of foreign debt, which was growing faster from year to year. During the meeting of Croatia's leadership with Tito on November 30, 1971, in Karadjordjevo, Tripalo, the leading figure in the national movement, declared that from 1965-70, Croatia had received only 10 percent of the loans granted by the International Bank while the republic had not got anything at all from the loans received from the USSR.[50] Still, the republic had to carry most of the burden in the repaying of these loans. Djodan, the leading economist, explained:

> Croatia is not legitimized to get international credits. But while others are spending the international loans, we, by our foreign currency surplus, are returning them.[51]

The financial relationship of the republic with the central agencies grew steadily worse, and the federal government's reluctance to resolve the issue became a major cause of the student strike in November 1971.

Self-Management

The proclaimed and much celebrated principles of self-management gave the Croatian politicians and economists an ideological legitimization to demand that economic, especially financial powers, be fully decentralized. It seemed at the time that even Tito was on their side. He declared:

> self-management has developed and affirmed itself so much that it began to clash more and more with the forces that alienate the surplus of labor. . . .[52]

The theory of self-management, however, was never fully implemented. According to the theory of self-management the workers' councils were supposed to control the fate of their enterprises and not some financial institution or the federal government. But, as a Croatian economist explained, "even after the economic enterprises were entrusted to the workers' councils, the sphere of financing extended reproduction remained mostly in the hands of the state."[53] For example, in 1952, the economic enterprises controlled 22 percent of the investment. Ten years later, the percentage was 32. According to the projected reforms, the economic units should have controlled 70 percent of social production by 1970. In that year, however, only 56 percent remained in the hands of the economy which the rest was controlled by the state. Clearly, the federal control of the economy was still overwhelming. In fact, economists complained that the "state structure and control of the federation had remained more or less untouched" ever since 1945.[54]

Because Tito also openly complained about the banks and other central financial institutions, Croatians gained a false sense of hope that finally these problems would be resolved by a full implementation of federalism and self-management. Those hopes, however, were shattered in December 1971, when Tito condemned the Croatian national movement as counter-revolution and called the Party leadership in the republic "rotten liberals."

Croatian economists and the republic's political leadership were accused of egotism and nationalism because they heavily stressed republicanism and the decentralization of the economy. As a result, the centralists accused them of being selfish and of not being willing to help the less developed regions.[55] These accusations, however, were rejected as a willful misinterpretation of Croatian complaints and proposals. The major issue was not whether the less developed areas should be helped or not—everyone agreed they should get help—but the question of how this should be done. Croatians also asked that Serbia proper should be considered a developed region and should, therefore, contribute her share in this common effort.[56] After all, it was argued, Slovenia and especially Croatia had some under-developed areas and no one was helping them to improve their fortune. (For example, in 1970 out of 150 communes [općine] in Croatia 41 were considered under-developed).[57] Without abandoning the less developed areas, Croatia asked for a break up of the existing financial maze which pushed them more and more into a colonial position.[58]

It was argued by the centralists that the more developed republics used the rest of the country as a market for their products and thus extracted money from the less developed regions. Therefore, it was also their duty to give some of that money back. But the Croatian economists made an effort to clarify facts about the markets in the country. They pointed out that Croatia had a trade deficit with all of the Yugoslav republics. In 1968, for example, Croatia had trade deficits with other republics that were as much as billions of old dinars: Bosnia and Hercegovina 51, Montenegro 4, Slovenia 32, Macedonia 7, and Serbia 36 billion dinars. Thus, it was a false presumption that Croatia had an advantage in being a part of the unitary market or that it exploited the other republics. Most of the Croatian trade was done with foreign countries where the republic had a positive balance of 350 million dollars annually.[59]

Djodan, the leading liberal economist in Croatia at that time, stressed that the development of some republics should not tie down the progress of others. He said that the economy should be determined by the market and not by political forces. A special fund outside the economy as a whole, however, should be established for less developed areas, and it should be located outside the federal capital.

> According to our opinion, a bank should be organized for less developed regions, with its headquarters in Sarajevo, because the republic of Bosnia and Hercegovina is the largest under-developed region and the least developed republic. That bank should control about 2 percent of the SFRY's income. It should invest in all under-developed regions in the next planned period, according to the

principles of best economic interests and optimum economic integration of all regions in the SFRY and to the best economic growth of Yugoslavia as a whole.[60]

As far as Serbia was concerned, Croatian economists indicated that Serbia proper developed more quickly than any other region. For quite some time, it had been stronger than Croatia in such economic fields as industry and agriculture, for example. But because it actually controlled the investment capital its exceptional strength was in credit potential.[61] All economic elements considered, Serbia was the "strongest republic" in the federation. Therefore, it was only just that it whould also share the burden of helping other regions, especially since "Croatia and Slovenia were too small to carry [alone] the burden of the development of other republics."[62]

There were two basic views on the economic development of the country as a whole: one advocated a decentralized and open market, while the other defended a centralized and autarchic economy. Most Croatian economists advocated an open economy in which the economic forces would determine economic development, and not the federal bureaucracy, the Party, or any other group. The Yugoslav economy, as a Croatian economist put it, should "face the world market where there is no mercy but the results are achieved only by work."[63] This way, enterprises would keep most of their profits and would be able to control their own fate. The polycentric economy would be a result of the free market economy. The role of the banks in that system would be one of service and not of dominance. The final result of this process would be self-rule of the republics, real federalism, and an open economy in an open society. One contemporary commentator argued:

Escape from the present situation has to be found in the consistent implementation of self-management in economy and transfer of profits to the immediate producer. Then, the implementation of the principle of self-management and sovereignity of the socialist republics should follow, with the special emphasis that every republic has the right to dispose its surplus of labor as it sees fit . . . . Our demand must be for an immediate equilibrium between the productive and financial potential in a single republic. That means liquidation of the existing monopolies of financial power in one of the republics. This is the essential question of national inequality in the SFRY's frame.[64]

In the name of Party leadership, Tripalo explained the problem in the following words:

> The key question is giving back the immense centralized funds to the economy. What we need is modernization of existing facilities and not building of vast new projects. . . . We have a central fund, budgetary subsidies, favored interest rates for credit, etc. But we must put an end to parasitism. Those who are able to earn cannot be penalized all the time. . . . As to nationalism, the only solution is that our multi-national Yugoslavia must be based on the full equality of each nation and not on some being more equal than others, on socialist self-government and not on bureaucratic centralism[65]

Social and political changes were to be part of economic reforms, because "without the reform of society there cannot be an economic reform either."[66] But at the same time, economic changes were supposed to be the essential condition of all other changes in the country, because "there is no independence or freedom of expression without the material basis."[67] Or as a leading Croatian Party official pointed out, "A nation which does not control its own income is not a free nation either in the class or national sense of the word."[68]

The forces opposing this kind of change, however, were stronger than the advocates of market economy and liberal socialism. The opposition to the liberal tendencies advocated a more autarchic form of economy, which would be less open to the world market and more under administrative control, as it had been in the past. The proponents of this view looked at the economy from the centralist point of view and not from the local interests. The main justifications for this approach were unity of the country and the assumption that "the bigger the better."

In response to the accusations that the implementation of liberal proposals would lead to a fragmentation of the country and to a weakening of its economic potential, Croatian economists said that centralism, and not republicanism, was causing the country's political and economic instability. In their opinion, a free association of nations, built on genuine self-rule would be the starting point of stabilization and not the cause of its disintegration. The new relations would be based on common political and ecnomic interests, not on ideology, on Slavism, or on some uncertain ideological vision of the future. According to Djodan, it was up to every republic to "decide what form of union it wanted" and no one had "the right to predetermine the form" of the new intra-national relations in the country.[69]

Some opponents of the market economy argued that republic economies would be too small in order to be efficient and compete in the world market. The liberals, however, regarded this argument as invalid because "no one could prove that the efficiency of an economic system is proportionate to the size of the state."[70] On the contrary, small countries in Europe such as Norway and Switzerland, for example, had a more efficient economy than most of the larger countries in the world, including Yugoslavia.

In the struggle for national emancipation and sovereignty, Croatians thought that a favorable resolution of economic issues was an essential pre-condition for a change in the federal system as a whole. At the Karadjordjevo meeting on November 30, 1971, the President of the Croatian *Sabor* (Assembly), Dragutin Haramija, summarized the underlying Croatian complaints as follows:

> We do not have enough capital because of the federal banks' organization and concentration in one region. Neither do we have a fund for under-developed regions as some other republics do. We do have surplus in foreign currency, but the policy on foreign currency is not being changed.[71]

Thus, it was the economic issues that greatly helped to stir such strong national feelings in Croatia. Further, it was the economic issues that helped to unite different national elements and bring about the mass movement of 1971.

Croatia Without Croatians

One of the most important effects of the extreme drain of the Croatian economy was a large number of emigrants. The constant flow of people across the border started in the middle Sixties and became a major concern for the Croatian national leadership. Too many Croatians were leaving the country; most of them went to Western Europe, especially to Germany and Austria, as temporary "guest workers" (Gastarbeiter). But since they stayed in the West European countries for quite a number of years, they really can be regarded as emigrants. Then, there were also thousands of Croatians who decided to move on to other continents and leave their homeland for good.

Such population movement had serious demographic, social, economic, and political effects on the Croatian nation. In order to prevent the steady decrease of Croatia's population and the national suicide (as some called it), the Croatian national movements made it one of its major goals to stop this population outflow.

Croatians, the only Slavic nation with a long maritime tradition, and had long been going out into the world either as sailors, merchants, or as permanent settlers in the New World. On the other hand, their society also had a tradition of stability and strong family ties; leaving the homeland was not an easy decision. The reasons for Croatian massive emigration were not just rumors that life was better abroad. Usually there were some strong political and/or economic pressures that caused their leaving the country.[72]

In the early Sixties, especially after the introduction of the 1965 economic reform, Tito opened the borders not only to the influx of western tourists but also to allow the flow of his citizens to the West. By making this move, he scored several points for his regime. Letting people work in other countries helped ease the high unemployment rates at home. Although the "guest workers" in the West became exposed to different political systems, the risk was worth it, because the political advantages for the regime were greater than the risks of "bourgeoisie influences." Finally, letting people out served also as a safety value for political and economic pressures in the country. To prevent internal political pressures, people were given passports, and in this way most of the real or potential enemies were neutralized. But the workers outside the country were not left alone. They were under constant pressure from the regime and its secret police which made sure that their citizens in foreign countries stayed clear from any political activities. One of the ways to control the political activities of the "guest workers" was the threat to take away their passport. By exporting workers to the West, Tito and his form of socialism gained praise on the international scene. The flow of people became one more "proof" of Yugoslav "liberalism"; many in the West considered it as a major step in the process of democratization. But the economic gains were the most significant aspects of the "open door" policy. Not only did the country's unemployment rate drop radically, but the workers outside the country became the single most important source of foreign currency, even more important than the tourist industry itself.[73]

It is very hard to determine exactly how many people left Yugoslavia in search of work in the West. A leading Croatian weekly lamented at the end of 1970:

> We do not know even today the exact number of workers or members of their families who are outside the country. We do not know in what country or [even] on what continent they are.[74]

The population census taken at the beginning of 1971 indicates that there were about 682,000 workers from Yugoslavia in Western Europe.[75] Official and unofficial experts, however, declared this number as unrealistic because the census, among other discrepancies, did not include families who had been outside the country for a relatively long period or families who were unavailable at census time. There was even the suspicion that the census had been done carelessly and even with some ill intentions.[76] Therefore, other statistical sources had to be used in order to find at least an approximate number of total workers outside the country.

Domestic and foreign experts agree that the number of "temporary workers" reached its peak in the early Seventies. At that time, there were more than one million workers from Yugoslavia abroad.[77] Whether this approximate number included children and other family members is not clear. It seems more likely that the number indicates just the work force, of which 70 percent were men and 30 percent women, mostly between the ages of 20 to 40.[78]

In a multinational state like Yugoslavia, massive migration can easily become a very delicate political and national problem. It can change the country's demographic, economic, and political balances, especially if the migration happens primarily in one of the nations. The fact that the number of emigrant workers from Croatia was much above that of the other nations became a major political and social issue during the Croatian national revival. The following table shows the share of each republic in the country's total number of "guest workers."

TABLE 7

Share of the Republics in Total Emigration in Percentages

Republic	Year and percentage	
	1968	1970
Bosnia and Hercegovina	22.1	24.0
Montenegro	0.2	0.5
Croatia	50.1*	46.0
Macedonia	3.1	4.5
Slovenia	15.1	12.0
Serbia	9.4	13.0

Source: Zvonimir Komarica, "Neka obilježja suvremenih migracija," *Kritika* Vol. 3, No. 13, 1970, p. 561.

* Another source states that 52.3 percent of all Yugoslavia's emigrants came from the republic of Croatia. See Šime Djodan, "Osvrt na savjetovanje o stanovništvu, emigraciji i zaposlenosti," *Kritika* Vol. 4, No. 17, 1971, p. 295.

"Croatia, [however], did not only have the highest absolute number of emigrant workers but also the country's highest rate of emigration." In the early Seventies, 8.2 percent of the republics total population had emigrated; by that time Croatia had the highest emigration rate in Europe,[79] and also the highest emigration rate to Western Europe of all Southern European nations, and Turkey. At that time, 5.93 percent of all emigrants were from Croatia and 5.57 percent from Portugal, while the emigration rate for Yugoslavia as a whole was only 3.19 percent. And if overseas emigration were included in this figure, then the Croatian percentage would be 7.3 percent.[80] One more factor should be kept in mind: the above percentages refer only to the present day republic of Croatia.

But if the Croatian emigrants from other republics, primarily Bosnia and Hercegovina, were included the percentages would be much higher. Obviously, then, Croatian share in the total of the country's emigrants was unusually high. The total number of emigrants and their descendants from today's territory of Yugoslavia was estimated to be around 2,200,000, and out of that number 1,500,000 were Croatians.[81] At the same time, their share of total population in the country was 23.20 in 1961 and in 1981 19.7 percent.[82]

The causes for this massive external migration were of political, social, and psychological nature; but the most important ones were economical, such as the lack of employment in their own country and better opportunities in the West. The economic Reform of the early 1960s had a negative effect on the Croatian economy. For example, there was more work available in 1965 than during the period from 1966 to 1969.[83] While employment opportunity increased from 1959 to 1969 by 34 percent, in the country as a whole, in Croatia it increased only by 24 percent.[84] On the other hand, there was an increasing number of job seekers. Thousands of young people were finishing their education and coming to the job market. Those who could no longer make a living on their farms were in search of work. Also many of the "small bourgeoisie" who had private shops were squeezed out from their private employment by high taxes or ideological pressures, and had to look for state controlled jobs.[85] The main reason Croatia could not provide jobs for all her people was because the Croatian economy could not expand. Money earned by Croatia and Croatians was taken in one way or another by the central agencies and was invested in other parts of the country. As a result, the republic's inability to create new work places and the increasing number of those who were looking for jobs were clearly in direct correlation to the massive migration of workers abroad.[86]

The country's economic problems, however, could not have been the only, or even the primary, reason for the massive emigration of the Croatians. Strangely enough, the more developed regions in the country suffered a higher emigration rate. Although 83.8 percent of the total number of emigrant workers came from the western parts of the country, which had a relatively high annual income per capita.[87] In other countries of Southern Europe, however, most of the emigrants came from economically less developed areas.[88] This unusual fact implied that there was some other reason for the high emigration rate from Croatia. Indeed a large number of Croatians had been leaving the country even before the decline of job opportunities.[89] Demographic statistics indicated that this increase of migration was not just part of the Croatian tradition to venture abroad, as some claimed.[90] It was quite obvious that there must have been a different cause for this kind of massive migration.

Without expressing it openly, Croatian experts pointed to the country's political development as the real cause for such massive Croatian emigration. These experts supported their opinion with the fact that emigration was clearly more related to ethnicity than to profession, to education, or to any other factor.[91] Also, the "1,300,000 names in UDBA's files [in Croatia alone] had not been gathered in vain."[92] Thus, the Croatian emigration on such a large scale was primarily a reflection of their adverse political and national situation in the Yugoslav state.

Among the numerous effects of "temporary" employment abroad the most evident consequence was the rapid decrease in the Croatian population. Decline of birth and fertility rates, depopulation of whole regions, and high mortality rates were causes for alarm. For example, in 1969, the population growth rate in Croatia was 3.9 per thousand and in 1970 it was 2.7 per thousand. At the same time, the republic's emigration rate was 5.5 per thousand.[93] A high number of qualified workers and individuals with university degrees joined the exodus, and most of these would never return to their homeland. This kind of "brain drain" was sure to hurt the existing Croatian economy and its future development. Also the money invested in the education of those who left the country had been wasted.[94]

Croatians traditionally had a strong and patriarchal family life. However, about 70 percent of the "temporary" workers were men from 20 to 40 years old. In many cases, father and mother were in the West, while the grandparents were taking care of the children. What the short and long range effects of this kind of "unbalanced" family life and social life were going to be, it was hard to say. Social, psychological, physical, and moral problems were definitely higher among these families and individuals than among those who remained at home.[95]

Yugoslavia as a country had major financial benefits from those citizens who had jobs in the West. The workers sent home millions in hard currency; but because of the complicated system of dealing with foreign currency it was impossible, even for the experts, to determine exactly how much money was remitted. At the end of the Sixties, the number was roughly 500 million dollars a year, and out of that amount, 300 million were sent by workers who came from Croatia.[96]

When it came to the "guest workers," Croatian national leaders considered their nation to be doubly exploited: there was a flow of its work force to the West, while the money made by this work force was taken by the federal government, the central banks, and by the re-exporters. There was no way, however, for Croatia to prevent this from happening. Its leadership neither could create suitable jobs so that those outside the country might return nor could it stop the outflow of its republic's earnings. Federal agencies, central banks and re-exporters had a virtual monopoly on hard currency and the economy of the country.

As a first step in solving the emigration problem, Croatian progressives demanded an "implementation of changes in political and economic systems, especially in monetary and fiscal areas. . . ."[97] Most of all they demanded that the remittance of the Croatian emigrant workers be invested directly in Croatia. This would help create new jobs, ensure a better and more stable life in Croatia, and would stimulate the return of those abroad. The progressives also proposed more liberalized private investment laws to stimulate investments in profitable private enterprises.[98]

Nothing, however, came out of these proposals, except the accusations that they were an expression of nationalism and "rotten liberalism." A certain percentage of "Gastarbeiter" finally returned, but only because Western Europe experienced an economic decline and was forced to cut down on their work force.

In the late Sixties and early Seventies, Croatian intellectual elites and political leadership were caught between a feeling of emergency to stop the massive outflow of their population and the impression that the federal government did not have any real concern for Croatian economic and national problems.[99] Milutin Baltić, a conservative Serb from Croatia and the president of the Sindicates, openly stated,

> The more of them go abroad, the more foreign currency we will get. In that way it will be better for us too. Above all, by their leaving we are solving our unemployment problem.[100]

Statements like this from high officials, and especially from Serbs, did not ease the growing national tensions. The feeling that the national fate was in somebody else's hands became increasingly stronger. Therefore, political and economic self-rule was seen as the only answer to the national problems.

CHAPTER V

CULTURAL NATIONALISM

After the creation of Yugoslavia in December 1918 some pro-Yugo-slav enthusiasts among the Croatians declared that East and West had finally met. They believed that the cultural, religious, and historical differences between the peoples in Yugoslavia would eventually disappear and the true national unification would follow.[1] But contrary to these hopes, the gap between the individual nations of the country grew steadily as political and economic struggles constantly caused new collisions between the various national groups. Also, cultural and ethnic differences were not erased as had been expected. On the contrary, the growing oppression of non-Serbs by the Karadjordjević ruling elite only strengthened the emphasis on cultural individuality among the national groups.

The same negative intra-national sentiments continued in Tito's Yugoslavia. Non-Serbs felt that their culture was being sacrificed in the name of "Yugoslavism" because Serbian cultural influences were expanding. While Serbs, and even some foreign observers, found it natural that Belgrade, the country's capital, be dominant politically and culturally, the Croatians and other non-Serbs, thought that Belgrade did not have that right. The non-Serbian nations argued that they had their own national capitals and centers of culture. Zagreb, for example, they argued, should not be regarded simply as the number two city in the country. Indeed, it was the capital of Croatia and the cultural and political center for all

Croatians. After all, Yugoslavia had not one single national culture; each of its nations had its own name, its own heritage, language, and cultural institutions. Therefore, their cultural centers should be of equal importance. The emphasis on national individuality and cultural rights was one of the strongest elements of the Croatian national movement in the Sixties and Seventies. The main reason for such emphasis was the strong feeling that federal forces, namely, the Serbian controlled bureaucracy together with Croatian "Yugoslavs," had been trying to neglect and "provincialize" the Croatian cultural heritage.[2] The evidence for this accusation was quite obvious to the Croatians. A close look at the curriculum of Croatian schools and at the low number of Croatian students in higher education, the neglect of Croatian national monuments and the lack of money for the arts, all of this proved that the government did not show much concern for preserving the national identity of the non-Serbian cultures.

A good example for the Croatian complaints concerning their national heritage was the question of textbooks in the republic. It was pointed out that Croatian literature was minimized and not properly presented to the new Croatian generations. Students were learning much more about foreign writers and about the literature of other nations in Yugoslavia than about their own national literary heritage.[3]

Another regular school policy was to avoid the words "Croatia" or "Croatian" in lessons on national culture; instead the unspecified pronoun "our" was used. Thus, instead of talking about Croatian culture, authors of the textbooks and school teachers were pressured to talk, for example, about "our language," "our history," "our literature," or "our people." Also terms like "Yugoslav," "among us," "domestic" were substituted for Croatia and Croatian because they implied that the peoples in Yugoslavia were one nation culturally. A Croatian intellectual once observed:

> On about fifty pages [of the book] pertaining to the chapter on 'Serbian Medieval Literature' it is customary and normal to use the possessive adjective 'Serbian' at least thirty or forty times in all its variations. But, on the other three hundred and fifty pages of the book, which deal with themes from older Croatian literature, we find specific lexical-semantic play of words: our, domestic, old, Dalmatian, of Dubrovnik, of Hvar, Littoral, Slav, Yugoslav, Slavonian,

Bosnian, of Split, [etc.]. Only one small word—Croatian—is not allowed to be mentioned. And it is not there.[4]

Another intellectual concurred:

As something very normal, many of the professors and authors dealing with older Croatian literature have written and are still writing thousands and hundreds of thousands of words about Croatian literary heritage but without using the attribute 'Croatian.'[5]

Those who did dare to use the adjective "Croatian" were regarded as anti-Yugoslav nationalists and chauvinists. Croatian intellectuals, thus, thought that putting away with the term "Croatian" was just another proof of Belgrade's unitaristic tendency and that its goal was to weaken Croatian national identity.

Similarly, Croatian intellectuals objected to the practice of dividing Croatian culture into its regional components and they rejected any direct or indirect Serbian claims on some Croatian cultural treasures.[6] A number of Croatian intellectuals also complained about the persistence of some Belgrade authors in negating Croatian individuality.

It is unbelievable but unfortunately true that even today students in Serbia are getting a completely false interpretation of Croatian history. . . . The whole school and scientific apparatus has been put in the service of Garašanin's old expansionistic idea. And a significant portion of Croatian cultural heritage is being claimed in the name of that idea. (And not only cultural heritage, for certain!)[7]

Another practice in post-World War II Yugoslavia was fragmentating the Croatian heritage into its regional components. The authors would talk about Dalmatian, čakavian, kaykavian, Dubrovnik, Littoral literature and art.[8] For example, one primary school textbook stated that

the ekavian dialect is spoken in the largest part of the SR of Serbia. The ijakavian dialect is spoken in Dalmatia, Croatia and Slavonia, and southwest of the [Adriatic] sea.[9]

Dividing the Croatian culture and history into these individual "subcultures" meant destroying the image of Croatia as a culturally unified nation and taking away its national heritage. After all, this was regarded a continuation of the old Austria-Hungarian and Karadjordjević political methods of weakening Croatia's national integration and her political strength. A prominent Croatian intellectual referred to the educational policies regarding Croatian culture as "Yugo-chauvinism":

> The term 'Yugo-chauvinism' [forced Yugoslavism] was supposed to be a consolation to those peoples in Yugoslavia, first of all to Croatians, who have been losing their [national] individuality and uniqueness. In return, they were offered a certain wide perspective [a vision] that we [peoples in Yugoslavia] would be bigger; that we would be stronger; that we would be more bound together, as though that made the strength and unity of Yugoslavia.[10]

Furthermore, this artificial unification meant Serbian cultural domination in the name of Yugoslavism, which was seen as "colonization of the Croatian national being."[11]

Among the numerous cultural issues that were raised during the Sixties and early Seventies by the Croatian cultural elites two stood out the most. The first issue was that of the Croatian language and its unification with the Serbian language. The second issue was official Yugoslav historiography and its treatment of Croatia and Croatians.

Language

Language is not only a means of communication, but it is often a reflection of the political, social, cultural, and even economic reality between various nations. Generally, it can be said that with the growth of political, economic, and military power of a particular nation, the importance of its language also increases. Language can be a useful tool in achieving strength and domination, but it can also be a very important instrument in the hands of the opponents of that domination.

The Habsburg empire is a good example of both the offensive and defensive role of language. German and Hungarian were the privileged languages; German in the Austrian and Hungarian in the Magyar half of the empire. Clearly, language in this empire was used not only for communication purposes but also for political reasons. Furthermore, all non-Germans in the empire, or non-Magyars under the Hungarian crown of St. Stephen, used language during the awakening of national consciousness, in the 19th century, as a major tool against Habsburg centralism or the Hungarian policy of Magyarization.

Among the Croatians, language codification was very important during the process of national revival in the last century. One might even highlight the major points of Croatian modern political history by studying the history of their language development. The measure of Croatian political self-rule within the Hungarian kingdom after 1868, for example, is clearly reflected in Hungarian language policies. Similarly, as a result of the Illyrian movement in Croatia in the mid-19th century, which envisioned a unification of all South Slavs, a language agreement was made in Vienna (1850) between some of the Croatian "Illyrian" visionaries and Serbian cultural representatives. This agreement set the stage for the "unification" of the two languages; however, the political reasons for that Agreement and its consequences were much more important than its linguistic implications.

Most probably, the signers of the Agreement had the same political message they intended to send to Vienna and their own people, but their undertaking did not mean the same thing to each of them. The Croatian Illyrians and their "Yugoslav" inclined successors thought that the similarities of South Slavic languages could be the basis of their cultural and perhaps political unification. On the other hand, to the Serbs the same similarities constituted a justification for their national expansion. To Vuk Karadžić (1787-1864), who was a leading figure of the Serbian national revival and co-signer of the Vienna Agreement, all those who spoke the štokavian dialect were Serbs and had to be "liberated" and unified into a Serbian national state.[12]

The Vienna Agreement, for certain, was not a linguistic success. The Slovenes rejected it completely for fear of losing their own identity and went their own way. Serbians and Croatians did not hold to the agreement either. Politically, however, it did have considerable significance, especially in Croatia. It established yet another demarcation between those who stood for Croatian self-assertion and independence and those who cooperated with the existing government. Nationalist forces rejected the Agreement as a political move of those who wanted to weaken their movement. Clearly, they had good reasons for their accusations. Both those intellectuals in Croatia who cooperated with the "Magyarons" (Magyarophiles) and those who looked for a solution of the Croatian national problem in the unity of South Slavs, advocated the unification of the South Slavic languages. It may seem contradictory that the once ruling "Magyarons" (at the beginning of this century) would favor a Serbian and Croatian language unification lest there be an anti-Magyar backlash. But because the Serbian minority in Croatia was their major political ally, supporting language unity was a handy way of weakening the Croatian national movement and, as a result, undermining Croatian opposition.

The peak of the language unification fever was reached in 1913. The anti-Habsburg movement was growing among the Slavs in the Monarchy. Serbia was a winner in the Balkan Wars and as such became even more attractive to the Serbs in the Monarchy and some younger Croatian, and even Slovene intellectuals as well. The idea of unification of the South Slavs was growing. Each nationality, however, had a different idea of how this unification should be accomplished and what form of state they should form. Many enthusiasts of the unification believed that the South Slavic peoples were "tribes" of a single nation which by the misfortunes of history had not been able to re-unify themselves.

As far as language was concerned, the formula "one nation one language" was applied. The creation of a linguistic unity was to serve the desired political and national unification. For that purpose, a compromise language proposal was made by a Serbian scholar, Jovan Skerlić: Serbians would give up the Cyrillic script and Croatians would accept Serbian "ekavica." Slovene was not to be considered a literary language at all; neither were the languages of the Macedonians and the Montenegrins considered separate languages.

The political unification of the South Slavs, except the Bulgarians, into a single state in 1918 only exacerbated the language question because the Serbian royal regime favored the advancement of Serbian in the "liberated territories."[13] As a result, the country became "not only a prison of nations but also a prison of languages."[14]

As the Croatian political struggle increased during the Twenties and Thirties, so did its emphasis on the individuality and preservation of the

Croatian language. The struggle for language rights became a symbol of national resistance against Serbian oppression, just as it had been against the Hungarians a few decades earlier. In 1941, when the Croatian independence from Serbia was established, new standards for the Croatian language were formulated which rigorously emphasized differences between the Serbian and Croatian languages.

After World War II, Tito's language policies were constitutionally similar to those of political federalism. Officially, Yugoslavia had four languages: Serbian, Croatian, Slovene and Macedonian.[15] However, because of unitaristic policies during the after-war years, a "unification" of Croatian and Serbian was fostered as a major political and cultural basis for, what the Party hoped to be, an emerging "Yugoslav" nation. A result of this political and linguistic process was the Novi Sad Agreement of 1954. The document, which was clearly politically inspired, declared that the Serbian and Croatian literary languages were one (jedan) and uniform (jedinstven).[16] The newly unified language was named "Serbo-Croatian" or "Croato-Serbian." The document, however, recognized that they were two "variants" of the same "standard language."[17]

The Novi Sad Agreement created numerous practical questions. One was the definition of "variants." What were they? Were they just dialects, languages, or temporary "inconveniences" which would disappear in time? The answer to these and similar questions usually followed national lines. Croatians emphasized and Serbians played down the role of the "variants." But whatever the answers were, one things was certain: the Novi Sad Agreement created more problems than it solved.

In the mid-Fifties the ideology of "Yugoslavism" and unitarism was at its peak. The Novi Sad Agreement was clearly an expression of the Party's desire to create a single nation in Yugoslavia. In order to achieve this goal, the unity of the Croatian and Serbian languages was essential; however, the Novi Sad Agreement de facto has the opposite effect. Croatians regarded the Agreement and the forced language unification as a pretext for a slow but steady Serbianization—first of their language and then of their culture and national identity. A leading Croatian writer emphasized that

[in intra-national relations, there is] a systematic penetration, which could be called even an ideology. It is organized and operates 'scientifically' in an orchestrated manner. Unfortunately, it is tied to national motives and not to socialist conceptions, no matter how much it is veiled with socialist language. That planned penetration comes through efforts to create a single literary language, through spoken language, the school system, textbooks, school programs, [federal] administration, etc. In Croatia, this is seen as part of a single, well planned political program which already has been publically called: cultural imperialism.[18]

On the other hand, Serbians saw in the Croatian resistance to the language unification "clear" signs of Croatian separatism and, therefore, a threat to the unity of the state.

Already at the time of the Novi Sad meeting, there had been disagreements, which became public knowledge only a number of years later.[19] Because of the political situation in the country, Croatia's complaints about the language issue were not made public until March 17, 1967, when the Declaration concerning the Croatian language was published. The fall of Aleksandar Ranković, in July 1966, and the victory of the Party liberals assured Croatian intellectuals that the time had come to clarify not only economic and political but also language issues. It is quite certain that most of the Croatian intelligentsia and its cultural institutions stood behind the Declaration and de facto renounced the Novi Sad Agreement. Although the Party swiftly condemned those who dared to raise the touchy language question, language discussions increased in frequency and intensity between Belgrade and Zagreb after 1967, and even extended to the republics of Bosnia and Hercegovina and Montenegro.

In retrospect, one could say that the 1967 Declaration was a visible turning point in the history of language relations between Croatians and Serbians. From the time of the Illyrian movement (1840s) until 1967 there had been a constant push toward a fusion of the two languages, except during World War II, of course. But as far as Croatians were concerned, after the Declaration, the process began to develop in the opposite direction. All major Croatian cultural institutions, linguists, and even young Party leaders began to emphasize the differences between the two languages and also stressed the right of each nation to develop its own language within its national and cultural tradition. They demanded the equality of all the languages in the country and, most of all, the right to call each language by its national name.[20] For example, almost every issue of the *Hrvatski književni list* (HKL) had an article on the Croatian language. In a series of articles, the paper made an effort to point out Serbian words, terms, and expressions that had crept into Croatian language usage. At the same time, language specialists were encouraging the use of Croatian words which had before been rejected by the regime as anachronisms or which in Ranković's days were considered chauvinistic.

One of the constant complaints of Croatians, in the late Sixties, was that the equality of the two "variants" existed only on paper. In practice, the Serbian "version" was patronized by the federal government as the official language, while Croatian was being treated as a disappearing dialect of Serbian. To prove these allegations, Croatians pointed to numerous examples of inequality between the two officially equal "variants."[21] There was the case of the notorious dictionary of "Serbo-Croatian" prepared by Dr. Miloš S. Moskovljević, a member of the Serbian Academy of Sciences and Arts and once a high Party official, published in 1966. It was clearly compiled and edited in the Great Serbian and even royalist fashion. It did not even have an entry for the word Hrvat (Croat) or any of its derivatives. Serbs were honored by various entries, while Slovenes and other nationalities were ill-defined or underrepresented.

While Moskovljević's dictionary was dismissed as the work of only one individual; another dictionary created many more problems in Croatian-Serbian relations. The first two volumes of the "Serbo-Croatian" or "Croato-Serbian" dictionary appeared in 1967. The dictionary was compiled in collaboration with Matica hrvatska and Matica srpska. The reaction of Croatian cultural institutions, however, and the public as well was furor. Both "variants" were supposed to be equally represented in this monumental work, but the dictionary was openly one-sided. Croatian words, expressions, and terminology were treated as provincial or archaic in nature, while the Serbian "variant" prevailed as standard language.[22] Because of this controversy, Matica hrvatska unilaterally withdrew from the project in January 1971. Since it considered the Dictionary to be solely Serbian, there seemed no point in collaborating in the project any longer. Croatians began to view the federal government as the major obstacle to the equality of languages. On the surface it seemed that the Croatian "variant" was being treated as equal; however, most central agencies used the Serbian "variant" as official language for the republics of Serbia, Bosnia and Hercegovina, Montenegro and Croatia. In many areas, such as in the legal profession, in banking, traffic, in medicine, railroads, post office, army, and even on the Red Cross posters the Serbian terminology was favored and it replaced the Croatian equivalents even in Croatia.[23] A Croatian writer wrote about this issue to a Serbian friend in Belgrade:

> You belong to people who are numerically larger than mine. You live in a city which is the economic, administrative, political and increasingly the cultural center of the whole country. The language of the people of that center is the language of our administration, our army, generally of our television, radio, and the language of a tremendous amount of books which are overflowing the markets of my nation. The existence of your language is not threatened. . . . But you are surprised that others are not happy about the flourishing of your language.[24]

As a result, the Matica hrvatska officially renounced the Novi Sad Agreement on April 16, 1971, and other Croatian cultural institutions followed its lead.[25]

Complaints regarding official language policies came not only from the republic of Croatia. Voices of protest were also heard in Bosnia and Hercegovina, where there were basically two different reasons for rejecting the Novi Sad Agreement of February 1971. One voice came from the newly recognized Muslim nationals who complained that the Novi Sad Agreement did not take into account their national language rights. The second voice came from Croatians (Muslims and Catholics) who protested against the language discrimination and its Serbianization in the republic. The late Mehmedalija Mak Dizdar, poet and editor of the literary journal *Život*, declared that "protagonists of the eastern variant [Serbian] had done everything in order to impose it . . . on the territory of Bosnia and Hercegovina."[26]

An even stronger debate developed, in the late Sixties, about the language status in Montenegro. There were basically two sides in that controversy which, again, went much deeper than the issue of language. Generally speaking, Serbs considered Montenegrins and their language as part of the Serbian ethnic unit. Among the Montenegrins, however, some considered themselves part of the Serbian culture, while others rejected that position and argued for Montenegrin national and linguistic independence. Montenegrin nationalists finally opposed the Novi Sad Agreement because it simply declared that their language was to be "Serbo-Croatian" or "Croato-Serbian," without even asking the Montenegrin people. To the Montenegrins this was a clear violation of their national and republican rights. From the linguistic perspective, Montenegrins maintained that their language was neither Serbian nor Croatian, but a language of its own. While their nationality had been officially recognized, the right to their own language was denied. Thus, they too, joined the Croatians in rejecting the Novi Sad Agreement.[27]

As a result of the language controversy and the renunciation of the Novi Sad Agreement in spring of 1971, a new Croatian Orthography was printed at the end of 1971. But even before it could be distributed, its 40,000 copies were destroyed by the regime because it considered the manual to be an expression of nationalism.[28] The Croatian national movement was violently stopped and the Croatian Orthography had been just another victim of the Party's counterattack.

After the linguistic arguments failed to convince Croatians that their language was supposedly one with Serbian, some Serbian intellectuals who had previously been stressing that the two languages were one, raised the question of the language rights of the Serbian minority in Croatia. According to them, it would be discriminatory against Serbs if the official language in Croatia would be called Croatian only. Thus, in order to do justice to the minority, its name should be "Serbo-Croatian" or "Croato-Serbian." On the other hand, Croatians justified their position by pointing out that Serbs in Croatia had been using the Croatian language as their own for centuries and that Croatians, as a majority in their own homeland, had the right to identify their language according to its national name. As far as the Serbs in Croatia were concerned, Croatian linguists and the political leadership acknowledged the right of Serbs to give their own language the name they pleased. Clearly, linguists and politicians from Serbia were using the appeal of Serb minority rights in Croatia as an excuse for not resolving the basic political and linguistic issues concerning the Serbian and Croatian languages.[29]

Viewing the history of the unification and separation processes of the Croatian and Serbian languages, it is clear that political motives played more important roles than linguistic issues. Each time the idea of language unity was in the winning position, there was less freedom of expression in Croatia. The Vienna Agreement of 1851 was made at the time of Bach's absolutism.[30] At the time of Khuen's terror in Croatia,[31] the advocates of unified Serbian and Croatian languages, known as Vukovci (followers of Vuk Karadžić) triumphed over those national forces which had fought for Croatian national and linguistic individuality. Similar parallels can be found after 1918. Discussions about the freedom of language corresponded to the political atmosphere in the country. The 1954 Novi Sad Agreement was a result of the political strength of centralist forces. Its rejection by the Croats and some others, in 1971, was possible because of the decentralization of political power at that time. But a return to a stronger Party role in 1972 stifled the separation process of Croatian and Serbian languages. The issue was put under administrative control again and the Novi Sad Agreement became sacrosanct once more.

But, as in the past, language controversies did not disappear from the national scene. Even the removal of the liberal Croatian Party leadership, at the end of 1971, the closing of the Matica hrvatska, and the jailing of a number of intellectuals could not suppress all the voices.[32] The language issue is still an important part of the unsettled national relations in the country. As far as Croatians are concerned, it is clear that they are not willing to accept a language union, regardless of what might be the relative distance of closeness of their language and the Serbian. They believe that their language de facto exists even though de jure it is not recognized.[33] Furthermore, to them the language question transcends pure linguistics; it is a question of national and cultural identity.

> Serbian and Croatian languages . . . are the languages of two [different] literatures, the languages of two nations. They are, thus, the means of these peoples in their life struggle, in the affirmation of their [national] being.[34]

Obviously, the more the Croatians are pressured to give in to the language question, the greater is their resolve to preserve it.

Historiography

One of the most important features of the Croatian national movement in the Sixties and early Seventies was its contribution to the rediscovery of the national past and to the revision of the national official historiography. In the popular press and among the younger generation there was a strong element of romanticism in the newly discovered national history. But on the whole, leading historians and other intellectuals tried to look at their national past in a new light in order to assess Croatia's place in the world and in history.

A basic problem in Croatian historiography after World War II was the unofficial requirement by the regime to avoid certain subjects. A leading Croatian weekly pointed to this problem in the late Sixties:

> There have been the so-called undesirable themes in Croatian historiography which historians were not supposed to touch if they were wise. Some of those themes or historic figures were most often ignored for political reasons. A good portion of Croatian national history has been drastically belittled.[35]

A Croatian intellectual in the country also complained:

> Croatian historiography, especially in the post-war period, suffers from minimizing, ignoring, and even consciously falsifying historical truth concerning the Croatian people. For this reason, we lately hear public cries that those shortcomings. . .have to be corrected as soon as possible.[36]

On the forbidden list were a number of historic figures, events or themes from all periods of Croatian national history. Those from the Nineteenth and Twentieth century, however, were especially numerous. For example, Ban Josip Jelačić, Ante Starčević, Stjepan Radić, Frano Supilo, and Andrija Hebrang,[37] were rarely even mentioned in history books or classrooms. One Croatian historian wrote:

> We have excluded [from our history] a number of dukes, kings, and [feudal] lords who preserved what we have; they [too] fought for Croatian autonomy and the state, without which we can hardly understand today's quest for Croatian statehood. We have removed some monuments, changed names to some streets and squares. We have disregarded the graves of some historic persons, and declared

that some people and phenomena are revolutionary and others counter-revolutionary as if the first and second do not belong to the history of the Croatian people.[38]

One of the better known controversial figures of the past was Josip Jelačić. He was condemned as a counter-revolutionary and his monument was removed from Zagreb's main square immediately after World War II. Jelačić's name, however, remained symbolic of Croatian resistance to all foreign oppression. In the late Sixties, there was a growing demand for the return of his statue. Croatians accused the Party of having destroyed national relics in the name of the working class. However, even ill-famed *ban* Khuen Hedervary in his twenty year reign had not dared to touch this statue.

Those who began to address such "unpleasant" subjects or "counter-revolutionary" personalities were usually accused of nationalism, romanticism, and idealism. But Croatian historians began to challenge such condemnations by arguing that there was no reason to ignore any period, event, or personality related to their national history. A Croatian intellectual argued, "if we have recognized nations [within Yugoslavia] we then have to accept their history too."[39] The new historians stressed that things could not be taken out of their historical context and be judged solely by Marxist revolutionary standards. They also considered it hypocritical of the Party to expect Croatians to renounce some of their national history while it was acceptable that other nations in Yugoslavia (and in the world) not only respected but glorified their national past and their real or mythical figures.[40]

The basic demand at that time was for freedom to deal openly with all subjects and periods of Croatian history. At a meeting of Croatian historians, in 1971, the participants declared that there had not been "freedom or real possibility for a development of [Croatian] national historiography" till 1969 or 1971.[41] One publicist stressed:

History cannot be negated. That is why it should all be brought to our knowledge no matter what that [history] might have been. Only in that way will we be able to prevent the repetition of blunders and errors of the past. As a result, we would fill the present moments, which are in the making, with true human relations . . . .[42]

Another goal was to free historiography from ideological determinism.

The historian, if he wishes to be a scholar and make a permanent contribution to the study of history, cannot be constrained by any ideological and party commitments, even less by any exclusivism, while engaging in the process of comprehending and evaluating historical events.[43]

An important aspect of the quest of Croatian historians for professional freedom was their desire to disseminate their findings and knowledge to a wider public, especially to students. Just as in the case of Croatian literature and other cultural matters, charges were made that school textbooks had "completely eliminated the national component of [Croatian] history, even to the point that some hardly mentioned the Croatian name."[44]

Another goal was to present national history in a synthesized manner. For centuries, different Croatian regions had been under the direct or indirect rule of different foreign powers, such as the Habsburgs, Turks, and the doges of Venice. Furthermore, even those regions of Croatia which had been tied to the Habsburg empire had different relations with the crown.[45] Thus, in order to subdue the Croatian national resistance and make their rule easier, the foreign rulers divided Croatia into several smaller semi-independent regions. This method of strengthening regionalism and thereby weakening Croatia's national unity was also the policy of the central government in Belgrade. Croatian historians had been fully aware of this kind of ruling design and finally in the Sixties they began demanding the end of such tactics and called for an integration of Croatian national history. The integrity of Croatian nationhood, they emphasized, should not be sacrificed for the sake of some imaginary "Yugoslavism" or socialist internationalism.[46] It was also for the same reason that Croatians objected to the proposed regionalism during the 1971 census. The federal government had suggested that a person could declare his regional affiliation as his nationality. Croatian leadership, however, saw this as just another element of the government's anti-Croatian tactics. They fought against this issue and the federal government gave in: regional "nationalisms" were not acceptable in the 1971 census.[47]

In the Sixties, Croatian historians began to pay special attention to the national history of the post-1918 era. They believed that this epoch of

Croatian history was the most distorted and that historians needed to give a more balanced view of Croatian national development during those turbulent years. Actually, one of the first and most significant historical controversies was caused by a history of the Communist Party of Yugoslavia, published in 1963. At that time, the Institute for History of the Workers' Movement in Croatia strongly opposed the Party's historiography. The Institute together with some other Croatian Marxist intellectuals organized a symposium at the end of 1963 in which the newly published *Pregled istorije SKJ* (A Review of the History of the LCY) was thoroughly scrutinized. The book was criticized not only from a historical but also from a theoretical point of view.[48] The main targets of criticism were the Party unitarism and the pro-Serbian views that were expressed in the book. Although the institute and its leader Franjo Tudjman were chastised for their actions, the fact that Tito himself addressed this problem of historiography and nationalism at the Eighth Congress of the LCY in 1964 indicated the importance of the dispute.[49]

Croatian historians pointed out that official Yugoslav historiography had over-emphasized the destructive role of Croatians in the First Yugoslavia and during World War II, without trying to analyze why the Croatians reacted in the way they did. The Croatian nation as a whole had been condemned, implicitly or explicitly, as Fascist and had been accused of being bloodthirsty. Furthermore, they had been held responsible for the breakup of royalist Yugoslavia in 1941 and for innumerable war crimes. While the Serbs had been presented as state makers and were portrayed in a much more positive light, post-war historiography treated the Croatians as a "guilty" nation.

Traditional historiography both in the First and in Communist Yugoslavia started with the premise that the creation of the common state of Serbs, Croatians and Slovenes, known as Yugoslavia after 1929, was a positive historical event; that it was the fulfillment of the national desires of all those who found themselves within that state.[50] All subsequent historical events and movements in that country were evaluated in that context. Croatian Marxist historians in the late Sixties, however, highlighted the other side of the Yugoslav state.

Regarding the international circumstances [during which it was created] and by its internal structure, [the old Yugoslavia] was a reactionary creation. With reference to the national question, for some peoples [that state] was even worse than the one before it [the Habsburg Monarchy]. Only with this in mind, one can understand all that took place in the framework of [Yugoslavia's] history from 1918 to 1941.[51]

All peoples—except the Serbs—were oppressed, and the situation they found themselves in was in many ways identical to a real occupation.[52]

In 1918 Croatia lost all the prerogatives of statehood, which it had had since medieval times under the crown of St. Stephen. The loss of this political status, no matter how fragile it may have been at different times, was considered by the Croatians a major blow to their national existence. The struggle against Serbian centralism and for Croatian statehood within and outside the Yugoslav state started immediately after the country's unification.[53] Aspects of this on-going struggle between Serbian hegemonism and the Croatian desire for self-rule were reflected in the politics of the Croatian Peasant Party (the most powerful political party during the inter-war period), in the creation of the revolutionary Ustasha movement in 1929, in the Croatian-Serbian Agreement in 1939, and in the break up of the state in 1941, as well as in the policies of the Communist Party in Croatia.

Yugoslav "court" historians blamed Croatians for the collapse of the common state in 1941 and, therefore, for all calamities of the war.[54] According to the Croatians, however, the Belgrade regime and its oppressive rule were the real cause for the break up of the state. Although the internal policy did shift from open Serbianization (1918-1929) to a policy of Yugoslav integralism (1929-1939), and although there was the attempt of a Croatian-Serbian compromise (1939), the essential aim of Belgrade's internal policy continued to be that of Serbian domination. For example, official historiography emphasized the coup of March 27, 1941, as a major sign of Serbian democratic opposition to Yugoslavia's ties to the Central Powers. The main goal of the coup, however, was the annihilation of the Croatian-Serbian Agreement (1939) and a return to the more traditional Great Serbian policies; the external dimensions of the coup were only of secondary importance.

Croatians further pointed out that official Yugoslav historiography did not make any distinction between the Ustasha movement and Croatian patriotism or between the regime in Croatia from 1941 to 1945 and the state itself. Even a former Partisan general acknowledged that

the declaration of an independent Croatia [1941], following the collapse of Yugoslavia, meant the realization of goals held dear not only by radical, separatist currents in Croatian political life but also by the majority of the Croatian people. . . .[55]

Croatians as a nation had also been blamed for the Ustasha alliance with the Axis and for war crimes committed during the war, while Serbian Chetniks, their collaboration with the Axis powers, and their crimes had been minimized.

To neglect that fact that historical causes for the Ustasha movement were in the hegemonistic oppression of the Croatian people in monarchist Yugoslavia, and also that the Chetnik movement had been no less dangerous for the Croatian population than the Ustasha movement for the Serbian citizens—results in holding onto unscientific and hegemonistic positions.[56]

One of the most sensitive ghosts of the past touched upon during the Croatian national revival was the issue of war victims in Croatia. Ever since the war, official Yugoslav propaganda had it that the Ustasha had killed hundreds of thousands of people, mostly Serbs. But no one came up with concrete evidence for such enormous numbers. Until 1965, when Franjo Tudjman openly challenged such official propaganda, no one had dared question those numbers. According to Tudjman, the Statistical Institute of Croatia, in Zagreb, calculated that the total number of those killed in prison camps and prisons in general on the territory of the Socialist Republic of Croatia was 59,639[57] and it was also stressed that those who were killed in the camps were mostly Croatian liberals.[58] Similar findings were published for the first and only time in 1969 by the late Croatian publicist Bruno Bušić in HKL.[59] Although Bušić and Tudjman, and their articles came under sharp Party attacks, nobody even tried to challenge their conclusions on a scientific basis.

The current Yugoslav government has yet to publish full information about war victims, nor has it permitted historians and other scholars to research the available data in order to authenticate the number and nationality of those killed. Some feel that the government is more concerned with the Partisan war record and especially with the killings that took place right after the end of the war.[60] Other reasons for keeping the true number of victims unconfirmed and so highly inflated were perhaps to use those numbers as propaganda in order to blacken the Croatian name abroad, to create a guilt feeling in the new generations of Croatians, to justify centralist policies, and to condemn all signs of Croatian patriotism as remnants of the Ustashe movement. A leading Croatian writer and Partisan war veteran commented on this kind of anti-Croatian propaganda:

> I know that those who are making the number of killed in Jasenovac ten times bigger than it is, simply know well that those who were killed in that camp were mostly Croatians. But they want to cash in on someone else's blood; and they are dragging it around for their own dirty interests.[61]

Younger Croatians in the early Seventies were asking for an open inquiry of all war victims and war crimes, including those which were committed by Tito's Partisans. But this was anathema to the Party leadership, and Tito reacted by saying that the killings done by his forces were not sin, they were part of a struggle for life and death. He even stressed that "during the war time there was no concern what someone else might say in the future; one fought and destroyed whomever he could."[62]

Another major effort made by Croatian historians in the 1960s was to bring to light the Croatian contribution to Tito's forces. Along with this, questions were raised about the ideological differences between the Croatian Party leadership and the Politbureau of the CPY and how these differences had affected war efforts. An important goal was to uncover and make public the true political and national goals of the Croatian Party leadership and other Croatians who had fought for the re-creation of Yugoslavia.

One of the beliefs of the Croatian historians was that while Serbian contributions to the war had been over-emphasized in the official historiography and Party documents, the Croatian role had been minimized:

The dissemination of the theory of the enormous historical guilt of the Croatian nation also serves to cover up the truth that in World War II Croatia was not only on the side of the Axis Powers but was also one of the firmest footholds of the anti-Fascist movement, giving not a smaller but larger contribution in blood to the victory of the democratic forces over Fascism than other Yugoslav nations.[63]

Croatian revisionists pointed out that the uprising in Serbia, in the fall of 1941, did not succeed. Partisan efforts in Croatia, however, were quite successful, and so much territory was under their control that it was possible to hold the First Croatian Partisan Sabor (ZAVNOH) in the Spring of 1943.[64] They were especially proud of the Third meeting of the ZAV-NOH (May 1944) and the Congress of Croatian Cultural Workers (June 1944). These meetings had been, according to them, a true expression of a newly forming "democratic state" and a major sign of liberal pluralism.[65] One of the participants proudly pointed out that the cultural Congress

> was the largest, most varied, and liveliest Partisan meeting. It not only carried on cultural work in the midst of the hardest wartime conditions, but it was also a sign and pledge of the creative possibilities in the still-to-be liberated nation...I was surprised at how much the pre-War Revisionism was still around.[66]

Furthermore, two traditional Party tendencies surfaced at the Congress: "one group wished to demonstrate its fidelity to Marxism-Leninism; for the other, the success of the National Liberation Struggle dictated a much broader approach to cultural issues."[67] For the first group, among which were followers of Tito, Djilas, and Kardelj, the meeting was "merely a political tactic to deceive the Allies and the citizens so they would support the Partisans."[68] The other group, headed by the Croatian Party leadership, accepted the proclaimed pluralistic principles as the basis of the future state and society. And it was this second faction that organized the war efforts and was dominant in Croatia.

The partisan mass uprising in Croatia had been a little slower than in Serbia but it was much better organized and had a better ideological structure than the partisan movements in the eastern parts of the country.

Neither did it suffer major setbacks as did the uprising in Serbia. Most of all, however, Croatians wanted to be assured that the new state would be organized on an equal national basis and would not be a copy of the First Yugoslavia.

> Only when the Communist Party in Croatia . . . succeeded to convince the Croatian people that the Communist Party was fighting for the freedom and equality of Croatia, not only for its liberation from the occupators and the Ustashe, but also for a full equality of Croatia within a new and socialist community of nations in Yugoslavia, only then was the Communist Party able to attract the Croatian people to the National Liberation Movement. . . .[69]

According to the liberal Croatian Marxist war participants, "the nationalist question was one of the essential issues of the socialist revolution" in Croatia. Many Marxists believed that nationalism, although "non-essential to the substance or to the victory," can be used as an ally of the revolution. In Croatia, however, according to the liberals, the national and class questions were genuinely united, and only on that basis could the Party attrack the mass following.[70] Thus, the main reason for Partisan war successes in Croatia was the ideological difference between leading Communists in Croatia and those who were with Tito in the High Command. The Croatian Party, headed by Andrija Hebrang, based the national struggle on the broad ideology of the National Liberation Front, which included a wide variety of national, social, and political segments, but most of all a large portion of the Croatian Peasant Party. Leading Communists in Serbia and Montenegro, on the other hand, emphasized class war, which did not find a favorable response among the population.[71] As a result, their efforts failed. During the war, Croatian Party leadership followed its ideology of the inter-war period and stood for a pluralistic society. The ZAVNOH was a reflection of this ideology, and it actually had a multiparty character.[72]

The ZAVNOH and the Party in Croatia also proclaimed that the aim of war and revolution was to establish a free Croatia together with other free nations united in a federated Yugoslavia. They believed that the new state would be federal not only in name but in reality. The promise of autonomy and democracy had a strong effect on the population, especially

on the Left wing of the Croatian Peasant Party, whose war participation
had been essential to Partisan successes in Croatia.[73] Indeed, it was the
Partisan war successes in Croatia and the political coalition of the National
Front which were seen as a major reason for the Allied support of Tito
rather than the Great-Serbian Chetnik forces.[74]

As post-war experiences indicate, the promises, however, were not kept.
There was no democracy, pluralism, or national self-government and Tito
together with the radical wing of the Party had the upper hand in these
decisions. Moreover, Hebrang, the man responsible for war successes in
Croatia and the number one man in the Croatian Party, became a Party
victim because of his political and national views. The hegemonistic and
centralistic forces could not tolerate what they called Croatian nationalism
and revisionism in the Party. In 1948, Hebrang, was accused of Stalinism
and of being an Ustashe as well as a German agent. But his main sin was
that he stood for full national equality and freedom in a confederated
Yugoslavia. Stalinism was just an excuse to condemn and liquidate him.
Ivan Supek claimed that the political system that Hebrang and his followers envisioned and promised to the people had the "essential features
of today's Eurocommunism."[75] But nothing of this had been realized
because of the ideological radicalism of Tito and his men at the top of
the Party hierarchy. Hebrang and a large group of Croatian Marxist intellectuals were wiped out during and after the war[76] and only those who
were true followers of Tito, Bakarić for example, became political leaders
in Croatia.

During the late 1960s and early 1970s, Croatian intellectuals pointed
out that their national history was misrepresented and that a major revision was needed in the official historiography, especially in that of the
Second World War period. They also demanded an open discussion of all
historical issues, but their attempts were suppressed by the centralist
forces at the end of 1971. Since then, continuous lack of access to archival
materials and official silence has prevented a re-examination of numerous
historical issues and events. Historiography, however, continues to play
an antagonistic role in the intra-national relations in the country.

CHAPTER VI

SOCIAL ELEMENTS IN THE CROATIAN NATIONAL MOVEMENT

The political and economic system in Yugoslavia has been complex and in many ways contradictory. Because of the diversity among its many nations and nationalities, the country has been organized on federalist principles. At the same time, there has been the Party's quest for homogeneity, and in order to achieve a national unification the Party promoted the principle of "Yugoslavism." This program, however, turned out to be a failure and was replaced by the principle of "Yugoslav socialist patriotism." But the balance between centralist and decentralist forces remained a constant problem for the ruling elites. Its delicate nature was especially exacerbated by the fact that these two forces were also very much influenced by national divisions.

In its first political and social phase of development, known as etatism (1945-1952), the country was controlled in a hierarchical fashion by a small group of Party functionaries. The state and society were in strict control of the Party, and there was no room for any other political or social group to stand between society and the state. After the introduction of the principles of self-management, political "pluralism" was supposed to be developed, but in a socialist fashion. The idea was to give different economic, territorial, and professional groups rights and obligations to participate in questions of economical, social, and even political nature.

126

Principles of self-management were supposed to replace centralism and lead to poli-centrism. It was in this way that a measure of political participation would be achieved and not through a multiparty system. But during the period from 1952 until 1966, the Party conservatives were in full control and the system continued to run basically in the old "etatist" fashion. After the victory of the liberals, the system was somewhat loosened up and poli-centrism began to emerge, but the Croatian national movement in the late 1960s and early 1970s put the principles of self-management and poli-centrism to the real test. The different social elements of the movement began to demand personal, group, and national rights in the name of those principles. The result was that the Party would not allow its monopoly of power to be challenged. The principles of self-management had to be interpreted according to the Party's views only, and there was no room for any outside interpretation of these principles. In order to preserve its role as the only guardian of the state and socialism, the Party was ready to crush all other political and social currents.

Although there were a number of socio-political organizations besides the Party in Yugoslavia, their political role had been insignificant. There was for example, the Socialist Alliance, the Sindicates, and the Youth Alliance, but they all were mere transmission belts for Party policies. In Croatia, in the late Sixties and early Seventies, however, other groups began to play an important part in society. Intellectuals, students, workers, peasants, people of all ages became more and more involved in the ongoing national revival. The more strength they gained, the more the Party saw them as a real threat to its power. As a result, the movement was on a collision course with the Party from the start. In order to get a better understanding of the national movement, it is, however, necessary to take a closer look at the Communist Party in Croatia and its relationship to the movement.

Factions in the LC of Croatia

At the peak of the Croatian national movement in the early Seventies, there were three major Party factions in the republic: conservatives, neo-conservatives, and liberals. At the time of the Tenth Session of the CC LC of Croatia, in January 1970, the Party was divided basically into liberal and conservative camps. At that meeting, the conservatives were defeated, although not destroyed, and a liberal Party platform was promulgated. But, not long after the Tenth Session, a number of leading liberals began to oppose the top republican Party leadership. In their eyes, the leadership was going too far in its demands for national equality and emancipation and was being too "soft" on the Croatian intellectuals and students in their national activities. These liberals became neo-conservatives. They moved closer to the old conservatives, while those at the top of the Party leadership moved closer to the humanistic intelligentsia. Gradually, this later group came to stand for humanist socialism and their goal was to change the Yugoslav federation into a confederation of fully equal nations. The best known exponent of the "conservative" Party faction in Croatia at the time was Miloš Žanko. His attacks on what he considered nationalist and anti-socialist forces in Croatia revealed the true nature of the conservative faction. In her speech at the Tenth Plenum of the CC LC of Croatia, Savka Dapčević-Kučar, President of the CC, pointed out the main characteristics of the conservative forces. She called the conservatives Yugoslav unitarists who believed that

concrete questions of national equality in intra-national relations had been definitely resolved by the constitution. [But] in reality unitarism is a mask behind which hegemonism is hiding its [true] face.

[They] completely negated the need for equality of nations.

The more intensive debates [that were taking place] about existing intra-national relations and inter-republican problems, [were considered by conservatives] as a danger threatening their cohesion, although those debates were strictly within the limits of Party principles.

Every national feeling they considered suspicious—and if according to them it existed—it has to be forbidden and destroyed. . . . They are stricken by panic only by hearing the words Croat, Croatian, Croatian language or the like. They consider it to be a revival of unhealthy ghosts of the past. . . . They do not wish to accept the fact that there is no such thing as a Yugoslav nation.[1]

The self-proclaimed defenders of the state and of the system labelled the whole spectrum of groups and individuals in Croatia as nationalist, and, therefore, dangerous. They did not even try to make any distinctions. The following excerpt is an example of the way Žanko and other unitarists were thinking at that time.

According to his [Žanko's] thinking, in the domain of the written word, on the pages of our many [Croatian] journals there is an orgy of nationalist frenzy. He unites, with a magic trick, a wide range of present literary and publicist activities of all of us [who are not in his camp]. All contradictions and polarizations in our activities he wants to obliterate in order. . . to silence once and for all 'the bourgeoisie elites' and 'the like'. In short, to silence 'tutti quanti.'[2]

In his blanket condemnation of activities in Croatia in the late Sixties, Žanko included the republican Party leadership as well. By doing so, he actually brought condemnation upon himself and his followers and from the Tenth Plenum (January 1970) till the purges at the end of 1971 the conservatives in Croatia had to keep a low profile.

The Party conservatives remembered the "good old times" when the Party had full control of the state and society. They thought that decentralization and self-management were the undercurrents that destroyed not only Party unity, discipline, and revolutionary idealism, but also most of all their own achievements such as the new Yugoslav state ruled by the Party. To them, the new and younger leadership was permitting too much freedom and therefore too many social, economic, and national conflicts came to the surface. They, on the other hand, advocated the policy of the "firm hand" and of old hierarchical order, where everything starts at the top circles of the Party. Also, they favored the old "centralized and dictated accumulation and redistribution of surplus of labor" and vehemently rejected decentralization.[3] As strongly as the conservatives felt about these issues, they never openly and outspokenly opposed the Reform because it was too dangerous to show direct resistance to Party policy. As a result, they paid lip service to the principles of self-management without ever really accepting and believing in these ideas. They did, however, try to slow the concrete realization of the Reform as much as they could. Surely, one should not forget the conservatives' personal interests in this intra-party struggle either. To allow more democracy and wider political participation would threaten their own positions and their economic and political powers. Thus, it was not just ideological principles that influenced the attitude of the conservatives. Personal interests played an important role because one of the goals of their economic policies was to "[create] a basis for themselves from which they drew their life juices."[4]

Even though the Tenth Plenum and the dismissal of Žanko was considered the final liberal victory over the conservative forces in Croatia, future events indicated that conservatism remained very much alive. Even the votes in the Croatian Sabor on April 8, 1971, by which Žanko was removed from his federal positions, showed that a number of delegates still had full confidence in him and in his political judgments.[5] The strongest supporters of the conservative Party faction in Croatia were found among the old partisans and among former army and police officers, especially if they were of Serbian nationality. These groups regarded the revival of Croatian national feelings and their national integration as a threat to everything they had fought for. They thought every national symbol or old patriotic song was a sign of chauvinism and condemned the Matica hrvatska as the "hot bed of Ustashism." Some former high ranking partisan officers even regretted that they had "laid down their arms," implying that the "enemy," Croatian nationalism, had not been destroyed and that the new blood should be shed.[6] Even the neo-conservatives admitted that

> there are individuals [among the old partisans] . . . who wished to ally themselves with foreign forces, to hold the flow of our revolution. They wanted such a Yugoslavia which would be a force above the people, a unitaristic and centralistic Yugoslavia. They would have liked to impose neo-Stalinist and cominformist ideas [on us] and to stop our progress.[7]

Finally, the conservative forces became political allies of the neo-conservatives in their common struggle against the progressive faction of the Party. The progressives later came to be known as the "nationalist faction" in the Party and they fully controlled the top leadership in the early Seventies. Jure Bilić, a prominent Party figure in Yugoslavia and Croatia in the post-1971 period, pointed out that the conservative partisan cadres would not have succeeded in their endeavors without the support of those who still had a powerful voice in the League.[8] Bilić's statements clearly indicate that, during 1970 and 1971, many so called liberals in Croatia had moved closer to the conservatives, and together they were able to change the course of events in Croatia at the end of 1971.

The neo-conservative Party faction came into existence after the Tenth Plenum of the CC LCC (January 1970) as a result of the differentiation process in Croatia's Party ranks. According to Miko Tripalo, the leading progressive in Croatia, the split of the liberals into the progressive and the neo-conservative factions came to the open in May 1971. It was at that time that "more important differences [between the two groups] came to the surface. . . and mutual mistrust was created" between them.[9] At the meeting of the Croatian Party leadership and Tito in Karadjordjevo, at the end of November 1971, Tito openly declared that the Party in Croatia was divided. Not only had the Party lost its internal unity, but the atmosphere of mutual distrust increased rapidly.[10] One of the basic disagreements between the two Party factions in the republic was the issue of nationalism. The neo-conservatives regarded the Croatian national movement as an enemy of Party, socialism, and state. They admitted that there was an economic exploitation of Croatia by the central financial and administrative agencies and they also agreed that there was a need for further changes in the federation. When looking for a solution to these and other problems they, however, were not willing to tolerate the participation of any forces which were not fully under Party control. The monopoly of Party power was simply untouchable. Although they admitted that nations were there to stay for a long time to come and although they admitted that intra-national problems did exist in Yugoslavia, they felt that all major problems facing Croatia had to be discussed in class terms rather than in national terms. The national forces claimed that many intra-national problems had their roots in inter-war Yugoslavia and that their solution was being either postponed, circumvented, or ignored by the Serbian controlled federal bureaucracy. The neo-conservatives, however, praised Party accomplishments and absolved all its failures with socialist dialectics; they saw all of these problems as a part of the evolving revolutionary process. Accordingly, they believed that the existing problems—no matter which nature they were—would be solved in due time without the "help" from ranks outside the Party.

The neo-conservatives' disagreement with the progressive faction in the Party, however, was more a result of practical questions than of socialist theories. The main cause for the split was the issue of how to handle the Croatian national forces. During 1970 and 1971, Croatian intellectuals and students were becoming more and more vocal on economic, social, cultural, and political issues and were proposing their own solutions to those problems, which they considered essential to the existence of the Croatian nation. To the neo-conservatives, these people were meddling with issues outside their designated domain, which was basically bourgeoisie liberalism. As Bakarić, the old Titoist in Croatia, stated at the Karadjordjevo meeting:

> We wanted to bring the working class from its work place to the political stage. We wanted to do this on the basis of self-management . . . . We did not want to lead the working class back where it would be led [by intellectuals].[11]

The neo-conservatives, thus, claimed that the Croatian "intellectual center," which meant Matica hrvatska, was becoming a political force which was "cultivating a deep process of political struggle with the aim of discrediting the Party and [different] individuals [in it]."[12] They thought that

> there was a plan to turn Matica hrvatska into a parallel organization to the Party or to Socialist Alliance, which would then have essential influences on political life in Croatia.[13]

In order to control these opposing forces, the neo-conservatives advocated a policy of the "firm hand." Jakov Blažević, a leading anti-progressive declared that,

> as far as papers like *Hrvatski tjednik,* then *Hrvatsko sveučilište,* and *Hrvatski gospodarski glasnik,* especially *Hrvatski gospodarski glasnik* and *Hrvatski tjednik,* are concerned, I think they have to be suppressed; they have to be hit hard. There is no single issue in which there is not an editorial or an article of counter-revolutionary nature, or which does not criticize our system which perfidiously uses this or that kind of language to attack us.[14]

Basically, the neo-conservatives thought that the executive progressive leadership in the republic was not decisive enough to put an end to the growing political opposition. What was even more confusing to them was that a good number of leading "counter-revolutionaries" were members of the League of Communists, which meant that the lines between the Party and the "opposition" were being blurred more and more. The neo-conservatives became afraid of a "mass movement" and more massive political participation. Not being able to take public criticism and scrutiny, they needed the protective shield of the Party to separate them from the masses. Moreover, they were afraid to lose their current political positions and economic privileges as well. In order to overcome the present state of confusion in the country, they demanded a cleansing of the Party from "rotten liberalism," and a return to the policies of a firm hand. In this, they found firm support among the conservatives in the Party, federal institutions, and Tito himself. At the present time there is no clear evidence whether the neo-conservatives in Croatia were asking for outside help in their effort to "clean up" their republican Party, whether they were executors of decisions made outside their republic, or whether both was the case. It seems more likely that they were basically an instrument of the federal forces. Whatever the case, the result was the same. The democratization process was stopped and Party discipline and control was reaffirmed.

The Tenth Plenum of the CC LC of Croatia (January 1970) admitted that the Party in the past had been more eager to crush any sign of nationalism as counter-revolution, while unitarism was acceptable because of its zealousness for the preservation of a unified state. But the Plenum declared that unitarism was just another form of nationalism and that it was even more dangerous in Yugoslavia's setting than Croatian nationalism.[15] It also asked for further and faster reforms by which Croatia was supposed to gain basic control of its own political, social, and economic affairs. It was at this Plenum that a liberal Party platform was promulgated and a young group of people became the leading force in the republican Party. These top officials of the Party differentiated themselves from the rest of the "liberals" and became the progressive faction which legitimized the Croatian national movement.

Ideologically, this third faction of the republic's Party was the heir to the strain of "nationally conscious" Marxism that had been present in

Croatia before, during, and after the Second World War. The young leadership was actually nurtured within the camp of the older Party liberals. They, however, had slowly begun to chart their own course under the influence of Croatian Marxist tradition, which had always been more anti-dogmatic, and had a wider and more nationally oriented platform than the bolshevized leadership of the LCY. As a result, one of the principal components of the Croatian national movement in the late Sixties had been an attempt to bring the Party in Croatia back to that tradition.

Instead of regarding themselves as the avantgarde of the working class and the guardians of ideological purity, the party progressives started identifying themselves more and more with the people and began to talk as leaders of the Croatian nation instead of just its "working class." They thought the traditional divisions of "class" and "nation" were artificial. Tripalo, the leading progressive, expressed this thesis by emphasizing that

> the national question is not some tactical move, in order to attract masses to the side of the Communist movement. . . . It is not a secondary question either, subordinated to the class problem. The national question is an integral and inseparable part of class struggle. It is an integral part of working class strategy in its struggle for socialism.[16]

The partnership of the national and class struggle was seen as an integral part of socialism. Tripalo argued further:

> A dominant position in Marxist theory is that every nation has the right to self-determination, which is expressed, first of all, in the right to organize a national state. Further, the relations among nations are based on the principles of equality and voluntary association. . . . [The struggle of the working class] is national in form, but international in context.[17]

It was also emphasized that it had been precisely the unity of national and class dimensions which guaranteed the victory of the Party in the Second World War. Savka Dapčević-Kučar, the head of the Party in Croatia, underlined the fact that the fear of emphasizing national pride, as something which could threaten the socialist unity of nations and nationalities in Yugoslavia, was not present during the peoples' war of liberation.[18]

It was not until after the war when the national dimension of socialism was declared dangerous. Unitarism and etatism had suppressed the national component in Croatian society and, according to the progressives, the time had come to make that component once more a part of the political, social, and cultural life of the Croatian people. It was this thinking that caused the Party leadership of the early 1970s in Croatia to be accused of a dualistic heresy: they were said to mix class and nationalism and even to give more importance to the latter. Tripalo responded to this accusation by pointing out that "class and national components [were] of equal, essential, and fateful importance for Croatia.[19]

This integration of national and class questions in the progressive platform brought the Croatian Party leaders closer to the national intellligentsia, to the students, and to the masses and finally made them an important part of the mass movement. By tolerating a wide range of opinions, by dispelling the old public fears of ever-present police might, and by allowing a relatively free participation of non-Communist forces in public discussions on important issues, the progressive faction of the Party in Croatia considered itself the founder of a new era in Croatian history. The main characteristic of that era was supposed to be humanistic socialism through which individuals and the Croatian nation as a whole would gain the desired self-rule, statehood, and full national emancipation. The main obstacles to these goals were the federally controlled agencies and institutions, the financial and exporting power centers in Belgrade, and the local conservative forces. The only way to overcome these obstacles, was through a massive participation of all national and social segments in Croatia on the platform of socialist self-management and under the leadership of the most progressive forces of the Party. Savka Dapčević-Kučar, President of the Party CC in Croatia, was convinced that the growth of the national movement in the republic was a positive force. In April 1971 she declared:

A certain national enthusiasm that we see in our own ranks in the League of Communists, and in our society, an enthusiasm that undoubtedly represents a very positive and important sociopolitical phenomenon, is a big moving force toward a quicker and more successful solution of our accumulated political and economic problems.[20]

Although it was a new and complex phenomenon for the Party to handle a "very massive" movement the progressive Party leadership was ready to work within such a heterogeneous force. Tripalo accused this former liberal colleagues of duplicity because, in the late Sixties, they were in favor of mobilization of the masses, but "while we [in the Party] were just talking about it, and while it did not appear in practice, everything was fine and dandy. When the movement appeared in its full complexity . . . and when it was clear that everything was not going exactly as we had planned and imagined, many comrades became scared of the movement." He further argued that the movement's "fundamental orientation" was socialist and even the Party itself should correct its own program under the influence of the new forces. Moreover, he stressed that the Party should be ready to accept new people *en masse,* give them a chance to prove themselves to be even better than its old members were, and those members who could not accept the progressive changes should leave the Party on their own.[21]

The Party leadership in Croatia, however, found itself torn between the demands of the masses and those of the old Party principles and power. Its solution was to balance the two, to incorporate new ideas and new people into an expanded old Party framework, and to come out with a more democratic and humanistic society. In order to achieve this the progressives urged the opening of Party ranks to the young people. "Only by joining [the Party] *en masse,* youth can make an alliance with the most progressive elements from former generations" and together they could move forward. But the newcomers were not trusted by the older Party members.[22] They saw them as a threat to their own positions and to the Party ideology and unity.

Beside the quest for a younger and more flexible Party membership, Tripalo and his followers counted on support from the majority of people outside the Party framework as well. He argued that all solutions in the country "had to be sought in an organized but democratic action—by majority pressure."[23] Srećko Bijelić, a leading progressive Serb from

Croatia also stressed the fact that even the strongest governments in history have fallen once they "lost their bond with the class and masses, or tried to construct economic and social relations for only their own interests, or just for a tiny segment of society."[24] This kind of advocacy of a wide political participation gave the young leadership massive support.

By getting closer to the people and by speaking on behalf of the Croatian nation, and not only in the name of the working class, the Party leadership in 1970 and 1971 also began to legitimize itself in the eyes of the Croatian people.

Shortly after the Communist takeover in 1945 the government lost its credibility in Croatia, even with many of those who once supported it. It had disregarded the promises of freedom and national equality and suppressed the voice of the Croatian Peasant Party, and other political parties as well. The Party tried to compensate the shaky grounds of its legitimacy by promises of a better future. For the Croatians, however, the "future" brought economic exploitation, cultural oppression, large emigration and, as many claimed, much uncertainty. Basically, it was a repetition of the experiences of inter-war Yugoslavia. Thus, when the Party leadership began to talk openly about the above problems and about revising the whole intra-national arrangement in the country, it began to receive public support from various national and social elements, and people like Savka Dapčević-Kučar and Miko Tripalo established themselves as true national tribunes.

Even before their fall at the end of 1971, Croatian Party leaders had been accused of "nationalism," "demogogery," and "personal ambitions."[25] But already in 1970 Tripalo had responded to those accusations by saying:

> We have been listening to such epithets already for a long time. The fact is, however, that most of our charges and arguments have been accepted [by the Party] at least in theory. The same thing happened when we raised the question of the material basis of self-management. We were accused of doing it out of nationalist motives. As soon as such 'arguments' are used, it is a sign that [our opponents] do not have real arguments.[26]

It is true that Tripalo's and Dapčević-Kučar's youthful and charming personalities did play an important role in their popularity. However, only when they began to raise essential issues and press for their solutions, did the masses begin to follow them. Such issues as finances, emigration, unemployment, investments, taxes, were very concrete and by no means demagogic. Also, if the progressive leadership had been primarily interested in its own ambitions and gains, it would have been more reasonable for it to follow the traditional and more secure Party path to power than engaging in new and unexplored experiments with the masses. There is no doubt, then, that the progressives' interest in improving the situation of the Croatian people was indeed sincere.

In retrospect, one can say that while the progressive Party leadership had the support of the majority of the people, even though that majority was not Communist, its strength in the Party itself was an shaky grounds. The Party membership was predominately of older age. For example, at one Party cell in Southern Croatia not a single young member had been accepted in the League for ten years.[27] A good proportion of the Party membership was made up of the Party apparatichiks and other poorly or half-educated professional career seekers. For example, in 1946 the "officials" (službenici) made up 10.3 and in 1966 39.1 percent of the total Party membership.[28] It is also interesting to note that less educated "officials" were more eager to join the Party.[29] Commenting on this situation and advocating a change, Tripalo stated:

> For today's leadership in all fields of social life there is a need of specific knowledge . . . . In sixty-four leading positions [in the metal industry] , for example, which presupposes high education, thirty-six of those in these positions do not have the necessary educational background. These people are under forty years of age. This indicates that under the formula 'workers-partisans' a new generation is appearing which is neither from the ranks of workers nor partisans.[30]

As a result, while the struggle at the top Party leadership was going on, many such administrative "officials" and those who owned their livelihood to the Party membership were on the side lines, awaiting the final outcome. And when the progressives lost their positions of power, it was clear that the loyalties of most of the bureaucrats was first of all with those who guaranteed their jobs.

The progressives based their arguments on "natural rights," the Marxist-Leninist theory of self-determination, and past Party declarations and principles (such as self-management and national equality), and on the support of the masses. Meanwhile, the conservative and neo-conservative forces in the Party turned to powerful allies outside the republic to get support. The progressives had the moral and ideological right and the support of the Croatian people; their opponents, however, had the political, military, and economic might in their hands. Tripalo was well aware of this power imbalance. In the summer of 1971 he foresaw the destruction of the movement and listed three reasons:

—First, because of major treason in our own ranks, which is possible.
—Second, because of lack of courage or wisdom.
- Third, because the balance of power is such today. But if we have to be defeated, we should be defeated only because of the third reason.[31]

The distribution of real power was indeed one-sided. The conservative forces thought that the movement was shaking the foundations of the Party and of the state and they believed it was better to destroy the "rotten liberals" than to change the traditional balance of power in the country and society. Moral and historical rights, or even mass support, had no importance in the struggle of power politics.

Intelligentsia

A humanist intelligentsia by its very nature is bound sooner or later to clash with a dictatorial regime, regardless of its ideological color. In modern Croatian history, like in many other nations, intellectuals traditionally have been a leading force in the quest for human dignity, social justice, and national freedom. This has also been true with most of the Croatian Left wing intellectuals during the inter-war period as well as in the 1960s and early 1970s. During the inter-war period, Croatian Left wing intellectuals stood not only against the Serbian royal regime but also against the bolshevization of the Party. Ivan Supek, one of the leading

contemporary intellectuals in Croatia, points out two major issues that
were debated between Croatian Left intellectuals and the advocates of
Party orthodoxy in the 1930s:

> The question of national equality and democratic freedoms pro-
> voked the fiercest debates. This was the start of Zagreb revisionism,
> the most heretical phenomenon in the Communist movement at
> that time.
>
> The liberal deviationism in Zagreb was looked upon there [Belgrade]
> as one of the greatest dangers to the Revolution.[32]

Even after the war, the national and the ideological elements continued to
play an important role among leading Croatian intellectuals. In fact, the
Belgrade centrists and unitarists from Croatia regarded them as the greatest
danger to the accomplishments of the revolution, and found it necessary
to shatter Croatian intellectual forces at the end of 1971.

Although many of the Croatian intellectuals had been Marxists before
World War II and actively participated in the revolution, they never lost
mistrust of the Party leadership. An older Croatian writer and a long time
Marxist cried in 1971:

> There is no true equality among us yet. There is an unbelievable mis-
> trust of some of us. The whole generation is considered half-suspi-
> ciously . . . .We have been pushed into a 'reservation.' This throws
> light first of all on those forces which have created the last Mohicans
> out of cultural workers, or even better, they have made out of [us]
> the first Etruscans among the masses who are condemned to share
> the Etruscan fate. This suspicion is even more obvious if seen in the
> light that a vast majority of the cultural workers is ready to support
> every constructive initiative, and it is without doubt socialist and
> democratic in its orientation.[33]

The reason for this kind of mistrust was the regime's lack of sensitivity for
intellectual life in general and for Croatian intellectuals in particular. Actually, never did the humanist intelligentsia feel an integral part of Yugoslav
society; they felt they were simply "an appendage, which is condemned
whenever there is a need to condemn somebody."[34] In fact, whenever the

regime wanted to "disqualify someone as a human being, to shut him up, and to portray him to the people as the biggest offender, he is usually denounced as an *intellectual,* or, what is even more popular—he is branded as a *nationalist.*"[35]

Although the progressive party leadership in Croatia accepted the intelligentsia's active role in the on-going political and economic discussions, it did not fully recognize the group's legitimacy to speak on behalf of the Croatiaan nation. To be the voice of the nation, that was a prerogative that belonged to the Party only. There never was a real coalition or even coordination between the Croatian Party leadership and the intelligentsia. But there was a mutual understanding about the goals of the mass movement. Both sides agreed that the movement's major goal was the full national emancipation, while other, related issues were those of national statehood, cultural freedom, new economic relations with the rest of the country, as well as the geographic and national integrity of the nation. The conservative Party forces on the other hand looked upon the intellectuals as anti-socialist "scribblers and loafers."[36]

The *Matica hrvatska* became the major focus of national revival during the late 1960s. It came to be the promoter of "political, economic, and national emancipation" and the defender of individual and national rights.[37] Because of these goals and activities, Party conservatives and neo-conservatives regarded the Matica as a potential political force and decided that it had to be crushed.

Apart from a small number of regime apologists, there were basically two groups among Croatian humanist intellectuals in the late Sixties and early Seventies: nationally minded and international Marxists. The members of the first group were Marxists and non-Marxists who gathered around Matica hrvatska and the Croatian University. This group had an overwhelming majority of Croatian intellectuals. It looked at the country's problems from a national point of view, but always with an eye on the class aspects of these problems. To them the traditional Communist division of "class" and "nation" was just another means of political manipulation. The working class was an integral part of its own nation, and, therefore, could not be separated from it. They stressed that "the national question, first of all the question of national statehood, was [also] . . . a principal question of the socialist revolution."[38] Although the Croatian intellectuals were strongly internationalistic, their goal was individual as well as national freedom. Vlado Gotavac, the leading ideologue of the movement, stressed the value of human freedom and dignity:

> The activism which I advocated should be understood . . . as resistance to falling into an apocaliptic voluntarism of the mechanical world. . . . [Resistance] to the raising of discipline above personal responsibility. . . . The highest ideal is the one which makes possible, which demands, which requires completeness of a human being in every moment. . . . Only one discipline should be known, the high sense (gordost) of personal responsibility in everything and to the end.[39]

As individual freedom was important for a human being and its dignity, so was national freedom for the life and fate of a nation. "The national question is not a speculative one. That is an existential question for every nation."[40] Without the solution of the national question "it was impossible to build socialism or undertake any progressive political moves. . . . The national question is always a social question. And for a nation which does not have its state, it is a class question too because the oppressed nation is related to the ruling nations the same as the exploited class to the ruling one."[41] Basically, this group of intellectuals felt that Croatian struggle was a part of an ongoing fight for freedom in other parts of the world, and that Croatian politics should be "deeply national, international, socialist and democratic."[42] To them a multinational and colorful world was positive and desirable mostly because it prevented global tyranny. Gotovac described the group's world view in the following way:

> I have never understood those who think that the rainbow should be of one color! A uniform world means a homogenized emptiness! The existence of different 'homelands' can only retain the beauty of the world—when the dedication to the world's future transforms its colors into a harmony. . . .[43]

As we can see in this quote, the *Weltanschauung* of these intellectuals was one of humanistic socialism. They described the individual nations in Yugoslavia and in the world as a rainbow of free and equal nations living in peace and harmony. No matter how big or small, each nation should be accepted by the world and also be responsible for the world; no freedom should be sacrificed for the sake of "greater good."

For the national minorities, for example the Serbs in Croatia, this message meant that Croatia had been their homeland for centuries and that they are and will always be an integral part of the nation, despite their minority status. Political forces outside Croatia had often tried to alienate the Serbs in order to prevent a united political and national front in Croatia. For example, before World War I Austria and Hungary kept emphasizing the cultural and religious differences between the Serbs and Croatians; later, during the inter-war and post-World War II periods, Serbia kept bringing up the differences in order to use the Serbian minority for their own advantages. Those Serbs in Croatia who had isolated themselves from the Croatian nation usually tended to be Party conservatives or neo-conservatives. Their political philosophy was "Yugoslav" and unitarist, which gave them the opportunity to link themselves with the "largest nation" in Yugoslavia, Serbia proper.[44] Because Croatian intellectuals wanted once and for all to get rid of unitarist Yugoslavism, they called upon the Serbs in Croatia to accept Croatia as their homeland. They stressed that the principles of individual freedoms and of "open pluralism"[45] would guarantee the rights of the Serbs and other minorities in the state. Although Croatia had to be the Croatian national state, it was also "the state of all its citizens, and all its citizens should be citizens of their state."[46]

The real issue, however, was not the oppression of the Serbs in Croatia, but their privileged status. The Croatian majority tried to divest the Serbian minority and the so-called "Yugoslavs" of their favored status in Croatia, and they tried to gain full equality with the Serbian minority. Jozo Ivičević, secretary of the Matica hrvatska, gave a few examples of how the rights of the Croatians were not respected in their own homeland: "Simple mentioning of the Croatian name elicited hysterical reactions . . . singing Croatian songs and wearing Croatian national symbols is punished by floggings . . . or punished by jail." On the other hand, he asked, "did anything similar happen in Croatia, let us say, because a Serbian name was mentioned or because Serbian symbols were displayed or songs were sung?" Furthermore, he concluded that "national minorities, in relation to the 'home' nation were usually under-represented in political functions and administration. Only in Croatia this was the opposite.

In this regard Croatia is a unique example in Yugoslavia!" Some of the crucial questions at the time were whether the majority, or "home" nation, had the right to name its language as it wanted, to develop its culture, and whether it should have full political rights. Other problems that had to be dealt with were whether the "home" nation should not be proportionately represented in the Party, the army, the police, and government administration and, most of all, whether the "home" nation should be granted the right to determine its own national future. Croatian intellectuals considered this to be the real test of officially proclaimed principles such as federalism, national equality, and self-management.[47]

The second group among Croatian intellectuals, the Marxist internationalists, was very small in number, but well known outside the country for its "humanist Marxism" and also for its criticism of Yugoslav bureaucratic socialism. These intellectuals, together with a number of others from different parts of Yugoslavia, especially from Serbia, came under fire by the regime several times, and their main voice, the journal *Praxis,* had been periodically suppressed.

The main positive contribution of the *Praxis* group to the development of the Yugoslav socialist system was that it raised a number of critical questions concerning Marxist ideology and practice and that it pushed for a better implementation of the Party proclaimed policies.[48] The role of these philosophers and sociologists in the Croatian national movement, however, was more of a negative nature. While on one side they were critical of the government and advocated more "liberal socialism," they differed considerably from the rest of the Croatian intelligentsia. First, the starting point of their world view was Marxist universalism. They thought that the national forces were looking at problems from too narrow a perspective.

> They, [the *Praxis* group], are unable to face our contemporary reality creatively. They have understood their philosophical mission as 'pure' critique of the existing reality based on the classical propositions of Marxism-Leninism. This 'creative inability' has pinned them down to citations and definitions . . . which become pure dogmas at the moment . . . when these definitions are applied to existing relations.[49]

But, as their critics pointed out, it was easy to stay aloof from concrete problems, and it was easier to philosophize on a universal level than to deal with complicated national problems. The *Praxis* group was, thus, accused of covering itself "with 'Left' and 'democratic' phrases" and that it was always ready to get involved "in so-called world and universal problems," but it did not "dare to bring out to the public its true position" on concrete problems of its own country.[50] The second major difference between the two groups of intellectuals was the fact that the first group stressed the national element to be at least equal to the class struggle, while for the *Praxis* group "proletarian internationalism" prevailed. They believed only the Communist movement could be the true "bearer, guarantor, and practical executor of the socialist revolution," and that the Party should "cleanse itself and eliminate from its ranks. . . all opposing and enimical elements." Thus, "the Communist movement could be the only ideological, integrating, and cohesive force in the Yugoslav community of nations."[51] The "international" and "class" positions of the group also led them to a certain kind of integral "Yugoslavism," and to a version of unitarism that was "beneath Bloch's utopianism."[52] However, this was unacceptable to the other national forces in Croatia. The one major inconsistency in this group's philosophy was that the freedom which they advocated for the world and for Yugoslavia as a whole, they were not willing to grant to the nations and individuals in Yugoslavia.[53] Another accusation made against the group was their dogmatism and their rigidity. As a contemporary Croatian intellectual pointed out, "if by some chance Prof. Kangrga (one of *Praxis* intellectuals and a Party official in the post-1972 period) were a leader of the Party, he would be just as merciless to those whom he considered enemies as Stalin was."[54] The *Praxis* group was basically regarded as a "philosophical sect which wanted to manage the meaning of the world and 'give order' to men's soul."[55] As a result, their place during the Croatian national revival in the Sixties and Seventies was closer to the regime than to the majority of the Croatian intelligentsia. As a foreign observer pointed out:

> Ironically, [the conservatives] found natural allies in the so-called humanists of the Praxis group, who felt an ideologically rooted antipathy toward decentralization, nationalism, and even federalism (which the humanists viewed as an unnecessary compromise with dogma).[56]

The above mentioned tendencies of the *Praxis* group had led some of them to condone the Soviet intervention in Czechoslovakia (1968) as well as the purges in Croatia at the end of 1971.[57]

The role of the nationally minded humanist intelligentsia had been indispensible to the Croatian national movement. It was these intellectuals who pointed out the problems facing the Croatian nation and also offered solutions to those problems. They bridged regional, ideological, and generational differences and thus, for the first time after the war, they brought about a Croatian national unity. Furthermore, they mobilized and integrated the younger generation and gave it a sense of direction in its search for personal and national goals.

Students

Ever since World War II, various Croatian student groups had been engaging in anti-Communist and anti-Yugoslav activities. The official student organizations were directly under Party control and were mere transmitters of the Party will. All social, political, and even cultural activities outside the existing organizational framework were considered illegal and dangerous. As a result, there had been an unbridgeable gap between the regime and the vast majority of Croatian students. However, in the late Sixties with the beginning restlessness in Yugoslavia's social and political life, the student groups became socially and politically very active and in 1970-71 they became independent from the Party's tutelage. Like the intellectuals, at that time, the students did not oppose the system itself but began to work through it, and soon they became the most active and most vocal part of the Croatian national movement, putting the proclaimed Party principles to a true test.

The student protests which started at Belgrade university in June 1968 "produced only a minor stir" at the Croatian university in Zagreb. The main reason for this general indifference was that the "majority of [striking Belgrade] students vigorously rejected national differences and problems, and shouted slogans of proletarian internationalism and Yugoslav unitarism."[58] Clearly, the students were the voice of those forces in Serbia which, under the slogans of radicalism and internationalism, wanted to save the old centralism, supposedly through a "purified" Marxism. A leading Croatian intellectual observed that most of the students did not even notice that their active dissatisfaction with the existing reality was being perfidiously manipulated [by some Serbian elements] against those forces and tendencies in our land which were working for radical changes in social, economic, and cultural spheres.[59]

The year of 1968, however, did not pass without commotion at the Croatian university in Zagreb, too. The first major uproar was caused by the election of Ivan Supek, a well known Croatian scientist, writer, and humanist as Rector of the Croatian University. Although a long time Marxist, but also known for his anti-bolshevism, he was elected without Party blessing, which created heated debates in University circles and Party ranks. Another important change were the plans for reforming and updating the University. These plans included such aspects as the improvement of educational standards, a better integration and upgrading of its different branches in other cities, but without over-centralization, and a plan to secure student participation in running the university.[60]

The biggest tremors among students, however, came two years later when, on December 21, 1970, Ivan Zvonimir Čičak was elected the first Student Pro-Rector (a student representative in the University government), and on April 4, 1971, when a new leadership was elected to the Zagreb Student Federation. Čičak was not only a non-member of the Party, but also he was not a member of the Student Federation. The Party thought he was a "nationalist" and "clericalist," because he was a practicing Catholic and defended the Croatian national issues; for some in the Church hierarchy, however, he was a "red Catholic" and a Communist spy.[61] Čičak thought of himself as a "Catholic by religion" but confessed that his "socio-political vision was self-managing Communism."[62] The Party would have liked to remove him from his position, but it was unable to orchestrate this removal, and at the same time, pretend to follow the principles of self-management. Thus, Čičak remained a controversial figure at the top of the student leadership.

Even more devastating for the Party than Čičak's nomination was the election of a new leadership of the Student Federation. The elections for president of the Zagreb Student Federation were supposed to take place in January 1971. However, because of divisions and ideological confusion within the local Party organizations, the elections were postponed several times. In anticipation of the annual student assembly to elect its leadership to be held on April 4, 1971, a group of students from various faculties (departments) at the University organized a mass meeting on March 27, without the Party's blessings. The purpose of the meeting was to elect a working presidency; all of this was done outside the Party framework, and was a clear challenge to the Party's supremacy.

Finally, at the official annual meeting, on April 4, the two contending forces clashed: the new national and progressive majority of the student body and those representing the traditional Party ideology. The national forces rejected the customary ceremony by which the Party's condidates simply got approved by the assembly. The Party candidates, however, objected to a democratic election, and, as a result, they were removed from the meeting hall. The elected new student leader was Dražen Budiša, an intelligent and eloquent philosophy student, who became a symbol of the student movement in Croatia. Soon after his election, he was joined in partnership by Ante Paradžik, newly elected president of the Student Federation for the republic of Croatia. These two young men and Čičak were the moving spirit of the Croatian national revival among the students, until they were silenced and jailed at the end of the same year.

The Party was very much embarrassed by the outcome of student elections but, at the end, it had no choice but to legitimize the new leaders. One of the main causes for the Party's losses among the students was the inability of the League of Communists at the University "to channel a positive political atmosphere among the students and to accept legitimate student demands as its own." Furthermore, the new student forces attacked the University Party organization for its conservatism and publically asked whether the organization stood "on the same [Tenth Plenum progressive] platform or . . . was it content with its bureaucratic work outside student masses."[63] It was obvious that the students were getting out from under Party control. The new leadership quickly declared that "the Student Federation cannot be anyone's transmission belt nor a tool of anyone from outside" the student body.[64] While the old student leadership had basically been a voice of the neo-conservative wing of the Party, the majority of the students now had been "inspired by the Tenth Plenum."[65] They supported the progressive Party leadership and worked closely with the leading intellectuals around the Matica hrvatska.

It seems that Supek's election as Rector, the election of Čičak as Student Pro-Rector, and the changes at the student leadership, all against Party wishes, were a clear message of Croatian students and university professors that they were dissatisfied with the slow implementation of "officially" inaugurated political and economic changes. But not less significant was the fact that the progressives at the top of the Party hierarchy were willing to accept the new forces at the University and even work with them. With the election of Čičak and with the consolidation of the new student leadership in April 1971, Croatian students became one of the firm pillars of the Croatian national movement.

The political and national activism of students was similar to that of their older colleagues, of the professors and of other intellectuals. A Croatian intellectual evaluated the student movement in the following words:

> This young generation [in Croatia] has initiated a new, autochtonous student movement. But, first of all, it accepts its share of responsibilities within the existing conflict of a much wider political movement for a further democratization of Yugoslavia's state system, for economic and cultural rebirth based on socialist principles and the platform of anti-dogmatism.[66]

In other words, the students' concerns went far beyond their own present interests; they were very much aware of and concerned about the economic, social, and political problems their nation had to face at that moment. Like so many other student movements at the time, they had a universal vision of a peaceful global community. At the same time, though, their concerns were very concrete, and thus they tried to solve the most urgent problems of their own national existence. In one sense, they could be compared to the American student movement in which there was much clamor about "peace on earth" but the main concern of which was the War in Vietnam; once the war was over the peace marches also ended. In their balance of universal and national concerns, the Croatian students wanted to be "deeply and sincerely Croatian and at the same time international and socialist in the best meaning of that word."[67] They were followers of their University Rector, Ivan Supek, who wrote in 1971:

In one of his novels, Dostoevsky observes with a wonderful insight
that the more his hero was zealous in his universal idealism, the less
were his concerns and love for those around him. One cannot know
those far away if one does not know those around oneself. By losing
his own human milieu or homeland a man finds himself in a vacuum,
often surrounded just by obstructions. Such an idealistic ideologized
'hermit' then negates everything around himself or what happened
before him: first of all history, nations, all past creativity or 'small'
human pleasures. Although I was one of the initiators of the movement 'Citizens of the World,' I have always been mistrustful of those
internationalists who were eager to reject national existence and
tradition, the same as I am mistrustful of those who raise their
nation above everything else . . . . Universalism is implanted in all of
us, and by immersing ourselves into those depths we lift ourselves to
understanding and respecting everything that is human.[68]

While the new student leadership was made of young people from different regions of Croatia and different social backgrounds, it was not an
accident that the "students who were the backbone of the movement
came from the socially most deprived elements of society and the economically least developed areas" in Croatia. At the same time, "it was
exactly those social elements and those regions that felt most of the yoke
of centralism and hegemonism."[69] This fact had an important influence
on the movement because its demands were not simply a "struggle for an
empty, formal and legal equality of nations" but they were "deeply class
and social demands."[70]

Those who opposed the movement very often asked whether the movement was truly socialist or nationalist. This was one of the ways to challenge the ideological legitimacy of the movement. But questions like this
were dismissed as "purely metaphysical."

When a farmer, because of centralist rule over the economy, has to
emigrate, and then wants to return to his homeland and to his own
farm, that is an existential question. Whether this is a class or national question it is a mere speculation. This is exactly what the
student movement in Croatia is seeking: class and national emancipation, as the only guarantee for tomorrow's individual, national
and class existence.[71]

The Croatian students proclaimed that because they were an integral part of their nation as well as a part of the working class, they were indeed a legitimate voice in society.

While the student movement's legitimacy had been accepted by the Party progressives, the rest of the Party saw the movement as a clear threat to traditional Party authority. Therefore, they demanded that it had to be dealt with with a firm hand. The conservatives and neo-conservatives considered the elections of the new student leadership to be a nationalist coup at the University and an expression of nationalist peril. Together with the intellectuals around Matica, students were also looked upon as a growing political force parallel to the Party itself and the conservative forces were just waiting for an opportune time to crush those threats to the Party's position.

The national movement among the young was not limited to the university students only. It spread to secondary schools and even to the Youth Alliance itself, which traditionally had been a hotbed for Party recruits. The Youth Alliance in Croatia wanted to get out of the traditionally subservient relationship to the Party and have its own voice in the political arena.[72] Its leaders stressed that the Alliance was "not above or below the interests of people in Croatia and its working class" and that the Alliance was "an integral part of the national movement as a whole."[73] The two papers published by the Youth Alliance in Croatia, *Tlo* and *Omladinski tjednik,* became the major voices of the young people in their active support of the Party's progressive leadership and of the national movement. But after the liberal movement was crushed in December 1971, both the Youth Alliance and the student leadership became once again the obedient tool of the Party hierarchy.

Workers and Peasants

It is very hard to find concrete data to give us an idea of what the majority of people in Croatia and Croatians felt about the important economic, social, political, and national issues at the time of the national movement. One reason for this problem is that the Croatian people, like others in Yugoslavia, never had the opportunity to express what kind of state, political system, or type of government they wanted. Most of these decisions had been made for them and without them.

The largest group in Croatia, the peasants, was not organized in any form or shape in the 1960s or 1970s, except that a small number of them were Party members. There were Sindicates, Socialist Alliances and Youth Alliances among the workers and partially in the villages too, but these organizations could not be considered as representatives of the people at large. Thus, the masses were truly a "crowd" without a specific political or even social framework. The social lines between peasantry and working class had also been very much blurred since many workers were peasants and vice versa.[74] The workers either lived in native villages where their wives and children farmed the land, or they moved to a town and still held on to their village possessions. In case the worker lost a factor job he had a place to return to and be a peasant once more. Also, a good percentage of students were from villages, and they spent most of their free time with their families in the country. Furthermore, many of the young people who did not finish their studies or who were unable to find jobs in their profession, became workers or they went back home to the village. Obviously, the group lines were not as clear cut as has often been presumed, and there were no free parties, organizations, or clubs through which this "crowd" could formulate or express their wishes or opinions. Thus, their voices remained unheard since there was no contact between them and the decision making levels of the Party.[75]

The relationship between the Party and workers and peasants had been a peculiar one. Although the Party had legitimized its rule by claiming to be the avantgarde of the working class, it was getting more and more alien to that class. It became the Party of the elites, where "a thin but very firmly intertwined layer of the 'consecrated' and 'pre-elect' individuals" were totally alienated from and ignorant of the needs and demands of the working man.[76] Furthermore, the workers' and peasants' share in Party membership indicates that the "avantgarde" was becoming more and more bureaucratized. In 1948, for example, workers represented 30.1 percent and in 1970 they made up 29.9 percent of the Party membership while the peasants constituted 47.8 percent and 6.5 percent of the membership for the same years.[77] The percentage of unqualified or semiqualified workers in the Party ranks was very low and so was that of young people especially women, from the working class and the villages.[78]

Despite the proclaimed policies of self-management, the workers' councils never became a true voice of the workers. The council members tended to be also an elite since they were usually members of the Party or Party-controlled organizations. For example, during one strike, workers shouted down a Sindicate representative who came to urge them to return to their work places. This is a clear indication of what they thought of the Sindicate.[79] A Croatian intellectual described the relationship between the regime and workers in the following way:

> The workers have comprehended that under the existing conditions they cannot find solutions to their vital problems. They do not want barricades. But the political leaders of this land gave them what is most necessary—they gave them a passport. They did not, however, go to Sofia but München. In this way, they are solving their problems. It is an illusion to think that the ruling class, who has done this, will make any radical changes on behalf of the working class.[80]

Going to the West became one of the main means for the workers and peasants to find some solution to their economic problems. For those who remained at their work places, strikes, officially called "work stoppages," were one way of expressing their grievances. Another response was absence from work. The slogan "Nobody can pay us so little as little we can work,"[81] is a true representation of the workers' mentality in Yugoslavia. Statistics indicate that

> about 700,000 workers were absent every day because of illness; each day some 600,000 were on vacation; and 400,000 a day were attending various conferences that kept them from work. With all this taken into consideration, the average Yugoslav worker was working 'only three hours and six minutes a day.'[82]

The workers' problems, however, were not only of a class nature. Questions were being raised, for example, as to why Croatians more than anybody else were leaving the country? It was the intelligentsia who began asking such questions first. A good number of people from its own ranks were also forced to look for solutions to their "vital problems" in some foreign country. Also, parents or other family members of many students were working outside the country. Looking for the cause and the answers to such vital national issues helped bridge the different social segments in Croatian society and mold them into one national front.

The growth of the Matica hrvatska and its publications is a good indicator of the support that intellectuals and students had among the people. For example, from November 1970 until December 1971 some thirty new branches of the Matica were organized in the republic of Croatia.[83] At that time it had forty one thousand members whereas only about a year earlier its membership was a little over twenty three hundred. Also the organization had thirty three steering committees and was publishing fourteen papers and journals when it was closed at the end of 1971.[84] Matica's main voice, *Hrvatski tjednik,* reached a circulation of over one hundred thousand copies in only thirty-three weeks of existence.[85] In 1968, *Vjesnik,* the best known daily newspaper in Croatia had a circulation of 90,000 while *Slobodna Dalmacija* had only 35,000.[86] Along with Matica's publications, a number of student, youth, and provincial papers also became voices of national ideas and the "counter-revolution," as the conservatives in the Party called the movement.

The workers and the peasant population had been definitely influenced by the revival of national ideas among the intellectuals and the students. It is hard to say, however, how strong nationalism was in the villages before it gained a legitimate voice. The Croatian peasantry as a social group had never supported the Yugoslav idea as can be seen in peasant politics and their fervent support of Stjepan Radić during the inter-war period. Yugoslavism and Communism remained alien to them; those were ideologies of the elites. It was in the villages where the elementary national identity had been preserved and where it germinated during the post-war years. Furthermore, many of the students and intellectuals also came out of villages, all of which indicates that the role of the village in the Croatian national revival was greater than had been visible on the surface.

Statistics about the Party members against whom "measures" were undertaken at the beginning of 1972 indicate that the movement had roots in all segments of society and regions of the republic. Out of 741 dismissed Party members before April 1972, 228 were from Osijek (North), 171 from Split (South), and 213 Zagreb (capital). Out of the total number, 85 were workers, 80 "technical intelligentsia," 96 "humanist intelligentsia," 288 leadership officials, 17 paid officials, 144 administration officials, 56 students, 43 retired personnel, and 25 with undefined status. As far as their Party membership was concerned, 643 of those dismissed became Party members after 1949, 2 were pre-war members, 31 were received into the Party during the war, and 63 had joined the Party during the period of 1945 to 1948.[87] These are clear indications that the movement was of massive and not just of elitist significance. In one of his interviews, Tripalo emphasized this popular aspect of the movement:

> One of the characteristics of this movement . . . is the fact that it did not begin in one place. It appeared in different places and then it became one strong river. Its elementary strength, which has surfaced in this last year, was most probably preconditoned by the fact that the movement has not been bureaucratized.[88]

Indeed, he claimed that "never before in history was there such unity between the [Party] leadership and the people" than in 1971.[89]

The students and the youth were, as Miko Tripalo said, the "core"[90] of the national movement. They were its most dynamic part, but the intellectuals, especially those around Matica hrvatska, played the most important role in it: they were its brain.[91] The workers and peasantry gave it the popular support and served as legitimacy to the progressive leadership in the Party. Through its tolerance of relative pluralism, the Party leadership in return provided the space the movement needed to flourish and expand.

The Role of the Catholic Church

It is commonly agreed that the Catholic Church played a major role in the development of Croatian national and cultural orientation. By accepting Christianity from the Roman West, the Croatian nation found a permanent place in the Western cultural sphere. But it has been often wrongly concluded that religion and national identity for the Croatians were synonymous and that the Church had been the main pillar of modern Croatian nationalism.

On the contrary, for the most part the official Church had not been in accord with the major streams of Croatian nationalism. Under the Habsburg rule, the Croatian higher clergy had been very loyal to the dynasty and the Empire. On the other hand, people like Strossmayer flirted with the idea of Yugoslavism. After the unification of the South Slavic nations in 1918, the higher clergy took a pro-Yugoslav position. Also, the Church hierarchy had been very much opposed to Ante Starčević and his party, as well as to the Radić brothers and their peasant movement. Both of these main streams of Croatian national ideologies were strongly anticlerical. The lower clergy, however, was mainly of national orientation.

It seems that the main source of the existing confusion about the role of the Church in Croatian nationalism comes from the fact that the Catholic Church in Croatia welcomed Croatian independence in 1941. Archbishop Aloysius Stepinac, the head of the Church in Croatia at the time, was brought to a rigged trial in 1946 and sentenced to sixteen years in prison because he publicly proclaimed that Croatians have the right to a national state. Thus, it was in the post-war period that the Church as a whole was looked upon as the bastion of Croatian nationalism, and Stepinac became a symbol of this apparent symbiosis. Because Stepinac and his successors had refused to denounce or distance themselves from their past stand on Croatian statehood, the Church was constantly accused of nationalism.

It is true, however, that the Church did and to a certain extent still does, serve as an institution that has been attracting many anti-Communists and nationalists as well. In Yugoslavia, as in other Communist countries, there is not an organizational alternative to the Party or its affiliates. The Church became the only channel through which one could give a visible sign of opposition to the existing state and regime. But it never became an organizational framework for national struggle. The militant anti-Communism and passive resistance lasted in the Church from 1945 until the early Sixties. Then came a period of adjustment and stable relations with the ruling regime. The signing of the Vatican-Belgrade Protocol, in June 1966, was the high mark of this rapprochement. These changes, however, corresponded to the Vatican's ideological and political shifts toward Eastern Europe in general. There had been little concern how these policy shifts would affect Croatian national interests. Good relations with Yugoslavia primarily were to serve as a model of the Vatican's adjustment to the new political and ideological reality.

The direct role of the official Church in the Croatian national revival in the late Sixties and early Seventies had been of minimal nature. It seems that there had been an ideological truce between the progressives in the Party and the higher authorities of the Croatian Church. Since the Church was not sure of the outcome of the mass movement, it adopted a policy of wait and see. It is interesting to note that some of the more conservative members of the Church hierarchy actually were closer to the neo-conservatives in the Party than to the progressives or nationalists. They thought that their role in the Church was very similar to the Party's role in the state: both hierarchies had the duty to protect society from the liberal "anarchy" and lead it to higher pastures.[92] Even after the purges in Croatia, at the end of 1971, the Church was reluctant to offend the regime over the imprisonment of Croatian students and intellectuals.

Generally, one could say that the Catholic Church in Croatia had a positive role in the development of recent Croatian nationalism. The Chuch had been among the Croatians for over 1300 years. While living and growing as an institution, it guarded and contributed to the preservation and development of Croatian culture and its people. Its history was an integral part of the Croatian national past and through its annals it helped to sustain the national consciousness of its members. The Church also served as an ideological counterbalance to Communism, and as such it stood as a major obstacle to the Party's desire to have full control of the society. It should be kept in mind, however, that the Church as an institution benefited from the fact that Croatians do not regard the Party as the true spokesman for their national interests and that there were no other institutions which were able to fulfill that role.

Apart from the positive side, there were some other negative aspects regarding the Church in Croatian nationalism. There was the way in which the role of the Church was perceived by Croatian non-Catholics or atheists, and there was the fact that some Croatians put too much hope in the political role of the Church. However, the most important negative effect in the long run was that the Catholic Church in Croatia, as in many other countries, had a depoliticizing effect on its membership. It directed the hopes of its believers from the immediate political goals to the eschatological sphere, to the life thereafter. In this way, it indirectly provided a good service of social control to the existing regime, because it was not in the interest of the regime to have the masses politicized. Otherwise, the Party might have been shaken from within, from without, or from both sides. And this was what happened in 1970-71, when the Party as a whole became afraid of the mass movement, a movement which did not grow within the Church but among the liberal intelligentsia and the progressive wing of the Party.

CHAPTER VII

ROAD TO KARADJORDJEVO

In Croatia, as in all other Communist lands, every major Party decision was considered of "epochal significance." The zig-zagging of Party policies were always justified by the latest "historic" Party plenum or document. Thus, everything that took place in Croatia from January 1970 to December 1971 was done in the name of the Tenth Plenum of the CC LC of Croatia. Allegedly, the meeting was of historic significance because it brought to the surface the "most important questions in Yugoslav socialist reality and it also [raised] some fundamental issues in international socialism."[1] It was believed the Plenum put the republic as well as the country on the road to liberal socialism and national equality. However, the now famous Twenty First Session of the Presidium of the LCY in December 1971 that ended the process begun by the Tenth Plenum, has been acclaimed by the Party to be of even greater historical importance because it purged the Party of "rotten liberalism" and Croatian nationalism.

The "epoch" of the Tenth Plenum began with the defeat of the conservatives and the unitarists in Croatia, and with the legitimization of the national element in the "revolutionary" process. But once the liberal platform was accepted, its supporters disagreed on its interpretation and implementation. As a result, two factions emerged soon after the meeting. The first faction was known as the progressives. Among it was the top leadership in the republic and it focused its attention on the major

Croatian national problems. Some of the issues which occupied this faction were: economic relations in the federation, emigration, current federal and republican constitutional amendments, proportionate national representation in various federal and republican agencies and institutions,[2] and the full implementation of the principles of self-management. The progressives also considered it very important for the Party to move closer to the people, as it once happened, they claimed, during the time of the National Front, in World War II. Although not accepting everyone who acted in the name of the Tenth Plenum, the progressives did believe that their platform should include a wider cross section of people and opinions than was the practice in the past. It was at this point that the national dimension of the progressive platform was manifested. The Party wanted to be a part of the people and of their nation, and it even wanted to step into the forefront of the growing national movement and direct its course. However, in order to achieve this goal, it was necessary for the Croatian people to gain a sense of freedom and equality. It was also necessary that they did not perceive the Party in their republic to be primarily in the service of the federation, namely Belgrade, and of the "working class." Savka Dapčević-Kučar, President of the CC LCC and a leading progressive, said that

> there cannot be socialism without the support of the people. But there cannot be support of the people if they do not have full national equality and affirmation. No socialism in the world can bring about its class emancipation if it does not solve the problem of national affirmation either.[3]

It was believed that the Tenth Plenum provided the necessary conditions for the Party to achieve its unity with people and to become the main spokesman for the Croatian nation.

In dealing with their opponents, most of them conservatives and unitarists, and even some nationalists, the progressives advocated "democratic means of struggle, fostering especially an open way of work."[4] While at the top of the republican Party hierarchy, the progressives did not use a "firm hand" with Croatian intellectuals or students, nor with the unitarist opponents. They believed that the main danger to the state and its system was not a Croatian national revival or some marginal "excesses" but in unresolved national, political, and economic relations in the country. They also thought that time had come to resolve those basic problems not only in theory, as in the past, but in a real and fundamental way. The main obstacle to this, however, were the central federal forces and the unitarists in the republic.

The other faction, the neo-conservatives, who shared the power with the progressives, looked at the situation and at Party policies from quite a different perspective. Although they accepted the Tenth Plenum platform, they thought it contained a "negative germ:"[5] it opened the door for nationalism. For the neo-conservatives, the platform was too broad and they thought that the national movement was not only altering the Party's activities but also threatening its monopoly of power. According to them, the ideological lines between Marxism and nationalism were being blurred, and worst of all, the progressive leadership was not decisive and firm enough to control these developments.

Differences between Party views, as represented by the two factions, were already evident in 1970. However, the Party was not just losing its unity. With the events at the university in Zagreb, it became clear that it also had lost control over the different oppositional forces. In February 1971, the political situation in Croatia became very fluid which was of major concern for the republican neo-conservatives. Party control became the main topic at top leadership meetings,[6] but Savka Dapčević-Kučar, Party leader and progressive, claimed that the neo-conservatives and the federal centralists were overexaggerating minor nationalist "excesses" in order to minimize the major questions. Although Dapčević-Kučar criticized the Croatian national forces, she agreed with the representatives of the movement that the neo-conservatives in their battle against nationalism were overlooking the fact that the real problems were caused by federal centralism and not nationalism.[7]

From mid-February to the end of April 1971 events in Croatia were evolving at full speed. The old student leadership, controlled by traditional Party loyalists, was unimaginative and did not understand the meaning of the events that were taking place around them.They lost the elections to a new, progressive, and dynamic group of young people, who wanted to play an active role in the society and in their nation. Also, the number of members in the Matica hrvatska began to grow rapidly. At this time, Matica began to publish a weekly paper, *Hrvatski tjednik*, dealing with "cultural and social" questions. Other papers and journals began to participate openly in political and economic discussions. Among the student papers, *Studentski list* and *Hrvatsko sveučilište* became especially active. In the past important economic, cultural, and even political questions were published only in intellectual or Party journals and thus reached only a very limited number of people. At this time, however, information dissemination began to take place on a massive level. Even the Party controlled papers in Croatia changed their tone and began to write plainly on different issues, without the traditional Communist phraseology.[8] The publishing activities of the Matica hrvatska and other cultural organizations were the major means of mobilizing the masses and of enlarging the national movement. The younger generations of Croatians began to wear old national emblems and sing the Croatian national anthem and other old patriotic songs. There was a new interest in the national past, in its culture, and in its historic figures. Beside this emotional side of the national revival, those young people were also very much concerned about their own present and future. They were raising vital economic, political and national questions which in the past were considered the Party's domain only. The movement was becoming more and more massive. The voices for a change were becoming louder. Meanwhile the Party conservatives and neo-conservatives, as well as the centralist forces in general, were becoming more and more paranoid. They began to see ghosts of the past in the Croatian national emblems, in the patriotic songs, and in the national movement as a whole.[9] But most of all, they were concerned for the Party's leading position; at least this ideological principle was used by the conservative and centralist forces in order to defend their position of power.

Attacks on the movement in Croatia, thus, came from two fronts: one from within Croatia the other from Belgrade. Although the local counter-forces were more visible and vocal, their outside (federal) partners were detrimental to the crash of the movement. Different political and cultural circles in Serbia interpreted Croatian national revival as purely separatist, counter-revolutionary, and even fascist in nature.[10] They often refused to see the movement as part of the country's progress toward full federalization because further decentralization meant that their political influences and their share of the economic pie would shrink.

Intra-Party Struggle in Croatia

In the summer of 1971, the political situation in Croatia was full of unrest. The main struggle was going on within the Party itself. The progressives and conservatives were trying to discredit each other. Progressives were accusing their opponents of being essentially Yugoslav unitarists and of being more interested in the preservation of their own privileged Party positions than in the fate of Croatia and her "working class." As such, the conservatives said to be against a full implementation of the Reform previously chartered by Tito and the Party. On the other hand, the conservative and neo-conservative forces accused the progressives of permitting the nationalists to attach themselves to the Tenth Plenum platform, and instead of exposing them for what they were, namely counter-revolutionaries, the Party leadership was accepting them as partners. Both sides were looking for allies. The Progressives found their support among the intellectuals around the Matica hrvatska, at the university, and among the Croatian population in general. Their opponents, conservatives and neo-conservatives now together, looked among the Veterans' organizations, among the Socialist Alliance, and among the federal institutions for help. Both sides courted Tito's good will and patronage; he was the ultimate arbiter at the republican and federal levels.

A major problem involving Party leadership in the republic and also on the federal level erupted when the Presidium of the LCY at its meeting on March 23, 1971 discussed "anti-Yugoslav activities" and concluded that there was an organized action to disqualify the political leadership of the SR of Croatia by spreading rumors about its connections with the "Ustasha" emigrants.[11] The central bureau of the Socialist Alliance of Yugoslavia, in its circular at the beginning of April 1971, also implied that the Party leadership in Croatia was collaborating with a Croatian emigrant organization centered in West Germany.[12] The implications of the accusation went even further. It was alleged that through an émigré organization the top Party leadership was in touch with the Soviets, through which, as the allegation went, Croatians were trying to gain their full independence.

To clarify the confusion[13] created by this report, the Nineteenth (closed) Session of the CC LC of Croatia was held on April 6, 1971. After many speeches and long discussions in its communique, the Croatian Party leadership pointed to "some organs of the federal authority" as the source of the rumor.[14] It was well known that unitarist and centralist forces wanted to abort the ongoing democratization process. The insinuation that the whole republic and even its Communist leadership was chauvinist, separatist, and even fascist was just another means toward that end. A leading Croatian intellectual, an old Marxist, characterized the case as "insinuation as a political method at the highest levels."[15]

The subject of the émigré connection was so sensitive and critical that Tito called the 17th Session of the Presidium of the LCY "to clarify the political situation."[16] It met on the Brioni islands at the end of April 1971. What exactly happened at that meeting is still a secret. After the meeting, Tito explained that the proceedings had not been published because they would "have created much more confusion than that which now exists."[17] In its final communique the Presidium stated that it "had accepted the conclusion of the Federal Executive Council that no federal administrative agencies and none of their services or officers had taken part in any kind of plot."[18] This conclusion, however, was just the opposite of the findings of the Party's CC in Croatia. As a result, the Croatian public was very interested to see how the Croatian Party would react to this discrepancy. Tripalo, a leading Party progressive in Croatia, admitted:

> We are quite often asked: who said what in Brioni, who won, who was on trial. Although this might seem a rhetorical answer, the real answer is: the League of Communists had won . . . .[19]

However, by stopping any further pursuit of the culprits in the plot, by granting a blanket absolution to federal agencies for any wrong doing, and without openly expressing confidence in the Party leadership in Croatia, the Presidium Session was a defeat for the Party progressives in Croatia. A Croatian publicist involved in the movement concluded that Savka Dapčević-Kučar, the President of the CC LC of Croatia, was most responsible for the outcome of the Brioni meeting because "she overestimated her forces" and, most of all, she overestimated Tito's support for the progressives.[20] In accepting the decision of the Presidium the Croatian progressives also lost the offensive initiative and gave the conservatives the opportunity to claim victory.[21] A number of things point to the fact that somewhere at the end of April or the beginning of May 1971, the Party progressives were put on the defensive and the conservative forces were becoming more and more vocal and open in their opposition to the top Party leadership in the republic. Clearly, they were encouraged by the results of the 17th Session and the republican Party meeting that had followed.

In mid-May 1971, the Party in Croatia held its Twentieth Session of the Central Committee and drafted an "Action Program" against all forces which 'started from [the platform] of nationalist, chauvinist, unitarist and bureaucratic tendencies and interests."[22] The conservatives were demanding action against the "petit-bourgeois, nationalistic and chauvinistic current whose final goal. . .was the separation of Croatia from Yugoslavia."[23] A month later, on June 22 and 26, there was a meeting of top republican and federal Party officials in Zagreb who discussed the two factions in the Party and the situation in Croatia in general. This meeting was one more confrontation of the two factions in the Party, and it did not resolve any intra-party problems. Only a few weeks after that meeting, however, two leading Croatian intellectuals and leaders of the Croatian national movement, Šime Djodan and Marko Veselica, were thrown out of the Party. Their political stands and activities were considered "harmful and unacceptable, as well as outside and contrary to the political line of the LCC and LCY."[24] Jure Šarić, a member of the Nationality Council in the Federal Government, an official in the Socialist Alliance in Croatia, as well as a World War II partisan in Serbia, was also removed from his post. General Ivan Šibl, president of the Veterans' organizations in Croatia and some other old partisans became special targets of the conservatives for their alleged nationalism. These and less known Party expulsions clearly indicated that the conservatives were gaining ground.

At the August 2, 1971 meeting of Party Presidents and Secretaries of all communes in Croatia, another Action Program was adopted. The neoconservatives complained that the nationalists insisted on a "unified national movement" and a "general reconciliation of [all] Croatians." Further, their complaints were that the nationalist forces, "among whom there were members of the LC," did "not start from the interests of the working class," were "silent about and ignored" the "Party decisions," and were "trying to create a political platform" of their own.[25] At the same meeting, Savka Dapčević-Kučar again emphasized the progressive platform, and at the same time, further distanced the Party leadership from the nationalists:

> The difference is that we see full national affirmation and strengthening of equality only on a platform of self-management socialism and in the context of the development of national equality, now of Republican and national statehood, in the context of socialist Yugoslavia. They [nationalists] are outside of that. That is the line of demarcation.[26]

But the progressives did not succeed in proving to the Party centralists and unitarists that they were not nationalists. Thus, during the summer of 1971, the conservatives and neo-conservatives came to the point of openly accusing the progressives of "moving into the swollen waters of counter-revolution." Jakov Blažević, an old Croatian Communist who was well known for his loyalty to the Party, stated in one of his speeches:

> I would not say that here is merely a question of Party factionalism. I would rather say we have here [among the Party progressives] the foundations of the counter-revolutionary movement. They have linked themselves with the counter-revolutionary movements outside the country and have organized themselves in the country in the same fashion.[27]

Blažević also accused the leaders of the movement, which included many members of the Party progressives, that "they had linked themselves with espionage agents and through those channels they were looking for help in order to create their own [political] bases."[28]

By emphasizing the so-called nationalist "excesses," conservatives were trying to prove that the national movement was basically the same as the old Croatian separatism and that it was even identical with Ustashism. The "excesses" were also useful in demonstrating to Tito that he should intervene and help the conservatives in their efforts. However, Stjepan Ivić, a progressive member of the CC, pointed out to Tito that the conservatives in the CC "were giving those excesses more value and attention than they deserved." Ivić mentioned that only 10 out of the 105 communes in Croatia had had problems with excesses, and out of those 10 only 5 or 6 were brought in front of the republican Executive Committee. Furthermore, other republics had at least as many problems with nationalist excesses, but there it was no big deal.[29]

The Veteran's organizations became especially active in attacking the national movement and the top Party leadership in the republic. Veterans wrote a letter to Tito early in the summer of 1971 demanding the replacement of the Party progressives in Croatia.[30] In June of the same year, they distributed a leaflet demanding the "heads of 2,500 Matica'a activists in order to return peace and order in the land."[31] The neo-conservatives were not only pleased with such activities, but they were courting the old Partisans by stressing the dangers the Croatian national movement supposedly brought to the achievements of the revolution. Jure Bilić, one of the leading neo-conservatives, declared in a speech to the Veterans in July 1971:

> They [leaders of the national movement] are criticizing the League of Communists because they want to behead this nation and this Party, in order to take over power. . . . They have organized a special political command center in Matica hrvatska. Why? To create a counter-revolution.[32]

Bilić, threatened the members of the movement that the conservative forces were ready to defend their goals. He even used the motto of the Spanish Republicans: "You will not pass!" in order to tell the leaders of the national movement that Bilić and his followers were ready to fight.[33]

Tito himself came to Croatia three times between the end of April and September 1971. He gave, however, mixed signals to the Croatian Party leadership. On May 1, a day after the 17th Session of the Party Presidium, during a major speech in Labin (Istria), he stressed that there were many problems in the country and the Party itself, but he claimed that the Party was still in "full unity" concerning "all questions facing the League of Communists." Finally, he promised that "from words about our unity" the Party would "pass to deeds."[34] But when Tito came to Zagreb, two months later, he sounded very critical of the Party in Croatia and the political situation in the republic as a whole. In a closed meeting with the republican leaders he declared that "the League of Communists was not ideologically unified. It had to be cleansed of everything which was not ideologically correct." Tito stressed that "in the LC there must be unity of ideas and unity of action" and that the "democratic centralism must be firmly respected." Furthermore, he demanded that Party forces "had to move against the class enemy."[35] At the same meeting, Tito condemned the nationalist activities of the students, of the Matica hrvatska, and of the *Prosvjeta,* a Serbian cultural organization in Croatia with the following words:

> Come on, comrades, wake up! . . . The roots of everyone who is anti-socialist have to be cut. And these [people in Matica] want to divert the whole flow of our development.[36]

Clearly, Tito demanded a firm hand against all those who deviated from or worked against the Party line. He even threatened to use the armed forces and declared that the old partisan veterans were ready to take arms one more time, in order to restore socialism in Croatia.

But in mid-September during his third visit to Croatia Tito was received warmly by the people at all his stops. The masses believed that he was fully supporting the progressive leadership in the republic and that, by his visit, he was helping them in their struggle against their opponents.[37] In a toast in Zagreb he said:

> This time I have seen that all kinds of stories [that are being circulated] about Croatia are real absurdities—that there is no unity here, that people think differently, that here chauvinism exists, and flowers, etc. That is not true. I saw the contrary wherever I have been [the last few days] . . . . Here in Croatia, I have seen and learned a lot. That is, next time I will know much better how to assess different news and stories than I was able to do in the past.[38]

These were definitely words of support to the progressive Party leadership in the republic; however, only two months later he would condemn the same leaders as "rotten liberals."

Tito's visit to Croatia did not reconcile the progressives and their opponents, nor did it stop the on-going debate in the media on the question of nationalism and unitarism. The climax of the intra-Party friction in Croatia was reached at the 22nd Session of the CC LCC, which took place during November 5-6, 1971. The conservative forces were planning to take this opportunity and turn the Plenum against the Progressives. Their plan was to discuss "the report on work" of the top Party leadership "in which the situation in the LCC and in its leadership was objectively presented."[39] The President of the Party, Savka Dapčević-Kučar, however, prevented this by using her own opening speech to the Plenum as the basis for discussion. She argued that the political climate in Croatia was positive, that the movement firmly stood on the platform of the Tenth Sesssion and that it had the full support of the masses. She stressed that a "unity of nation and Party was forged and sturdily grew into a mass political movement." However, she strongly disagreed with those who thought that the Party "should behave with reserve toward the mass support or even reject it in the interest of some abstract revolutionary 'purity,' and who considered the progressives dubious as Marxists. . . precisely when they had the support of the people." Furthermore, Dapčević-Kučar accused her opponents of hypocrisy because they wanted people's support only in theory and only in Party proclamations but not in practical politics, as if "the working people exist for us and not we for them."[40] Her 118 page report was accepted by the majority as the official Party document and it served as "the basis for further activities of the LCC."[41]

Realizing that things were not going the way they had planned, Dušan Dragosavac, a leading conservative and vice-secretary of the Executive Committee, delivered an opposing speech at the Plenum. This, however, had not been customary practice in any Communist Party, and his action caused a strong irritation at the meeting. While Savka's conclusions were positive, Dragosavac emphasized that "on the edges of our socialist self-management and the Party. . . attempts are being made to create some kind of movement."[42] For him the leaders of "the other movement" were the intellectuals whom he called "literal descendants of nazism, Chetnikism, and Ustashism."[43] Moreover, he declared that "on some points foreign ideologies are creeping into the LC."[44] There was nothing new in what he said, but his rebuttal to the speech of the President of the Central Committee was a clear sign that the two factions were reaching a breaking point. The road to Karadjordjevo was thus all prepared.

A few days after the 22nd Plenum, Dragosavac went to Tito to report on the events in Croatia "since [Tito's] meeting with the CC LCC in July" 1971.[45] It is not clear if Dragosavac asked for the meeting at Bugojno

(Bosnia), or if he was invited to an already arranged larger secret gathering with Tito. There are indications that, at this meeting, Yugoslav army leaders were also present to report on the situation in Croatia.[46] From the events which followed, it is clear Tito accepted Dragosavac's and the military's interpretation of events. Even the general public had become aware that there was a firm resolve on the side of the conservatives to remove the progressives from power. A leading political commentator in Croatia openly asked:

> Is Haramija's [the President of the Croatian Assembly (Sabor)] government in danger today . . . is it someone's goal to remove this [republican] government and impose another . . . ?[47]

On November 22, 1971, the students decided to go on strike and express their support for the progressives in the republican Party. But their move was just another "proof" for the conservatives that the Party was not in control of the events in Croatia and that a "counter-revolution" was in the making. There are suspicions that the strike was encouraged by the conservative forces in order to speed up the end of the Croatian Spring.[48] Tito, as the ultimate arbiter, finally took the side of the conservatives: he had the Party purged and fully restored democratic centralism.

The Constitutional Amendments of 1971

At the end of 1970, the LCY decided to amend the 1963 federal Constitution yet another time.[49] The amendments were formally proposed in December of the same year and drafted by a Constitutional Commission at the beginning of 1971. After the proposed constitution changes were approved by the Presidium of the LCY, at its 16th Session on March 2, 1971, the amendments were submitted for public debate and finally promulgated by the Federal Assembly on June 30, 1971.

There were three underlying points that the new amendments addressed. First, the "working people and organizations of associated labor"[50] were assured more voice in the decision making processes, which was supposed to ensure "the practical and political victory of self-management."[51] Second, the republics and autonomous provinces were guaranteed more self-rule, because the republics were "states based on the sovereignty of people. . . ."[52] Thus, the national character of the republics was re-emphasized. The federation was to be a "community of equal nations and nationalities constituting a self-managing community of working people and citizens."[53] In the decision-making processes on the federal level, the principle of parity among the republics and autonomous provinces was to be applied. And third, the collective Presidency of the SFRY was officially promulgated as the executive body to succeed Tito.

The debate on the proposed amendments, which lasted from March to June, proceeded along two traditional lines. One was centralist, the other federalist. The first group considered the amendments to be a danger to Yugoslav unity, while the other group stressed that the country's unity was only as strong as its components and advocated a loose federation. The latter group believed that such a federation should have a Council of nations and only three other common government agencies which would deal with common foreign policy, defense, and the federal budget.[54]

The centralist forces were concentrated in Belgrade, among unitarists in other republics, as well as among some of the left intelligentsia.[55] Supposedly, their main concern was the future of the country and of socialism. Tito himself emphasized in his speech on May 1, 1971, that "there was an opposition which was trying to prove that with the [amendments] Yugoslavia was falling apart."[56] One proponent of centralist thinking was Professor Jovan Djordjević, a leading Belgrade authority on Constitutional Law. He argued that the strength of the federation could not be based on the "interests and opinions of the republics" and rejected the "confederative elements" in the amendments.[57] Belgrade's reaction to the amendments was overall negative. They saw in them a threat to the political and economic position of Yugoslavia's Serbs. For example, a number of Serbs from Belgrade were concerned that a further decentralization would put the future of Serbs in other republics in jeopardy. Some even considered the amendments nothing less than a "Croatian plot."[58] The Serbs in Yugoslavia were especially sensitive to the growing independence of the autonomous provinces. The point in the amendments that "the surplus of labor" should remain with the immediate local producer was understood in Belgrade as an anti-Serbian move, which, at that time, was the center of financial and economic power.

The federalist forces in other republics, especially those in Croatia and Slovenia, however, considered the amendments to be one more positive step in the on-going process of federalization. They considered the economic implications of the amendments as being of primary importance. Some Croatian economists, however, pointed out that the amendments did not go far enough in affirming the economic independence of the republics because, to them, "economic independence was the foundation of state and constitutional sovereignty."[59] On the one side, the amendments proclaimed republican sovereignty, but on the other side they limited their power to protect their economy in the name of a united market.[60] The republics were not allowed to get involved in foreign trade or make any credit arrangements on their own. Only that republic which controlled the financial capital would have economic advantages and, consequently, would have more political power than the others. In practice, this meant that major banks and re-exporters, located in Belgrade, would continue to be centers of the financial and also of political power. Šime Djodan, a leading Croatian economist, argued that, in accordance with the proclaimed sovereignty of the republics, the Constitution should allow the republics to "protect themselves in case of misuse of the united market. Otherwise, the 'outflow' of capital from Croatia to the East and of its working class to the West will continue," and thus republican sovereignty would continue to be without substance.[61]

Strengthening of the republican "statehood" and "sovereignty" was welcome news in Croatia, because it was seen as a possible fulfillment of the Croatian national dream of renewed national statehood. A well-known Croatian historian cautiously greeted the amendments by saying: "It seems that slowly we are now approaching the goal [of statehood].[62] To those in the federal establishment, however, who questioned the wisdom of the amendments, every sign of "national interest was seen as a black demon which would swallow up the class" and its self-proclaimed avant-garde.[63]

To the leading intellectuals in Croatia, the federal amendments created a 'historic chance' for the "creation of Croatian state sovereignty,"[64] and it was the responsibility of the Party in Croatia to incorporate into its platform the Croatian national interests and achieve political autonomy.[65] The progressives in the Party were in full support of Croatian statehood. The following words of one of those progressives are an example of the group's positive reaction to the Croatian national statehood.

> So, we want everyone to know that we are fighting for and will direct our political organization toward the achievement of Croatian statehood as an equal union of Croatians, because here is a unique chance that Croatia, that Croatian people create their state which they have sought throughout history, and if they do not get it now, it seems to me, we will never again get the Croatian people to support the Communist movement.[66]

To the Croatians the amendments were not a question of nationalism but a "principal question of the socialist revolution."[67] They argued against those who considered the nations in Yugoslavia as "some kind of half-nations, which were condemned to be tied to somebody like the Siamese twins," that "the nations in SFRY are no less nations than any other nation [in the world]."[68] Furthermore, they accused their opponents of using a double standard in being vocal advocates

> of full sovereignty in the socialist world while they were against sovereignty of the republics in their country. They were against supra-national blocs in the world, but they did support its variant at home. They were bitter about the [Soviet] intervention in Czechoslovakia but were wishing for one in Croatia. They said that they were for freedom and independence of every nation in the world— except in Yugoslavia—as if these nations were less nations, or some other kind of nations than all others.[69]

The "internationalists" were dismissed by the Croatian intellectuals as traditional exponents of unitarism. They vehemently rejected the argument that the dying out of nations was part of the international revolutionary process; to them it was only an excuse for a national assimilation in Yugoslavia. In this sense, the intellectuals pointed out that the USSR and China, "which considered themselves the two beacons of world socialism," were fighting over a small island on their eastern borders. "An insignificant island was much more important than world socialism. But 'internationalists' in Yugoslavia ask us Croatians to die out, so that we may be the guinea pigs, and our homeland a lab [for the sake of world socialism]."[70]

To achieve national sovereignty within the existing state framework, Croatian intellectuals advocated a major change in intra-national relations.

Instead of the existing federalism, they proposed confederalism. They thought that federalism did indeed contradict the sovereignty of nations, which was proclaimed by the amendments. The amendments implied a "supra-national community." In a federal set-up, "citizens participated directly" in decision-making processes and not only through federal components, which meant that "the federation could make decisions even against the will of its individual components."[71] This fact, that there was always the possibility of surpressing the rights of the individual components in a federation bothered the Croatian intellectuals. Therefore, they advocated statehood and sovereignty of the republics with full powers for decision-making; then as free and sovereign nations the republics should become part of a common state as "an alliance of the republics" and a community of "equal states."[72]

The amendments to the Constitution of the republic of Croatia became especially controversial. The main issue was the proposed First Amendment in which the rights of Serbs and other nationalities in Croatia were specified.

> The Croatian nation (*narod*) in harmony with its historical aspirations, in community with the Serbian nation (*narod*) and nationalities in Croatia . . . realized in the national liberation war and socialist revolution its own national state—the Socialist Republic of Croatia . . . .
>
> The Socialist Republic of Croatia is a sovereign national state of the Croatian nation (*narod*), the state of the Serbian nation (*narod*) in Croatia, and the state of the nationalities that live in it.[73]

While the 1963 Croatian Constitution did not specifically mention Serbs in Croatia as a constituent nation of the republic along with the Croatians, in 1971 this was done to guarantee the rights of the Serbs in Croatia.

Although to the Croatian progressive Party leaders the new formulation was acceptable, strong objections to this change came from the leading intellectuals, the students, and the Matica hrvatska. Their objections concentrated mainly on the following. First, it was pointed out that the Croatians had had a national state in the Middle Ages and that their statehood, no matter how limited, had been preserved until 1918.[74] The First Amendment implied, however, that the Croatians had never had a state. A second, and much more important, issue was the formulation which stated that Croatia was the state of the Croatian and Serbian nations. This implied much more than the equality of Serbs in the republic. Although there was no higher percentage of non-Croatians in Croatia than non-Serbs in Serbia, from this formulation it could be deduced that Croatia was not a Croatian national state, while other republics, except Bosnia and Hercegovina, were national states of their respective peoples. A Croatian intellectual at the time wrote:

> It is essential that Croatia be clearly defined as a sovereign state, but it is also essential that the position of the Croatian nation be constitutionally and politically defined the same as the position of the Serbian nation in Serbia, the Macedonian nation in Macedonia, the Montenegrin nation in Montenegro, and the Slovene nation in Slovenia.[75]

Because a different type of Constitutional formulation was applied only in Croatia, the Croatian national forces concluded that they were the only constituent nation in Yugoslavia without their own state. In effect, the Serbs had two states, one in Serbia and another in Croatia. Under the proposed amendments Croatia was also to be the "state of the Serbian nation in Croatia" which implied that

> any Serb who came to Croatia was a part of the Serbian nation, whose state was Croatia. Because there were more Serbs than Croats in the SFRY, this might mean that Croatia was a Croato-Serbian state and by possible demographic changes even a Serbo-Croatian state.[76]

An example of such an implied federalization of Croatia was one of the proposed republican amendments[77] which provided for the creation of a Commission for intra-national relations in the republics. It was designated that the Commission would be made of an equal number of Croats and Serbs, and a proportionate number of minorities. The Commission clearly would have had a touch of federalism, similar to the Council of Nationalities in the federal government. Thus, such a formulation could have easily put the Croatians into a minority status in decision-making.[78]

The Serb minority in Croatia had a special constitutional treatment going back to the war period. They had been treated not like other minorities but as an equal partner of the Croatian majority in the republic. The fundamental reasoning for this was expressed by Moša Pijade, Tito's constitutional theorist, during and immediately after the war. In 1944 he wrote:

> ...the Serbs in Croatia are not 'a national minority,' notwithstanding the fact that the Serbs in Croatia make up only a small part of the population in comparison with the Croats... because the Serbs are a 'ruling' and 'state-making' nation.[79]

It seems that among some circles this thinking prevailed throughout the post-war period, although it became unwise and dangerous to express it publically. It was for this reason that the Croatians demanded national equality and wanted an end of a practice in which some were more equal than others.

As a logical consequence of the desire for full statehood and sovereignty of every republic, some of the more outspoken Croatians in the movement asked for the following: the creation of a Croatian national bank, a "National Sabor of Socialist forces," Croatian membership to the United Nations, that young men drafted into the armed forces serve in their own republics, that the training of the armed forces be done in the language of the republic in which the soldiers were located, and that every republic has the right to its own legal system.[80] These proposals were meant to be applied equally in all other republics to prove their newly defined sovereignty.

The neo-conservatives considered the federal amendments essentially as "an excuse" used by national forces in Croatia for their ultimate goal—the "destruction of Yugoslavia."[81] The specific proposals convinced the neo-conservatives that their predictions were right. On the other hand, the progressive Party leadership considered these voices to be coming from the periphery of the movement and thought they were only a normal part of the on-going public debate. To them, their Party opponents were blowing the "radical demands" out of proportion in order to avoid other more important issues.[82]

The intellectuals associated with the Matica hrvatska based their proposals for the amendments for the republic of Croatia on three main principles: 1) that Croatia was a national state of the Croatian people; 2) that the republic was a "self-managing community of the working people"; 3) that equality of all citizens was guaranteed.[83] Thus, the republic was national in form but socialist in substance. National sovereignty was not to be shared by any other national group, just as was the case in other republics. The Matica and the national forces, however, lost the battle on this issue. The amendments were promulgated in April 1972, and the objections of Matica hrvatska were not taken into consideration. Moreover, the most controversial First Amendment remained, as the Party had originally proposed: that Croatia was "the national state of the Croatian nation," and "the state of the Serbian nation in Croatia."[84]

The Student Strike

At noon, on November 22, 1971, about three thousand university students in Zagreb gathered at the Student Center Hall to discuss the proposed republican constitutional amendments. Within an hour, they decided to take action and proposed a student strike for the next day.[85] The motion was enthusiastically supported not just by those present, but also by students from all the faculties of the University in Zagreb, as well as by those from university branches in different cities throughout the republic. Soon over 30,000 students in Croatia were on strike, while Faculty deans, professors, Native Student Clubs,[86] and all major educational institutions in the republic endorsed the students' decision. It is not certain whether Matica hrvatska was consulted before the strike was declared or whether it had wished such a strike, but once the students decided to intervene, the Matica supported them in their efforts.

One of the first moves of the Party regarding the strike was to prevent it from spreading to the workers. At the same time, however, they tried to turn the workers against the students. But this "counter-mobilization" did not succeed because the workers refused to be used simply as instruments in the Party's political power play. They had their own opinion about what was going on and were no longer blindly following the voice of the Party officials. The following was a response of a worker at one of the meetings urging the workers to condemn the strikers:

Time has passed when the workers were voting like monkeys, simply raising their hands [and accepting] whatever was read to them [by the Party officials]. Today the worker has his own opinion about everything. Nothing can be imposed on him.[87]

In general, the workers in the republic remained calm, awaiting the outcome of the events. They had much more to lose by leaving their work places than did the students. Still, a number of workers' collectives supported the strikers, thus openly opposing the Party's wishes. Interestingly enough, the most enthusiastic supporters of the students' strike came from the Čistoća, Zagreb's sanitation workers, who had the lowest wages and whose jobs were traditionally considered the most degrading. Not only did they support the students' demands, they even offered financial aid.[88]

The immediate justification for the student strike was the unresolved issue of foreign currency policy. In its message to Tito, the Presidency of the Student Federation of Croatia stated:

We have stopped work at the Croatian University in order to protest the unresolved [problems regarding] foreign currency, credit, and the financial system. We demand that these questions . . . be resolved as soon as possible.[89]

The feeling among the students was that political and economic changes, which had been promulgated by the federal Constitution and especially by the Constitutional amendments of 1971, were being frustrated. To them this was a clear "proof that bureaucratic-unitaristic forces" were still in power. Furthermore, they pointed out the inconsistencies between the proclaimed policies and implementation of those policies. In the case of foreign currency, for example, at the time when Tito himself stated that the foreign currency issue had to be resolved, "the very Commission which had been established at the [Federal] Assembly to resolve that problem was dissolved."[90]

The implementation of federal amendments, especially of those dealing with foreign currency, was a major political issue at that time. This can be seen also from the discussion of the CC LCC with Tito, in Karadjordjevo, on November 30, 1971. Some Party progressives openly complained to

Tito that "the amendments were promulgated at the beginning of summer, but very little of those decisions had been implemented until that day."[91] Tripalo, leader of the progressives in Croatia, admitted at the same meeting that it seemed to him that the Party was often "incapable" of implementing decisions.[92] While Dapčević-Kučar, President of the CC LCC, was stressing that foreign currency was an important issue which brought students and others in Croatia together, Tito, however, dismissed it as a mere ploy for counter-revolutionary activities at the university. He stressed that the students had no idea of what was all involved in the foreign currency system. Some of them may know, but not the masses.[93]

The masses, however, and especially the students, were aware of the economic issues, because those issues had been on the front pages of most papers in the republic for months before the strike. Those who were working in the West were dealing with foreign currency every day. They were surely concerned about what happened to the earnings they sent home. However, it is clear from the striking students' declarations that these issues were only part of a much more complex political situation. First of all, the students were dissatisfied with the slow progress of political change. To them it seemed as if the Party was deliberately taking its time to fulfill its promises. Therefore, they urged the progressives in the Party "to start in a concrete way to chip away and demolish the centralist system so that self-management would not continue to be just a nice phrase and a fiction."[94] Thus, beyond the issue of foreign currency, there was the underlying problem of centralist power, economical and political. Also, there was the on-going struggle in the Party of Croatia, in a way a reflection of the first problem. It must have been known to the student leadership, as well as to the Matica hrvatska, that the factional Party struggle in Croatia had reached an acute stage after its 22nd Session (November 5-6, 1971). It was clear that the clash was imminent and also that the progressives were losing the battle. The students, the most explosive segment in the Croatian national movement, decided to take dramatic action in order to express their support for the progressive Party leadership and to show to Tito that the conservative and neo-conservative forces in the Party did not have popular support in the republic. The Secretary of the Student Alliance in Croatia said in this sense:

At that moment [November 22, 1971] we considered giving not only verbal support, as until then, but by such an action [as the strike] we wanted to give support to all progressive forces in the LC in Croatia and in Yugoslavia.[95]

The students of the Law faculty even named leading conservatives and neo-conservatives in the CC LCC and openly called for their removal from their Party positions and from the Party itself.[96] Although the progressives did not solicit dramatic action, the students nevertheless stopped work at the university in order to make clear on what side they and the people of Croatia stood. The Party faction that was supported by the students was caught in the middle of the events. On the one side, it was clear to them that their opponents in the Party were on the offensive and that the end of their era was at hand.[97] On the other hand, they did not believe that the strike could help the situation. Savka Dapčević-Kučar, president of the CC, in her assessment of the situation considered the "motives" of most of the striking students to be "positive, well-intentioned, and progressive." She, however, thought that the way in which the students expressed their support for the Party leadership was an unacceptable method of political struggle.[98] Tripalo also believed "that the vast majority of the students and their leadership" was well-intentioned in deciding to go on strike, but he made a public plea to the students to end it.[99] Indeed, the progressives believed that the strike was actually having an opposite effect of that which the students intended. While acknowledging the "dilemma" of the progressive Party leadership, Budiša, the outstanding figure in the student leadership, called upon it to "step in the forefront of the radical, democratic, and socialist movement which is being born at the Croatian University." He also asked them not to side with the "forces which had been making that same leadership powerless." He pointed out that "if [progressives] wished to have the confidence of the people, they should have confidence in the people" and take an open stand on the side of the strike.[100]

Putsch in Karadjordjevo

While the strike was still on,[101] the entire Party leadership from Croatia was ordered to come to a meeting with Tito. The goal was not only to resolve the problem of the student strike but also to purge the Party of its progressive elements. The meeting took place on November 30, 1971, at Karadjordjevo, the old royalist hunting lodge near Belgrade.

The student strike in Croatia constituted a political crisis for the Party more in appearance than in substance. Although the situation was potentially explosive, the students themselves kept everything under control. The strike remained peaceful and within university limits. The real political crisis, however, was at the top of the republic's Party itself. Milka Planinc, neo-conservative member of the CC and successor to Savka Dabčević-Kučar, confirmed this at the Karadjordjevo meeting when she said the "central question where we differ is the assessment of nationalism in Croatia, its essence and its dangers. These few [striking] students are not the question."[102] Another proof that the strike was secondary on the Party's agenda is the fact that, in the midst of the student crisis, the Party leadership in Karadjordjevo was debating its internal relations while the strike itself was barely mentioned. Obviously, the meeting was the culmination of long intra-party struggle and not a result of the strike. The student protest was only its immediate cause.

Looking back at the events in Croatia in 1971, one can see that the road to Karadjordjevo was being prepared ever since the spring of 1971. The conservatives and neo-conservatives had been steadily gaining ground, not among the people or the Party rank and file, but with Tito and on the federal level. While the progressives were closer to the people, the conservatives were closer to the state power. For example, the military forces were eager to convince Tito that the Croatian national movement was a threat to the Party and the country,[103] while the state secret police was very useful in providing "proofs" for the arguments of the conservatives.[104] The conservative forces also had the advantage of constantly communicating with Tito, while the progressives were cut off from the country's ultimate arbiter. Bakarić, a life-long Tito loyalist, was the major contact between Tito and the Party opposition in Croatia.[105] After the Party top in Croatia had been finally separated during the 22nd Session of the CC LCC early in November 1971, Tito received Dušan Dragosavac and heard his side of the story. Tito, however, refused to receive the top three CC Party progressives, obviously he was not interested in hearing their views.[106] Instead, Tito decided to call together the entire Party leadership for a final showdown at Karadjordjevo.

This meeting with the Croatian Party leaders lasted 22 hours. The official, but edited Minutes, of the meeting show that the progressives did in the end accept responsibilities for events in Croatia,[107] but they also continued to defend their former actions and point of view. Dragutin Haramija, President of the Sabor, reiterated the economic complaints. Ivan Šibl, a retired general and president of the Veterans' organization in Croatia, emphasized that Croatian nationalism had been treated differently than other "isms," implying that the neo-conservatives considered Croatian nationalism much more dangerous than unitarism or Serbian nationalism. The progressives also pointed out once more the discrepancies between Party principles and practices. They stressed that the only solution to the problems in Croatia, and in the country as a whole was the full implementation of Party decisions so that the forces outside the Party would not have any reason to complain.[108] Furthermore, even the students' strike was part of the on-going political process of democratization and not a counter-revolution. The opponents of the progressives, however, accused them of seeking personal popularity, of deviating from the Party decisions. Among other things, the progressives were accused of tolerating nationalists and counter-revolutionaries.

Tito's meeting with the Croatian leadership was followed the next day by the 21st Session of the Presidium of the LCY, held at the same lodge. The date and place of the meeting which formally ended the Croatian national movement was highly symbolic to the Croatians as well as to foreign observers.[109] The First of December was the anniversary of the creation of the First Yugoslavia, and the name Karadjordjevo brought to memory the former royal regime and its policy of Great Serbianism. Thus, it was easy to associate the events of December 1, 1971, with former turbulent intra-national relations.

The major points of Tito's remarks at the meeting with the Croatian leadership and at the 21st Session of the Party Presidium consisted in acknowledging that the Croatian economic complaints were justified; at the same time, however, they should not be discussed as a national but rather as a class problem. Furthermore, other ideological, social or national forces, as well as a separate Croatian road to socialism would not be allowed. The role of the Party had to remain unchallenged. "The League of Communists [was to remain] the sole factor which [had] the right of ideological-political action within the overall Yugoslav framework."[110] Most of all, Tito stressed the need for Party discipline, for an ideological and organizational unity, and for a renewed democratic-centralism. The

Party unity and discipline were of utmost importance because of the Party's role as the guardian of state unity. A few days after the 21st Session, Tito stated about the problem of decentralization:

> If the League of Communists continues to move in [the current] downward direction, this Yugoslavia would break up. It would break up, or rather it would be prey to someone, and it is only a question of whose prey it would be. But the League of Communists must again become [the] cohesive force of our socialist community and a guarantee of its strength. It must not only be an ideological force, but at times must even be somewhat firmer toward those who fail to adhere to party policy, that is, the policy adopted and inaugurated by the top leadership.[111]

It seems that Tito even regreted the decisions of the 1952 Party Congress which had guaranteed the decentralizing measures. He thought that because of those decisions the Party had lost its true role in society.[112] Finally, to solve the Party's problems Tito proposed that "administrative" measures should be taken in order to achieve desired Party unity. These were his words:

> This democracy of ours has suffered too much abuse. I agree that democracy here is increasing. But when it comes to opponents who are working against such a community, a democratic community, the most effective measures must be taken, including the administrative.[113]

The 21st Session became a "historic" meeting which changed the course of the LCY once more. This time, however, it was a step backwards to the old times of Party purges, to disciplinary actions, and to arrests of those who were considered dangerous to the regime.

The Clean-Up

The top Party progressives in Croatia understood well why Tito had called them to Karadjordjevo and what his verbal chastising at the meeting meant. But interestingly enough, none of the progressives renounced his or her political activities in the Croatian national movement or the fundamental principles for which they stood. Tito himself complained in both his opening and concluding remarks of the 21st Session that there "was in fact little auto-criticism" especially by the "leading comrades."[114] However, the removal of the unwanted elements did not come immediately. First, the neo-conservatives went all out to orchestrate "popular" support for the Karadjordjevo condemnation of "rotten liberalism." Next followed party meetings, speeches, and telegrams in support of the new course. On December 4 there was a meeting of Zagreb's Party Presidium; it was still presided by a leading progressive, Srećko Bijelić, a Serb from Croatia, and there were no open confrontations at that meeting. Two days later, however, numerous Party gatherings took place throughout the republic, the purpose of which was to give members the opportunity to abandon the sinking ship of the progressives and jump aboard with the conservatives. The Executive Bureau of the LCY met in Karadjordjevo on December 8, and Tripalo was still one of two Croatian representatives. But, on the same day he informed Tito that he was resigning from all Party and government posts. Savka followed his example on December 9, the day when the 22nd Session of the Party Presidium took place. (Their resignation, however, was not made public until December 12.) On December 10, another round of Party meetings in Croatia was held. This was the time to condemn the progressives by name. Finally, at the 23rd Session of the CC LCC on December 12 and 13, 1971, a public show of the "friendly" departure of Savka Dapčević-Kučar was displayed. She actually opened the meeting and, after reading her letter of resignation and listening even to some praise from the leading conservatives, she left the meeting hall. The conservatives tried to display a "friendly" atmosphere while forcing the progressives out, because they were not certain how the masses would respond to the coup. It was with this Session that the neo-conservatives officially began to clean-up within the Party ranks.[115] Marko Veselica, a member of the national movement described the Party's actions as follows:

> After Karadjordjevo all those who had demanded the equality and sovereignty of the Croat people in the Yugoslav community were systematically purged as were those who only sought a greater degree of political or human rights as well as freedom in scholarly work and artistic expression.[116]

While the Party was preparing for self-cleaning and while the "friendly" show was taking place at the 23rd Session, the police and military forces were "cleansing" the streets of Zagreb of "undesired elements." Helicopters were cruising above the Croatian capital and tanks were stationed in its outskirts. Armed forces of the Zagreb district were stationed in and around Zagreb, and were commanded by a Serbian general, Djoko Jovanić. There was no counter-revolution. When after the beginning of the purges the students came out in the streets for a peaceful demonstration they were clubbed and jailed. Eyewitnesses reported that "many students were severely injured and some may have been killed. Police reinforcements were brought in from other republics and they had no regard or consideration for Croat students."[117]

From January until the end of April 1972, twenty-three Party organizations in Croatia were obliterated, 741 people were thrown out of the Party, 131 Party functionaries were removed, and 280 Party functionaries resigned.[118] The clean-up, however, was even more thorough outside the Party ranks. Workers' collectives, schools, the writers union, newspapers, TV and Radio stations, publishing houses, professional groups, the Youth Association, and even film makers in the republic had to go through the same process of denouncing the "counter-revolutionaries," of praising Tito and the Party, and pointing a finger at those who were on the side of the fallen leadership. This process continued for about two years. The ones who were hardest hit, however, were the Matica hrvatska and the students. The Matica was practically closed down, its branches eliminated, its periodicals shut down, and its leading figures tried and sentenced to many years in prison.[119] The entire student leadership as well as hundreds of students were tried and jailed. According to Veselica, "about 32,000 people were arrested, dismissed from their jobs, interrogated by the police or subjected to other kinds of persecution and pressure."[120] There were no higher Party officials among those who were tried and sentenced to prison. The highest sentence was demanded for the historian Franjo Tudjman; but, he received "only" two years in jail because his friend Miroslav Krleža, Tito's old confidant, appealed directly to Tito on his behalf.[121] The longest prison sentences were given to Marko Veselica (seven years) and Šime Djodan (six years). Both of them were former Party members, professors at the University in Zagreb, and leading figures in the national movement.

The conservative Party leadership made a strong effort to justify the purges and persecutions by projecting the former leadership and the Croatian national movement as a great evil. The national forces, according to them, would have brought a great calamity to the state, and even to humanity if the Party had not interfered in time. Jakov Blažević, best known as the persecutor of Archbishop Aloysius Stepanic in 1946, declared:

> We are faced with a Civil War which in fact has already started, if only in mild form. This is a counter-revolution which. . . would have led to genocide. The instigators wanted . . . to provide a pretext for those who wish to offer 'help,' that is, a brotherly intervention. Had we not restored the unity of our leadership, we would not be sitting in this air-conditioned hall but would have had to fight on the streets.[122]

Thus, the new leaders wanted to be seen as the "good guys" who had not only saved Yugoslavia and the world but who had protected the Croatian nation from itself. In 1981, Vlado Gotovac, a leading Croatian intellectual and former prisoner expressed this mentality in an open letter to Jure Bilić, President of the Croatian Sabor:

> A disobedient Croatian is a planetary danger: as a reckless fascist adventurer, he is a burning match near the 'Balkan powder keg'; and you (and the circle around you) are extinguishing that match for the general good! . . . And that is why: those for whom [your work] is good—are helping you![123]

Croatian intellectuals claimed that ever since World War II, conservative elements in the Party and the federal hegemonists had been "exorcising" Croatia from the "evil spirits," but, at the same time, whenever the Party needed to use those "spirits" it was more than eager to point out that the "exorcism" did not work.[124] The purges in 1971-1972 were one of those occasions when the Party needed to project itself as the only force which could keep the Croatian "evil forces" under control to justify its own power control.

Resignation and apathy in Croatia followed the Karadjordjevo coup. Many had believed that democratic changes in Yugoslavia were possible and that the late Sixties and early Seventies would bring "equality and democracy in a sovereign Croatia."[125] Those who were working for such changes, however, were denounced as "counter-revolutionaries." The Croatian national movement itself was crushed. By destroying the movement, however, the Party did not solve fundamental national problems, nor did the purges and the imprisonments in Croatia help improve the intra-national relations in the country.

In the post-Karadjordjevo period, Yugoslav internal policies developed in two opposite directions. On the one hand, the process of state decentralization continued; that is clear from the 1974 Constitution. On the other hand, "democratic centralism" in the Party was reaffirmed. With the Party purges, the "evil spirits" in Croatia were in the bottle once again. However, ever since the Belgrade regime has been plagued with severe economic, intra-national, and intra-Party difficulties. In fact, Yugoslavia finds itself in a much deeper crisis today than it had to face in 1971.

CONCLUSION

The Croatian national movement in the Sixties and early Seventies went through three major phases. The time periods were approximately the following: 1965-1968, 1968-1970, and January 1970-December 1971. During the first phase (1965-1968), two important changes took place which greatly affected the events that followed immediately afterwards. First, reformers at the top of the LCY, led mainly by the Croat and Slovene members, were victorious in their decentralizing efforts and in subduing the conservative forces led by Vice-President Alexander Ranković. Second, Croatian intellectuals, although mostly of Marxist orientation, became the leading spokesmen of Croatian national interests. Among other signs, the Declaration on the Croatian language (1967) clearly indicated that both Croatian Marxist and non-Marxist intellectuals were concerned about the future of their national culture and national well-being.

Neither of the two opposing ideological camps, the Communist Party and the religious institutions, were able to achieve national unity among the Croatian nation. It was the intelligentsia, which came from different social and ideological elements, that brought about some national unity in Croatia.

Although the intelligentsia lacked organizational structure, it managed to attract massive support because of its ideological tolerance and because it openly expressed national concerns and issues.

On the whole, the intelligentsia and the national movement did not challenge the state or the system itself, but they protested against the inconsistent implementation of the Party's basic principles, particularly where Croatian interests were involved. They put to a test the basic post-War proclamations on national rights, self-management, and on the so-called "liberal" Communism in Yugoslavia.

In the late Sixties (1968-1970), while the gap between Party conservatives and liberals was growing, the Croatian national movement entered its second phase. Now liberal party elements in Croatia began to raise the same questions as the intelligentsia. A major difference among them was, however, that the Party liberals were talking in class terms, while the intelligentsia used both national and class references. While the Party liberals tended to regard economic problems as the origin of all the tension in Yugoslavia, intellectuals maintained that the national problems had much deeper historical, political, social and cultural roots. Also during this period, the roles within the national movement became more clearly defined. The Matica hrvatska began to play an important part on the national stage. Its publishing activities increased, it became better organized, and its leadership became more nationally oriented. There were also some important changes at the Croatian University. Its leadership was slowly getting away from Party control, and the University began to chart a new course of liberal, humanistic socialism and national affirmation. This phase culminated in the Tenth Plenum of the CC LCC, in January 1970, with which a new period of the movement began.

The third and final phase of the movement lasted from January 1970 to December 1971. The Tenth Plenum at the beginning of the phase brought a defeat for the conservatives in Croatia and the legitimization of the Croatian national movement. During this third phase, the movement widened its basis and gained mass support. At the same time, the liberal Party leadership, which was victorious in 1970, split into two groups. One segment, the younger and more progressive members, drew closer to the intelligentsia. This group soon found itself at the top of the Party hierarchy in Croatia, it united the national and the class struggle and, in a popular alliance, made an effort to gain more freedom and self-rule in Croatia. The other segment of the liberal wing in the Party, the neo-conservatives, moved very close to the ultra conservative camp.

The national movement in Croatia was not an organized force but a combination of various national groups. The movement had three major centers: the Matica hrvatska, the top republican Party leadership, and the Croatian University in Zagreb. The soul of the movement were intellectuals

who had gathered around the Matica. The Party leadership stood somewhere between the Party and the masses, trying to influence both. University students were the true idealists of the movement. They enthusiastically supported the Party leadership and demanded full human and
national rights for the Croatian people.

Although the Matica hrvatska was undoubtedly the spearhead of the
movement, the role of progressive Party leadership was not less important. It legitimized the national element as an integral part of the class
struggle but lacked the power to bring about the desired changes. Its
influence in the republic was significant, even though it was unable to
transform the mass support into political action. The reason for the lack
of political power among the progressives was that the real power in the
country was in the hands of the military and police forces, of the banks,
and of the LCY—all of which were centered in the federal, Serbian capital
and which were ultimately controlled by Tito himself. The progressives
had become tribunes of the masses, but the only political weapon they
had were the unorganized masses themselves. Once Tito withdrew his
support of their endeavors their fate was sealed.

In the context of Croatian national history, the movement can be
viewed as a continuation of the Croatian national struggle, which began
with the national awakening in the mid-19th century. In the pre-World
War I period, while Croatia was still a part of the Habsburg Empire,
Croatian national forces fought Vienna's and Budapest's centralism, their
economic exploitation, and their cultural oppression. They demanded
political and economic autonomy, cultural as well as national emancipation, and the unification of all Croatian lands into a single political unit.
Similarly, during the inter-war period, the main issue was Serbian centralism and the political, economic, and cultural subordination of Croatia
to the Serbian royalist regime. Immediately after 1918, their goal was a
Neutral Croatian Republic. During the late 1920s and the 1930s, there
were two main political streams in Croatia: one was working for a Croatian statehood in a confederated Yugoslavia while the other demanded
complete independence. Even the Communist Party in Croatia flirted
with both ideas.

The Croatian mass movement of the Sixties continued in this same
tradition of struggle for Croatian self-rule. Its ideological roots were
Croatian Marxist revisionism of the inter-war period, which survived

among the Left intellectuals through the war and post-war periods. The movement, however, would not have grown nor spread so fast had it not found a fertile ground among the population in Croatia. In some respects the Croatian Mass Movement resembled very much Radić's Croatian Peasant Party from the inter-war period. In the 1920s Radić awoke Croatian national consciousness and politicized the Croatian peasantry. Similarly, the Mass Movement in the 1960s and 1970s, especially the Matica hrvatska, made the Croatian younger generations aware of their national predicament and mobilized the masses in the struggle for their national rights. In the dichotomy of two traditional Croatian national ideologies, Starčević's exclusivism (Party of Right) and Strossmayer's Yugoslavism, the movement, like Radić's party, stood somewhere between the two. It did not advocate the break-up of Yugoslavia, but it insisted on Croatian national rights, including the right of full statehood and self-determination. This is why Radić, his pacifism and his social and national policies were very much admired by the masses in the movement.

The most important objectives of the Croatian national movement in the Sixties and early Seventies was to gain hold of its national destiny and achieve full national emancipation.[2] Historically, Croatia has been one of those "small nations" whose fate has been shaped by wars, international peace treaties, as well as by international religious and ideological power struggles. In the Yugoslav state, contrary to all promises, the ultimate decision-making power for the Croatians was in Belgrade and not in Croatia. Also in the 1960s, there was a feeling among the Croatian intelligentsia and Party liberals that the existence of the Croatian nation was threatened by assimilation, emigration, and economic exploitation. Thus, the desire for a further decentralization of Yugoslavia and for Croatia's statehood became increasingly stronger. However, the goal was not just nominal statehood as in the past but the real one. This meant first of all full control of their economy. Without stopping the outflow of economic wealth from Croatia, there could be no new jobs, and the exodus of Croatians to the West would continue. In other words, without these changes Croatia would soon have to face national disaster. The leading voices of the movement also stressed that Croatians had their own ancient culture, language, state and political tradition. Therefore, they demanded the right to be directly among the "rainbow" of nations in the world and not simply a part of "Yugoslavism" which no one accepted anyway.

The means and methods of the Croatian political struggle in the Sixties were also similar to those in previous periods. They were based on historic rights, on natural and moral principles, on the emancipatory role of the Communist revolution, and on world opinion. Croatian national forces in the past had argued the historic rights principle by pointing to the continuation of Croatia's national statehood since the early Middle Ages and to its legal arrangements with the Hungarian crown of St. Stephen and with the Habsburgs. Similarly, the leaders of the national movement in the 1960s and 1970s stressed the Party's official proclamations on national policy in the 1930s and during World War II, according to which each nation in Yugoslavia was guaranteed self-rule and even the right to separation. By recalling these historical documents they were hoping to legitimize their national struggle. Also, like their forefathers in the past, they invoked the natural and moral rights of every nation to self-rule and self-determination. They were envisioning a world where every nation would be allowed to participate freely and fully. Despite the fact that many in the world, especially the larger powers, considered "small nations as a weakness" and as impediments in the power politics, they dreamed of a pluralistic society and of a world where all individuals and nations would be emancipated and would be positive contributors to the world progress.[3]

According to Marxist theory, nationalism was a product of capitalism, and thus its future doomed. Nationalism, however, can be progressive and useful before and during the revolution. Only after the revolution it becomes a counter-revolutionary force. Many captialists, on the other hand, believed that with the technological revolution and world progress, nationalism would lose all its attraction. Both kinds of internationalists considered nationalism essentially as a negative force in the world community, and as such it should be destroyed by a revolution or overcome by progress. It seems, however, that both kinds of internationalists have been wrong in their judgments. Modern nationalism is alive and well. This can be seen from the growth of a number of states and national liberation movements in the world today.

Intellectuals in the Croatian national movement strongly believed that the world should be peaceful and integrated. But, they thought that this integration should not be achieved on the basis of assimilation and Marxist or capitalist internationalism, because in every supra-nationalism or internationalism some are sacrificed for the "greater good." To them, the process of integration should be based on the respect of the individuality of every nation.[4] They were well aware that nationalism can be a positive as well as a negative force.

They, however, saw the whole movement in the positive light of defending the people's own rights and of working toward a democratization and humanization of their own society. Also, to them the movement was a part of the on-going process of humanization and decolonization of the world.[5] In that way, they believed, they were even contributing to the world as a whole.

There was also a belief among the Croatians in the Sixties that world opinion, especially in the West, was on their side, because their movement was liberal, humanistic, and freedom oriented. They still believed that the West was interested in giving at least moral support to such movements and that moral principles were above immediate political interests.[6] But all of these principles had very little, if any, political weight. Generally speaking, the movement did not find much understanding among the Western governments.

From its beginning, the Party claimed as its prerogative to label anybody as its "enemy," which usually is the first step in the process of discrediting and destroying the "enemy." In the case of the Croatian intellectuals, the Party used exactly these old propaganda methods and condemned the members of the movement as "counter-revolutionaries," "reactionary," "extremists," "separatists," "clero-fascists," "fascists," and as being in touch with foreign "secret services."[7] Also, during the post-1971 trials some of the members were accused of having planned to take over the political power from the Party. It is absurd, however, that such accusations were made by a ruling party which represents less than five percent of the people.

The fate of the LCY had been closely connected with that of the Yugoslav state itself. In addition to the class role, the Party traditionally has portrayed itself as indispensable to the unity of the country and peace in the Balkans. Thus, to preserve the country and its monopoly of power it needed to crush all forces which, in its eyes, became a threat to its unity and power and to the integrity of the state. The Croatian national movement was considered such a threat and it had to be subdued and crushed by any means.[8]

Besides being a challenge to the Party's monopoly of power, the movement in Croatia had been on a collision course with the Belgrade centrist forces on the issues of economic and political decentralization. It was not in the interest of Belgrade to fully implement decentralization, because this would divest the Serbian controlled federal institutions of much of their economic and political power; obviously, Belgrade did not want this to happen. Thus, one of the essential problems between the Serbians and Croatians lay in the fact that it was in the interest of the Croatians to keep their economic wealth and earnings for themselves, while it was in the interest of the Serbians to have a hand in Croatian economy.

It seems that the Croatian political and intellectual leadership in the late 1960s and 1970s did not pay enough attention to the effect of the movement on the country's international relations, particularly on the East-West balance of power. This was another factor that contributed to the movement's failure. It has been in the interest of both the East and West to support a centralized Yugoslavia in order to preserve Yugoslavia as a buffer zone between the two ideologically and military opposing camps. One of the unfortunate facts about the movement was that the political powers in the East and the West regarded it as potentially dangerous. To the Western governments and observers who started with the premise that Yugoslav unity was intrinsically good and politically beneficial, the movement was reactionary and negative, despite its socialist nature. To the Soviets the movement was ideologically and geo-politically dangerous. Therefore, the Belgrade accusations that the movement had gone too far, and that it had to be crushed for the sake of socialism, for peace in the Balkans, and for the balance of power in Europe, were readily accepted by other countries and their observers of Yugoslav events. Most probably it had not been by accident that Brezhnev was in Belgrade and Tito in Washington shortly before the Karadjordjevo coup of December 1971.

The Croatian movement in the Sixties and early Seventies can also be looked at in the light of the events in Eastern Europe in the post-World War II period. National Communism has been one of the most disruptive elements in the Communist bloc. For example, Communists with a national orientation played a major role in Hungary and Poland in the mid-1950s. But the events in Czechoslovakia during the Prague Spring of 1968 resemble most those in Croatia and Yugoslavia. In 1968, Czechoslovakia, a multinational country, was oriented both toward ideological liberalization and national equality. Like the Croatians, the Slovaks were struggling for greater autonomy and national rights. In both countries even the "liberal" members of the ruling nations,Czechs in Czechoslovakia and Serbs in Yugoslavia, had little understanding of Slovak or Croatian "nationalists." The main obstacle to the Prague movement came from external Soviet pressures and from military power. Similarly, the ultimate fate of the Croatian movement was in the hands of forces outside Croatia. The Croatian Spring was stopped by the Belgrade central institutions, including the military forces, and most probably with the blessings of both ideological blocks.

Although the movement had been subdued, the events of the late 1960s and early 1970s had a strong effect on the Croatian people, especially on the younger generation. By uncovering fundamental political, economic, cultural and national questions, the movement raised the national and political consciousness of the post-War generation. The movement had also an effect on the 1974 Constitution, which gave the republics more decision making autonomy than they had before. A major battle, however, is being waged at the present time for revision of that Constitution. Serbia is demanding amendments to the Constitution which would strengthen the central powers once again, while the Croatians and Slovenes are opposing these changes. Another positive outcome of the Croatian Spring has been that people in Croatia as well as in other republics also had a taste of pluralism which shook the Party's control.

By suppressing the movement, the regime "did not resolve a single major issue [raised] in 1971."[9] Despite some constitutional and structural changes (acclaimed inside and outside the country) in the mid-1970s, the basic problem of centralism remained. Purges, trials, and imprisonments pushed the Croatians into apathy and passive resistance, and even into a deeper nationalism. In the Sixties and early Seventies, Croatians believed that the system was somewhat flexible in allowing national and other problems in Yugoslavia to be solved through a peaceful process. But the events of December 1971 resulted in a further alienation of the Croatians and, as some feel, increased the threat of a more radical movement in the future.

Besides having severe economic problems, Yugoslavia continues to be plagued by nationalist problems. Serbian and Albanian relations in Kosovo have been rapidly worsening ever since 1981. While non-Serbs considered the issue of Kosovo to have been primarily a Serbian problem, the Slovenes have been lately raising their voices against the federal centralism. Ironically, the Slovene party leaders, although federalists, sided with the centralist forces in 1971, but, at the present time, their new and younger leadership demands are the same as those of Croatia in 1971. However, the Croatian question still remains the most important national issue in the country. The Belgrade unitarists and hegemonists still see Croatian nationalism as the most dangerous, because it is in direct opposition to their own interests. For example, there is much more political and national freedom in Slovenia than there is in Croatia. But, the Croatians, although relatively quiet at present, did not give up their national goals.

In the last issue of the *Hrvatski tjednik,* its editor Vlado Gotovac described the essence of the Croatian struggle in the Sixties and early Seventies as a struggle between the love of the Croatians for their homeland and "the integralists," for whom that love was "a ghostly spectacle from the past century, an archaic scene of fanatical nationalistic pettiness." It was also a clash between those who had a dream of "free men and just society" and the "dogmatists, mythomaniacs and apologists, all of whom were fallen spirits" and were "afraid of freedom." Although those "arrogant and cruel" "representatives of power" were victorious, Gotovac ended his last editorial with a message of hope. He commended his readers to keep the flame of hope burning.

> . . . We want a Croatia that will become a beautiful vision and a dream homeland to all [its inhabitants]. That is an impassioned dream, but it is the only dream worthy of being dreamed about this land! Dulcinea exists, though no one knows who she is and how she looks. The same is the fate of Croatia in our love . . . . [10]

Croatians had this dream of national freedom for a long time. Both the First and Second Yugoslavias did not fulfill it; instead they tried to crush it by all means. This is why the Croatian question and the national problem in Yugoslavia are as relevant today as they have been ever since the creation of the state in 1918.

POSTSCRIPT

At the moment when Tito shattered the Croatian national movement at the end of 1971, the internal and external advocates of the *status quo* and those who perceived the movement as a great danger for the country and its system were thankful that Tito was still alive. It was believed that the old man had saved the country once again. Some foreign observers went even further and hailed the purges and imprisonments in Croatia as a "thoroughly democratic step."[1]

The ultimate power in the country was still in Tito's hands and he remained the final arbiter until his death. But the fact that the fate of the country was contingent on the will and destiny of a single person has had a profound effect on the country, after he left the scene. Tito's absolutist powers covered up a multitude of the country's unresolved problems and weaknesses. And as soon as he died, the papered-over cracks began to appear and the country has been faced with severe economic, political, social, psychological, moral, and intra-national crises.

The events in Yugoslavia from 1972 until the present can be divided into two basic periods: before and after Tito's death. The overwhelming concern in the country during the first period (1972-1980) was to tighten Party discipline and Party control of society, and to devise an adequate mechanism that would insure a peaceful succession of power at the moment of Tito's death. In this respect the regime was successful. But the events that followed Tito's death indicated that the smooth transition of power in 1980 was deceptive. The country could not sustain itself on the basis of the inertia of the past. One could even say with some certainty that the post-Tito Yugoslavia has been on the road to the unknown. But more significant is the fact that the country's leadership has been moving in two opposite directions: namely, Serbs are pushing for recentralization of the country, while others, primarily Slovenes and Croatians, are defending their autonomies and advocating even more self-rule for the republics. Moreover, there are more and more of those who are even questioning the purpose of the Yugoslav state as such. Optimists outside the country seem to believe that the country will muddle through as it did in the past; presumably it has no other choice. For others, Yugoslavia of the 1980s did not enter a new, post-Tito era; rather, they have seen this decade as the beginning of the end of Titoism, and likely even of the country itself.

Political Developments, 1972-1980

From 1972 to the time of Tito's death, the main effort was made to secure the continuation of Titoism and the unity of the country after his departure. A collective state Presidency was introduced by the constitutional amendments in 1971 and then incorporated into the new Constitution of 1974. In 1978, a similar mechanism of collective leadership was devised for the Party. The collective state presidency was seen as a logical outcome of the principles of federalism by which the major decisions were to be made by the consensus of the republics and autonomous provinces. The unity of the Party and its basic principle of democratic centralism, however, seemed to be contrary to the idea of Party federalism. This problem was resolved in 1978 by the introduction of a merry-go-round Presidency of the 23-member Party Presidium, a combination of elected and ex-officio members. The mechanism was supposed to combine the two main, and at the same time opposing, principles: federalism and democratic centralism.

The creation of the collective leadership also points to the fact that Tito was the last "Yugoslav." No other person has been, nor most probably will be, acceptable to all republican parties as a single leader. Thus, the idea of personal leadership was not only discarded but has been considered even dangerous.

The top state and Party mechanisms were supposed to be completely independent of each other. No one could be in both structures at the same time. The Party, however, was to remain the magic glue to hold the federal parts together. Besides the fact that the top Party official meets with the collective leadership of the state, the ideological convictions of the state functionaries, all of whom are Party members, were to be stronger than their own regional or national interests or feelings. By adhering to the loyalty of the Party and its avant-garde role in society, the members of the state bureaucracy were also supposed to work together for the common goals of the whole country. This was a major reason for the LCY's reinforcement of Leninism in the immediate post-1972 period. While the state continued on the path of decentralization, the Party, through its own recentralization and clean-up, strengthened its unity as well as its control over the state and society in the 1970s.

Out of major political events that took place in the 1972-1980 period, the following were among the most important. After the crushing of the Croatian movement, there were Party purges in other republics, mainly in Serbia and Slovenia. The republican Party leadership was accused of "liberalism" and they were removed. However, there were no trials or persecutions. Centralization within the Party structure and, at the same time, continuation of the on-going decentralization of the state were furthered. Furthermore, the principles of self-management were strengthened and reaffirmed as the only path to communism. These political processes and principles were incorporated in the new Constitution, promulgated in 1974, and officially accepted by the Party as a whole at the Tenth Party Congress held in the same year. The last Party Congress attended by Tito and Kardelj, the two leading figures in Yugoslavia since the Party took power in 1945, was held in 1978. This congress was full of Party's self-praises and optimism. It appeared to be more a farewell party for the old leaders than a meeting of the avant-garde of the working class that was facing a number of major crises. Tito in his speech to the Congress expressed a strong belief that he had laid down firm foundations to the new Yugoslav state and that he was leaving the country in excellent shape. He enumerated the strengths of the country and, clearly, he was pleased with himself and his legacy.[2] It seems that everyone else, except Edvard Kardelj, was elated at the time. He shocked the optimistic Congress delegates by stating that "the political structure of the society [was] in many ways the same or similar to the one prevailing at the time of direct revolutionary conflicts."[3] His speech implied that the internal forces in

Yugoslavia and their relations at the end of the 1970s were not much different from those in pre-war Yugoslavia. But despite Kardelj's warning, the Congress and the 1970s ended on a high note. The Party's and the country's main preoccupation was Tito's departure and not the important issues which were swelling under a thin covering of optimism and self-praise.

Economic Crisis of the 1980s

After the political crisis in the early 1970s, it seemed that Yugoslavia's economy was doing exceptionally well. The new and (especially in Croatia) unpopular political leaderships in the republics and federation were eager to legitimize their reign by making sure that there were visible signs of economic improvement. This impetus was reflected mainly in two fields: huge investments and a rise in the standard of living. The investments were made regardless of their economic feasibility or of the real strength of the economy, and, at the same time, the overall standard of living improved in the country. Usually, if a country turns to heavy investments, the standard of living suffers, but in Yugoslavia both were expanding simultaneously. The solution to this apparent contradiction was found in foreign credits. Yugoslavia was borrowing billions of dollars from the Western countries and banks.

The mistakes of Yugoslavia's economic planning of the mid-1970s were already becoming visible by the end of the decade. But while the foreign debt was huge and still growing, inflation rapidly increasing, and the investments not making expected returns, the Party leadership turned to meetings and discussions on the economic problems. In 1981, a 300-member federal commission was created to find the cures for what they believed were only minor flaws in a still healthy economy. After two years of meetings and discussions, the commission came out with a long-range program of economic stabilization. It did not propose any radical changes in the economic system, but simply recommended firmer implementation of the existing economic mechanisms. This, and a number of other attempts in the 1980s to fix the system and get the economy on the tracks, did not work. On the contrary, the inflation continued to burgeon from 45 percent in 1980 to about 300 percent at the present time, and it is still growing. Industrialization and modernization were halted, the standard of living rapidly declined, unemployment rapidly increased, and the foreign debt remained around twenty-one billion dollars.

Despite economic hardships and constant decline of real salaries, surprisingly there were no serious social disturbances in the first half of the decade, mainly because of corruption and flourishing underground economy. These two things served as main vents to the social and economic pressures. It is a common belief that the state and Party bureaucracies are permeated with corruption. Strong indications of this belief are their lifestyles and almost constant corruption "affairs" involving people at the top Party echelons. It is believed that it is not the hard work but the membership in the Party or "good connections" that bring economic and social advancement. Thus, while the regime kept an eye closed, many turned to the underground economy in order to make a living, or even to enrich themselves. However, the longer the economic crisis lasted, the more people were squeezed out of the game. As a result, numerous strikes have been taking place in the last two years; there are more and more homeless and hungry people in the country, and the economy has not been able to turn around. The regime is trying to raise hopes again by proclaiming that the country needs yet another economic reform. But after the failure of sixty economic, political, social and other reforms in the country since 1945, there is a serious doubt that new reforms would succeed.[4]

One of the major problems of all Yugoslav economic reforms has been the umbilical ties of the Party to the economy. Although, on one hand, the Party has been constantly professing and even strengthening the principles of self-management, on the other, it has been nullifying those principles by its constant interference in all levels of the economy. For this reason, there is skepticism about the success of any future economic reform unless the Party lets the economy out of its grips. But if the Party should do that, it would mean the end of the Party's monopoly of power, which would usher in radical changes in the system itself. Although there are more and more internal voices suggesting that the Party give up its avant-garde role, one can seriously doubt that the Party will, out of its altruism, make such a radical move.

Worsening of the Intra-National Relations

Besides a deep economic crisis, during the 1980s Yugoslavia lost not only Tito but the old guard partisan leadership; divisions among the republican Parties reached the point of no return; ethnic distrubances were taking place among the Kosovo Albanians; unexpectedly, Slovenes began to oppose Belgrade policies and demand more personal liberties and greater autonomy; workers' strikes became common in the late eighties; intellectuals questioned everything, including Tito, his legacy, the legitimacy of the system, and even the desirability and legitimacy of the Yugoslav state itself. The Party leadership, however, at its two 1980s Congresses (1982 and 1986) and at numerous conferences and meetings, satisfied itself with identifying, analyzing, and discussing current problems. It gave an enormous number of recommendations for the economic, social, and political ills, but after the meetings were over, very little if anything was done. In the Party debates and documents, as well as among public discussions, three different approaches to the resolution of the country's problems have clearly surfaced. Some advocate the strengthening of democratic centralism and recentralization of the state; others advocate political and economic liberalism; and there are those who would like to keep the present federalist arrangements and Titoist legacy untouched. Opinions on this and other issues are split mainly according to the republican and national lines, and thus instead of giving a general overview of the current problems in the country, an attempt will be made to indicate the major trends in the individual republics.

It has been commonly accepted, with good reason one should say, that the Serbs have been the ruling nation in the country since its creation in 1918. But in the last decade or so, after some of the decentralizing reforms had been implemented, Serbians have been trying more and more to portray themselves as the victims of the first and second Yugoslavias.[5] While Tito was alive, such thinking was still marginal, or, more probably, it was not opportune to express it openly. In the last few years, however, this Serbian view has become prevalent in the republic, first among the intellectuals and then in the Party. Their immediate target has been the Constitution of 1974, which the Serbians considered to be the result of an "anti-Serbian coalition" within the Party itself, put together by Tito and Kardelj. They insist that the constitutional provisions paralyzed the central powers of the federation and created a policentric state; thus, the Constitution has become the major cause of the country's economic, political and social problems. Although the federal center still controls the legislative powers, military and secret police forces, fiscal and monetary policy, foreign policy, enforces justice against political offenders in any of the republics regardless of their sovereignty, and although Serbs still dominate the state and Party bureaucracy, military and police forces, foreign ministry, banking and other institutions, they believe that the 1974 Constitution has turned the tide against them.

The major Serbian concern in the 1980s, however, has been the growing autonomy of the two autonomous provinces, Kosovo and Vojvodina, which in their eyes were drifting away from the control of the Serbian republic. As a result, the Serbians' first goal has been to get the control of the autonomous provinces and secondly to recentralize the whole country. The discussion about limiting the powers of the autonomous provinces had already begun in 1977, but the issue became especially compelling after the eruption of the Albanian demonstrations in Kosovo in the spring of 1981. While the moderate forces in Serbia were advocating closer relations with the province to be developed on the bases of self-management and cooperation as provided by the 1974 Constitution, others advocated a "strong Serbia in a strong Yugoslavia."

The 1981 Albanian riots in Kosovo opened a major crisis in Serbia and in the country as a whole, a crisis that is still very much alive. The ethnic Albanians, who make up 87.4 percent of the population in the province (Serbs and Montenegrins comprise 11.4 percent), demanded more self-rule and even their own republic within Yugoslavia's framework. Demonstrations were condemned by the Belgrade officials as counter-revolutionary. Armed forces occupied the Province for a few months, the protest was subdued, a number of Albanians were killed and hundreds, mostly intellectuals and students, were imprisoned. But the Province has not been peaceful ever since. The Kosovo question has remained one of the hottest political and intra-national issues for the Serbs and Albanians, and it also has exacerbated the political and national crisis in the country as a whole.

Kosovo became a rallying point of the Serbian revanchism and it also gave an opportunity to the Serbian leadership to change the methods of the political game in the country. While in the past the political arena had been the Party forums, the latest Serbian leadership, headed by

Slobodan Milošović, has taken the struggle for Serbia to the masses. This struggle, however, has been seen by the non-Serbs as a resurgence of Serbian determination to tighten their hold on the whole country once again. In 1987, Milošević eliminated a more liberal Serbian leadership, including his own proteges, took control of mass media, and pushed out from the scene all those who disagreed with his goals and methods. It was in the Kosovo mass meeting in April 1987 that his star began to rise, and he continues to ride a high political tide in Serbia based on Serbian nationalism and anti-Albanian sentiments.

What began as meetings of the Kosovo Serbs and their small delegations to Belgrade, demanding help against the local Albanians, developed into an all-Serbian movement through which Milošević has crushed the provincial government in Vojvodina, forced political changes in Kosovo, and attempted to extend Serbian movement into Montenegro and even other republics. At these meetings, signs were displayed asking for the return of the Serbian kingdom, unification of "all Serbian lands," cries for arms to "defend Serbia," to get rid of all Albanians, and even calls for Russians were heard. While Milošević and his supporters claim that the meetings were a spontaneous expression of Serbian national dissatisfaction, and that he was merely expressing the wishes and frustrations of the people, non-Serbians see in him reflections of Mussolini, and they are also pointing out that his mass-meetings were the best organized "spontaneous" meetings ever seen. He is accused of manipulating the Serbian masses in order to put pressure on the rest of the country and impose his wishes in the republic and even in the country as a whole: to return the country to the Ranković type of rule.

An attempt is being made on the part of his supporters, however, to project Milošević as a "second Tito," as the only politician in the country "strong" and "popular" enough to get the country out of the present crisis. But to anyone who is famiilar with Milošević's activities in the last two years and with the history of intra-national relations in Yugoslavia, it is obvious that he has become a leader in the Serbian national tradition. Not only can he not be acceptable to non-Serbs, but he is seen as a symbol of the old sour grapes of Serbian hegemonism in new skins. It is true he professes to be for market economy, but his economic liberalism is coupled with political centralist and hegemonostic views, and the two in Yugoslavia's setting do not go together. Because he considers "democracy in which everyone can criticize everyone else" to be "in theory and in history" nothing more than anarchy,[6] his call for a reform is inspiring more fear than hope, at least among the non-Serbian population in the country.

From the writings of the leading Serbian intellectuals it is becoming more and more clear that the Serbs are dissatisfied with their present situation in Yugoslavia. A leading Serbian intellectual and one time Ranković protege, Dobrica Ćosić, expressed a belief that the recent events in Yugoslavia indicate the "fall of the existing system and the crash of the Brioni Yugoslavia."[7] According to him, despite the fact that the Serbs are "the most loyal to Yugoslavia, "Serbophobia" has spread among the Slovenes, Croatians, Albanians, Macedonians intellectuals, and the Muslims,[8] practically among all the non-Serbs except the Montenegrins. Reasons for "Serbophobia" as well as for other Serbian misfortunes, however, are not found by him and other Serbian intellectuals in Serbian policies in the first and second Yugoslavia, but, it seems, in the ungratefulness of the non-Serbs for the Serbian "selfishness" in their work for the country, and in anti-Serbian conspiracies stretching from the Comintern, Vatican, Tito and the present Ljublana-Zagreb-Sarajevo-Priština axis. It seems that Serbian intellectuals and the present republican leadership see two options in the Serbian national program. One is a strong and expanded Serbia (elimination of the two autonomous provinces and desirably united with Montenegro) in a recentralized Yugoslavia. The second option, although not openly expressed, is an independent Greater Serbia. It appears, though, that the second option has been also used as a political weapon to pressure others to accept the Serbian solution to Yugoslavia's problems. Serbia needs Yugoslavia more than the non-Serbs need Serbia. While the Slovenes and Croatians see no economic or other benefits in being a part of the Yugoslav state, Serbians would lose much by the break-up of the country. Also, in the case of the break-up of Yugoslavia, most likely the Serbians would not be able to create a Greater Serbia; thus, it seems that a recentralized Yugoslavia would be their priority.

Traditionally the Slovenes have not been considered as "trouble makers" for Belgrade. On the contrary, they have been cooperative with the Serbian controlled governments in the first and second Yugoslavia until recent times. They are the most western, the most advanced, and ethnically the most heterogenous republic. Their geographic position, cultural, and linguistic differences from the rest of the country have made them less susceptible to Belgrade's domination and influences. In the last few years, however, Slovenes have been reevaluating their position in Yugoslavia and as a result have become one of the strongest voices for change in the country.

The Slovenes have made some important shifts in their own republic, which also have influenced the rest of the country. For example, they have relaxed the Communist control in the republic; there is a stress on pluralism and individualism, while the role of the Party and its monopoly of power are being downplayed; an active cooperation and even a single national program have developed between the Party leaders and other segments of society, mainly the intellectuals; they stress that economic and political liberalism go together and, for that reason, they are more and more abandoning Yugoslavia's Third World political and and economic orientation, and are returning to their European tradition of political pluralism and market economy. While the Serbs and Macedonians, for example, usually compare themselves and their advancements to Bulgaria, Romania or Greece, the Slovenes, as well as the Croatians, look toward their western neighbors and in that way measure their progress or lack of it. But what they see is more and more Balkanization and not Europeanization of their republics. A leading Slovene intellectual, Taras Kermauner, expressed this attitude clearly in an open "Letter to a Serbian Friend" by saying:

> We Slovenes have proceeded along the path of European individualism which recognizes solidarity resulting from particular wills, and not [solidarity] of terror in the name of brotherhood. Our goal is to unite with the developed world; to move into the third or fourth technological revolution; development of knowledge and the person; respect of individuality and society under the law. To put it another way, [we are for] destalinization, rejection of the tribal society, [and] removal of the tyrants. . . . [9]

It seems that the Slovenes have been for a long time in a dilemma which is known as the "active" and "passive" Slovenism. In the second half of this decade, they have opted for their "active" nationalism. Many of the reasons for their national reawakening, or what is also known as the

"Slovene Spring," are similar to those that sparked the Croatian Spring in the early 1970s: a sense of economic exploitations, linguistic, cultural, and political Yugoslav unitarism, and a feeling that Yugoslavia has become a burden to their national development. Ironically, the Croatian national revival of the early Seventies did not find much sympathy among Slovene intellectuals at the time and even less among their political leadership. Edvard Kardelj and Stane Dolenc played a major role in suppressing the Croatian movement. But in the late Eighties, the Slovene demands are even more radical than those of the Croatians. Furthermore, their unsupportive attitude toward the Serbians on the issue of Kosovo has so infuriated Belgrade that it has caused a split in the traditional Serbian-Slovene political alliance.

The Slovene national platform at the present time is clear: either a confederated and pluralistic Yugoslavia which would guarantee them freedom to draw closer and closer to the West European community and away from the Balkan and the bankrupt Yugoslavia's policies; or, as a second option, a direct entry into the European political and economic community. As a result of the latest Slovene national awakening, Slovenes have begun to think of their nation as a fully independent political entity and not, as it has been in their tradition, merely a part within a wider Austro-Hungarian or South Slavic context. And that psychological change, the feeling that they can and have the right to be fully politically autonomous or even independent, might prove to be the most significant element of the "Slovene Spring" of the late 1980s.

As a result of the persecutions in Croatia that followed the crash of their national movement at the end of 1971, Croatia has been relatively quiet. The leading intellectuals were silenced, conservatives took control of the Party leadership, and major cultural institutions were curtailed or closed. Silence, resentment, and resignation fell upon the land. But while for some time Croatian national voices were forced to be silent, it seems that in the second half of the 1980s the silence became a part of the national strategy; while the others were crossing swords with Belgrade, Croatians were not eager to join the battle. The feeling was, let someone else take on the Serbians for a change. A number of reasons stimulated this approach in Croatia. Croatian nationalism has been traditionally treated much more harshly than other natonalisms in the country, and there was a fear of renewed persecutions. Croatian national forces have been disunited, and there was not a personality or institution that could be considered as a national voice around which different forces could gather. Mistrust between the Party leadership and other segments of society, especially the intellectuals, has not been bridged yet. Although the conservative post-Karadjordjevo Party leaders have been voted out of power by the younger cadars, the Party leadership in Croatia never gained a minimum of legitimacy in order to have self-confidence and to be considered as national leadership. Moreover, the Party itself in Croatia has been divided. While one wing is cautiously liberal and indicates a willingness to support further liberalization of the society and economy, the other wing supports the status quo and a continuation of Tito's legacy. Furthermore, one of the most resented men in the Party in Croatia, Stipe Šuvar, has now become the head of the LCY against the wishes of the Party in his own republic. He was sent to Belgrade as the republican representative simply to remove him from Zagreb, but by the help of the centralists he became the head of the Party. Thus, he has been considered in Croatia more a menace than help. He and Branko Mikulić, the head of the state, are the leading force of the status quo in the country. They oppose any changes in the system or in federal relations. But it is doubtful that these advocates of the balance of fear will be able to lead the country out of the present crisis.

Currently in Croatia, there are more and more voices critical of the system as well as demands for political pluralism and free economy; struggles for various national and human rights are going on; a number of Croatians have clashed with the regime and some have found "asylum" in Slovenia; and the press in Croatia is becoming more and more open in its support of the Slovene-like political platform. Their goal of national sovereignty has been clear for a long time, but there is not yet in Croatia a clear national leadership or program to achieve that goal under the present conditions. Their present defensive position is seen by some as the only logical choice because Croatian nationalist activities have been treated differently than those in Serbia or Slovenia. It would most probably be considered once again as "innate Croatian reactionism" and crushed by force. Thus, their attitude at the present time seems to be, wait and see.

The republic of Bosnia and Hercegovina, because of its delicate geographic and ethnic position, has been caught in a balancing act between different ethnic and political factions. In the 1970s, Yugoslav leadership strongly promoted the Muslim national consciousness and their role in the republic as well as in the federation in order to create a "neutral force" between the Serbians and Croatians. Only a few years later, however, Belgrade became suspicious of the Muslims and as a result their leading personalities were in one way or another discredited and removed from various important positions. A strong desire of Milošević's forces to cross into Bosnia and Hercegovina and spread the Serbian movement in that republic has been balanced by Mikulić's fight for the status quo. How long this stand-off will last is hard to say. One thing is clear: all the forces in the republic are reexamining their strengths and positions for possible different coalitions in the near future.

More than anything else at the present time, it is the Albanian question that allies two other republics, Montenegro and Macedonia, with Serbia. In all three republics there is a proportionately large Albanian population. But after Milošević's attainment of power, there is also more and more pressure on Montenegrins to come out and "freely" declare themselves to be Serbs and join the Serbian offensive. Although there are some open calls for unity with the Serbians, and Montenegrins have been most faithful to Belgrade centralism, Montenegrins are also proud of their own identity and their past independence, and it is doubtful that they will freely join the republic of Serbia. Macedonians, on the other hand, have a strong tradition of opposing Serbian hegemonism and centralism, but at the present time they are caught between the Serbian offensive for recentralization and the fear of Albanian irredentism. It seems they are cautiously siding with the Serbs, at least on the question of Albanians.

The question of Kosovo will remain as the most destabilizing factor for Serbia and the country as a whole. While in the first Yugoslavia and during the Ranković era, Serbs had dealt with the Albanians as they pleased, it will be impossible to revive those policies. Albanians have a nationally self-conscious and fast-growing population, educated elites, and a strong will to fight for their self-rule. Although the Serbs have scored some victories in the second half of 1988 by gaining more judicial control in the republic and removing a number of Albanians from the provincial leadership, it is strongly believed that the struggle for Kosovo is not over but is most probably just entering a new stage.

Post-Tito Yugoslavia has been plagued with numerous crises, most of all economic and intra-national problems. There are serious doubts about its future. What is holding it together, it seems, is not the strength of the shared interests of its peoples but more its geo-political position. How the changing relations between the East and West will affect that strategic area is not clear yet. Most probably it will lessen the importance of Yugoslavia, and that, too, will not help its internal situation. The Yugoslav regime has been constantly pointing to "external enemies" in order to gain at least a semblance of internal cohesion. But it is becoming clear that those "threats" and the Yugoslav strengths have been blown out of proportion. The latest events in Yugoslavia are showing that some basic predicaments have been with the country since its creation, and the remedies that have been applied to cure them have proved to be as bad if not even worse than the problems.

December 1988

NOTES

Notes to Introduction

1. Andrew Borowiec, *Yugoslavia After Tito* (New York: Praeger, 1977), p. 34.

2. Boro Krivokapić, "Pitao sam Krležu," *Reporter* (Beograd), No. 5, October 1982.

3. Frano Supilo (1870-1917) was one of the leading members of the Yugoslav Committee which advocated a unity of the South Slavs. Ante Trumbić (1864-1938) was President of the Committee and the first Foreign Minister after the Kingdom of the Serbs, Croats and Slovenes was created. Ivan Meštrović (1883-1962), the best known Croatian sculptor, was an enthusiastic supporter of Yugoslav unity, and also a member of the Yugoslav Committee. All three died as Croatian nationalists.

4. Ivan Mužić, *Hrvatska politika i jugoslavenska ideja* (Split: 1969), p. 96.

5. Stjepan Radić (1871-1928) was the leader and a co-founder of the Croatian Peasant Party.

6. The Ottomans defeated the Serbs and their allies at Kosovo field on June 28, 1389.

7. For further study see Franjo Tudjman, *Velike ideje i mali narodi* (Zagreb: Matica hrvatska, 1969), pp. 291-294; Petar Šegedin, *Svi smo odgovorni* (Zagreb: Matica hrvatska, 1971), pp. 28-29; Bogdan Raditsa, "The Disunity of the Slavs," *Orbis* Vol. 10, No. 4, 1967, p. 1087.

8. A. J. P. Taylor, *The Habsburg Monarchy 1809-1918* (Chicago: University of Chicago Press, 1976), pp. 260-261.

9. George W. Hoffman and Fred W. Neal, *Yugoslavia and the New Communism* (New York: The Twentieth Century Fund, 1962), p. 493.

10. Phyllis Auty, *Yugoslavia* (New York: Walker, 1965), p. 218.

11. George Klein, "Workers' Self-Management and the Politics of Ethnic Nationalism in Yugoslavia," *Nationality Papers* Vol. 5, No. 1, 1976, p. 4.

12. *Politika* (Belgrade), November 11, 1966.

13. Dennison I. Rusinow, *Crisis in Croatia*, American Universities Field Staff Reports. Southeast Europe Series, Vol. 19, Nos. 4-7 (June-September 1972).

14. Alvin Z. Rubinstein, "Whither Yugoslavia," *Current History* Vol. 64, No. 38, May 1973, p. 204.

15. For example see Pedro Ramet, *Nationalism and Federalism in Yugoslavia, 1963-1983* (Bloomington: Indiana University Press, 1984), pp. 104-143.

16. Cynthia W. Frey, "Yugoslav Nationalisms and the Doctrine of Limited Sovereignty," (Part II) *East European Quarterly* Vol. 11, No. 1, 1977, p. 102.

17. Ivan Perić, *Ideje 'Masovnog pokreta' u Hrvatskoj* (Zagreb: Narodno sveučilište, 1974); Ivan Perić, *Suvremeni hrvatski nacionalizam* (Zagreb: August Cesarec, 1976). The following are some of the articles on the subject: Ivan Perić, "Ideje 'masovnog pokreta' o odnosima u Savezu komunista i njegovoj komunikaciji s okolinom," *Naše teme* Vol. 16, No. 6, 1972, pp. 785-807; Ema Derossi-Bjelajac, "Karakteristika i dimenzije idejno-političkih devijacija u Savezu komunista Hrvatske," *Naše teme* Vol. 16, No. 1, 1972, pp. 1-20; Jovan Mirić, "Neke ideje protagonista 'masovnog pokreta' o državi," *Naše teme* Vol. 16, No. 10, 1972, pp. 1537-1561; Dragan Lalović, "O 'pokretu hrvatskih sveučilištaraca'," *Ideje* Vol. 3, No. 1, 1972, pp. 75-98; "Masovni pokret. Rasprava na temu 'masovni pokret' održana u Splitu 17. lipnja 1972." *Vidik* Vol. 19, No. 4-5, 1972, pp. 5-47.

18. One unpublished source used extensively is Ivan Supek's manuscript *Heretic on the Left*, an expanded version in English of his book in Croatian *Krivovjernik na ljevici* (Bristol: British Croatian Review, 1980).

Notes to Chapter I

1. Zvonimir's only son Radovan died as a child. Stjepan Trpimir came out of a monastery to the throne (1089) and died two years later.

2. After the fall of Napoleon's Illyrian Provinces in 1813, southern

Croatia came under Austrian administration. Military Border was also directly under Austrian jurisdiction. While Bosnia and Hercegovina were under the Ottomans.

3. Croatia had its own Sabor (Diet) and Ban (Vice-Roy). Some of the most important rights were: "jurisdiction in internal affairs, reduced taxes, special representation at the meetings of the Hungarian Parliament, maintenance of an independent military force, and independence of Hungary in decisions concerning religion and language." Elinor-Murray Despalatović, *Ljudevit Gaj and the Illyrian Movement* (Boulder: East European Quarterly, 1975), p. 12.

4. The movement was dominated by the liberal, radical democratic and anti-clerical elements of Croatian society.

5. Croatian cyrillic script, also known as Bosančica, had been widely used by the Croatians in the Middle Ages. See Stephen Krešić, "The Principal Characteristics of Croatian Literary Culture in the Middle Ages," *Journal of Croatian Studies* Vol. 25-26, 1984-85, pp. 37-46.

6. Slavic language combined with the Roman liturgy had been preserved in some parts of Croatia till the second Vatican Council. Church Slavonic in Croatia had been constantly enriched by Croatian vernacular, while the Orthodox churches prevented such a fusion.

7. Šimun Kozičić Benja in his speech to Pope Leo X (1513-21). Marin Franičević, "Razdoblje renesansne književnosti," in *Povijest hrvatske književnosti* Vol. 3 (Zagreb: Liber-Mladost, 1974), p. 9.

8. Petar Zoranić (born 1508). Ibid., p. 89.

9. Marko Marulić's (1450-1524) "Molitva suprotiv Turkom" (A Prayer against the Turks), and *Judita.*

10. In 1493 Martinac the priest wrote: "The Turks assailed the lands where Croatian was spoken." Marko Marulić stated that his *Judita* was composed in "Croatian verses." See "A Chronology of the Croatian Language," *Journal of Croatian Studies* Vol. 25-26, 1984-85, p. 247.

11. Antun Vrančić (1504-1573) wrote to an Ottoman official, Hasanbeg that both of them "belong to the same Croatian nation." Franičević, "Razdoblje renesansne književnosti," p. 9.

12. Vinko Pribojević's panegyric *De origine successibusque Slavorum* (1532), for example. Ivan Gundulić (1589-1638) in his *Osman* poured his love for Poland and its victory over the Turks at Choczin (1621). See also Jaroslav Šidak, "Počeci političke misli u Hrvata—J. Križanić i P. Ritter Vitezović," *Naše teme* Vol. 16, No. 7-8, 1972, pp. 1119-1120.

13. Croatian Catholic priest, Juraj Križanić (1618-1683) looked to the Russian tsar for leadership and assistance in the struggle against Slavic enemies, Turks and Germans. But instead of Slavic solidarity, Russia exiled him to Siberia, where he spent fifteen years. His best known work is *Razgoworie ob wladatelystwu,* better known as *Politika.*

14. They were especially influenced by the Croatian intellectual tradition from the XVI century on. Just to mention a few: Juraj Šižgorić, Vinko Pribojević, Mavro Orbini, Juraj Križanić, Pavao Ritter-Vitezović, Andrija Kačić Miošić, etc. See Šidak, "Počeci političke misli," pp. 1118-1135. About Vitezović's influences on Gaj, see Jaroslav Šidak, *Studije iz hrvatske povijesti XIX stoljeća.* (Zagreb: Sveučilište u Zagrebu-Institut za hrvatsku povijest, 1973), p. 9. A good summary on Slavism in Croatian intellectual tradition is found in Milorad Živančević, "Slavenska ideja od humanizma do Ilirizma," *Zbornik Zagrebačke slavističke škole* Vol. 1, 1973, pp. 137-146.

15. Dragutin Rakovac, *Mali katekizam za velike ljude* (Zagreb: 1842), p. 16 as cited in Jaroslav Šidak, "Prilog razvoju jugoslavenske ideje do g. 1914," *Naše teme* No. 8-9, 1965, p. 1296.

16. See Murray-Despalatović, *Ljudevit Gaj,* p. 134.

17. Good examples of such claims were Teodor Pavlović (1804-1854) and Vuk Stefanović Karadžić (1787-1864).

18. Croatian language has three dialects: kykavian, čakavian and štokavian.

19. Mirjana Gross, "Croatian National-Integrational Ideologies from the End of Illyrism to the Creation of Yugoslavia," *Austrian History Yearbook* Vol. 15-16, 1979-1980, p. 4.

20. Ibid., p. 11.

21. The Party of Right stood for Croatian state and national rights and should not be confused with right wing politics. Its ideology was regarded as left radical at the time.

22. Ante Starčević, (compiled by Blaž and Jurišić) *Misli i pogledi* (Zagreb: Matica Hrvatska, 1971), p. 244. Starčević's motto was "Bog i Hrvati!" (God and the Croatians!), which was a purely political and not a religious expression. It symbolized people's sovereignty.

23. The leading proponent of Greater Serbianism at the time was Vuk Stefanović Karadžić who claimed that all Croatians who spoke štokavian dialect were Serbs and the kykavian speaking Croatians were

Slovenes. Starčević counter-attacked by denying the existence of Serbs as "political people."

24.   It is a well-known saying by Starčević: "We all want to free ourselves from anyone's yoke, and we do not wish simply to exchange it." Starčević's speech in Sabor (1861) as in *Misli,* p. 62.

25.   Gross, "Croatian National-Integrational Ideologies," p. 11.

26.   Muslim nationality was created in Yugoslavia in the 1960s, but only for the Muslims from Bosnia and Hercegovina. It was actually Starčević who began the process of separation of religion and nationality in Bosnia and Hercegovina. At the present time that process has been reversed.

27.   Mirjana Gross, *Povijest pravaške ideologije* (Zagreb: Sveučilište u Zagrebu-Institut za hrvatsku povijest, 1973), p. 161.

28.   Some supported the Habsburgs and others promoted Yugoslav unity.

29.   Branka Boban, "Shvaćanja Antuna i Stjepana Radića o mjestu i ulozi seljaštva u gospodarskom, društvenom i političkom životu," *Radovi* Institut za hrvatsku povijest, Vol. 12, 1979, p. 271.

30.   Franjo Tudjman, "Stjepan Radić i hrvatska državnost," *Riječi* (Sisak) Vol. 3, No. 2, 1971, p. 13.

31.   Ibid., p. 15.

32.   Stjepan Radić as quoted in Stjepan Gaži, "Stjepan Radić: His Life and Political Activities," *Journal of Croatian Studies.* Vol. 14-15, 1973-74, p. 46.

33.   In contrast to Belgrade's centralist Vidovdan Constitution of 28 June 1921, which was promulgated against the will of most non-Serbs in the country, Radić and his party proclaimed in April 1921 *The Constitution of a Neutral Peasant Republic of Croatia.* For the text of the Constitution see Stjepan Radić, *Politički spisi* (Zagreb: Znanje, 1971), pp. 366-393.

34.   Vladko Maček, *In the Struggle for Freedom* (University Park: Pennsylvania State University Press, 1957), p. 100.

35.   For a full explanation of Radić's political goals, tactics, and activities see Ivan Mužić, *Stjepan Radić u Kraljevini Srba, Hrvata i Slovenaca* (Zagreb: HKD sv. Ćirila i Metoda, 1987), pp. 191-240. See also Franjo Tudjman, "Uzroci krize monarhističke Jugoslavije od ujedinjenja 1918. do sloma 1941," *Forum* Vol. 6, no. 1-2, 1967, pp. 73-111. Also by the same author: "Hrvatska politika u prvim godinama borbe protiv Vidovdan--

skog centralističko-hegemonističkog poretka," *Kritika* Vol. 3, No. 14, 1970, pp. 570-617; "Zaoštravanje sukoba i pokušaj nagodbe-izmedju pobornika centralizma i federalizma u Kraljevini SHS (1924-1927," *Forum* Vol. 10, No. 6, 1971, pp. 920-955; "Raspre o uzrocima sloma monarhističke Jugoslavije i o pretpostavkama razvitka narodnooslobodilačke borbe u Hrvatskoj." (Pt. I) *Kolo* Vol. 6, No. 8-9, 1968, pp. 201-218; Pt. II. Ibid., Vol. 6, No. 10, 1968, pp. 363-378; "Slom vidovdanskog parlamentarnog centralizma i državno-politička kriza Kraljevine SHS," *Hrvatski znanstveni zbornik* Vol. I, 1971, pp. 51-114. Bruce Bigelow, "Centralization versus Decentralization in Interwar Yugoslavia." *Southeastern Europe* Vol. 1, Pt. 2, 1974, pp. 157-172. About Radić's life see *Current History* Vol. 29, October 1928-March 1929, pp. 82-106.

36. The only exception to this were the followers of integral Yugoslavism.

37. See Mužić, *Stjepan Radić*, pp. 251-267.

Notes to Chapter II

1. *Osmi kongres Saveza komunista Jugoslavije* (Belgrade: Komunist, 1964), pp. 35-36.

2. It had changed its name in 1952 to League of Communists of Yugoslavia—hereafter LCY.

3. *Sedmi kongres Saveza komunista Jugoslavije: Stenografske beleške* (Belgrade: Kultura, 1958), p. 1058.

4. Viktor Meier, "Yugoslav Communism" in William E. Griffith, ed., *Communism in Europe* Vol. 1 (Cambridge, Mass.: The M.I.T. Press, 1964), p. 73.

5. *Politika* February 14, 1963 as cited in Meier, "Yugoslav Communism," p. 73.

6. Edvard Kardelj, *Razvoj slovenačkog nacionalnog pitanja* (Belgrade: Kultura, 1960), p. 42.

7. *Osmi kongres*, pp. 98-99.

8. Kardelj, *Razvoj*, p. 39.

9. Paul Shoup, *Communism and the Yugoslav National Question* (New York: Columbia University Press, 1968), p. 258.

10. In the newly organized country, different Social Democratic parties were united at the First Congress, held in Belgrade on April 20-23,

1919. The Slovene socialist party, however, was not represented at the Congress. From Croatia, only the left-wing of the party participated.

11. Gordana Vlajčić, "KPJ i nacionalno pitanje 1919-1941" in *Socijalizam i nacionalno pitanje* (Zagreb: Centar za aktuelni politički studij, 1970), p. 79. On the Party's changing view regarding the national question see also Franjo Tudjman, "Uvod u historiju Socijalističke Jugoslavije," (Part III) *Forum* Vol. 2, No. 4, 1963, pp. 702-712.

12. Vlajčić, "KPJ i nacionalno pitanje," p. 91.

13. Nerkez Smailagić, "Socijalistička revolucija i nacionalno pitanje," *Dubrovnik* Vol. 13, No. 3, 1970, p. 87. There was a strong opposition within the CPY to the idea of creating a Slovene and Croatian CP. See Tudjman, *Velike ideje*, pp. 270-272.

14. Edo Kunštek, "Interpolacija obračuna," *Republika Hrvatska* Vol. 34, No. 146, September 1984, pp. 58-59.

15. Tito, "Politički izvještaj Centralnom komitetu KPJ." *Peti kongres KPJ—Izveštaji i referati* (Belgrade: Kultura, 1948), p. 46. See also Kunštek, "Interpolacija," pp. 46-61. Edo Kunštek, Croat and Party activist in the 1930s, gives an account of Party changes on the national question and also of Tito's role, as Stalin's man, in the purges of the CPY leadership in Moscow.

16. Jack C. Fisher, *Yugoslavia: A Multi-National State* (San Francisco: Chandler, 1966), p. 24.

17. Jozo Ivičević, "Odrednice unitarističkog nacionalnog programa I i II kongresa KPJ," in *Hrvatski znanstveni zbornik* Vol. 1 (Zagreb: Matica hrvatska, 1971), p. 164.

18. Ibid., pp. 164-165.

19. Ibid., p. 165.

20. Gordana Vlajčić, "Kominterna i KPJ o državnopravnom aspektu rješenja jugoslavenskog nacionalnog pitanja (1919-1929)," *Naše teme* Vol. 15, No. 10, 1971, p. 1702.

21. Ivičević, "Odrednice," p. 165.

22. Out of 374 delegates only 115 of them voted for the centralizing Party program adopted at the Second Congress. A number of Slovene and Croatian delegates walked out before the vote was taken. For more details on the Second Congress see Neda Engelsfeld, "Centralizacija Partije 1920. i rasap—1921. godine," *Hrvatsko sveučilište* November 3, 1971. On disputes concerning the number of votes at the congress see Ivo Banac, "The

Communist Party of Yugoslavia during the Period of Legality, 1919-1921." in Ivo Banac, ed. *The Effects of World War I: The Class War after the Great War: The Rise of Communist Parties in East Central Europe, 1918-1921* (New York: Brooklyn College Studies on Society in Change No. 32, 1983), p. 224, n. 59.

23. Frits W. Hondius, *The Yugoslav Community of Nations* (The Hague: Mouton, 1968), p. 168.

24. Dušan Bilandžić, *Ideje i praksa društvenog razvoja Jugoslavije 1945-1973* (Belgrade: Komunist, 1973), p. 40.

25. Hoffman and Neal, *Yugoslavia*, p. 82.

26. Eric R. Terzuolo, "Soviet-Yugoslav Conflict and the Origins of Yugoslavia's Self-Management System," in Wayne S. Vucinich, ed., *War and Society in East Central Europe* Vol. 10 (New York: Columbia University Press, 1982), p. 198.

27. Ross A. Johnson, *The Transformation of Communist Ideology: The Yugoslav Case, 1945-1953* (Cambridge, Mass.: The M.I.T Press, 1972), p. 76.

28. Terzuolo, "Soviet-Yugoslav Conflict," p. 202. That Tito was looking for a reconciliation with the USSR can be seen from his speech at the Fifth Congress of the CPY (July 1948). See Branko Petranović and Momčilo Zečević, Jugoslavia 1918-1984—Zbirka dokumenta (Belgrade: "Rad," 1985), pp. 777-778. On how much affection there was for Stalin and Stalinism in the CPY immediately after the 1948 break see Bruno Bušić, "Raskid sa Staljinom nije bio raskid sa staljinizmom," *Poruka Slobodne Hrvatske* (London), No. 5, 1978 and "'Naš dragi druže Josipe Visarionoviću Staljine'," Ibid., No. 6, 1978. Both articles are reprinted in Bruno Bušić, *Jedino Hrvatska* (Sabrani spisi.) (Toronto: ZIRAL, 1983), pp. 594-600.

29. Jozo Tomasevich, "Immediate Effects of the Cominform Resolution on the Yugoslav Economy," in Vucinich, *War and Society*, p. 121.

30. For detailed statistics on collectivization see Tomasevich, "Immediate Effects," p. 123.

31. Vladimir Bakarić, Report to the Central Committee of the LC of Croatia on February 24, 1966. In *Aktuelni problemi sadasnje etape revolucije* (Zagreb: Stvarnost, 1967), p. 246.

32. Veljko Vlahović, "Značaj afirmacije antidogmatskih gledišta i prakse Saveza komunista Jugoslavije," in *Naš put* (Belgrade: Komunist, 1969), pp. 165-175.

33.   Tomasevich, "Immediate Effects," pp. 118-119.

34.   Smailagić, "Socijalistička revolucija i nacionalno pitanje," *Dubrovnik* Vol. 13, No. 4, 1970, p. 118.

35.   *Vjesnik u srijedu* (VUS) September 7, 1966; Miko Tripalo, *Bez kompromisa u ostvarenju samoupravnog socijalizma* (Zagreb: Naprijed, 1969), p. 130.

36.   R. V. Burks, *The Removal of Ranković: An Early Interpretation of the July Yugoslav Party Plenum* (Santa Monica: The Rand Corporation, RM-5132-PR, August 1966).

37.   Third Plenary Session of the Central Committee of the League of Communists of Yugoslavia, *Socialist Thought and Practice* No. 21, January-March 1966, pp. 86 and 95.

38.   *Peta sednica CK SK Jugoslavije* (Belgrade: Komunist, 1966), p. 59.

39.   See Dennison I. Rusinow, *Yugoslavia: 1966* Southeast Europe Series, American University Field Staff Report, Vol. 13, No. 6, 1966, p. 1 and *Croatia Press* Vol. 20, No. 4-6, 1966, p. 2.

40.   *Komunist* July 28, 1966.

41.   *Socialist Thought and Practice* No. 23, July-September, 1966, p. 110.

42.   Svetozar Vukmanović Tempo, *Revolucija koja teče* Vol. 2 (Belgrade: Komunist, 1971); Paul Lendvai, "National Tensions in Yugoslavia," *Conflict Studies* No. 25, 1972, p. 6; *The Guardian* October 6, 1966.

43.   *Socialist Thought and Practice* No. 23, 1966, p. 106.

44.   Some have suggested that Ranković was planning a coup d'etat for the fall of 1966 when Tito was to be abroad. See Francois Fejtö, *A History of the People's Democracies—Eastern Europe Since Stalin* (New York: Praeger, 1971), p. 138.

45.   *Croatia Press* Vol. 20, No. 4-6, 1966, p. 7.

46.   Ibid., p. 12. Yugoslav efforts to build an atomic bomb was also seen as a part of Ranković's desire for power. He was the head of the project. See Ivan Supek in *Hrvatsko sveučilište* April 8, 15 and 22, 1971; Supek, *Heretic*, pp. 340-347.

47.   *Croatia Press* Vol. 20, No. 4-6, 1966, p. 13.

48.   *Socialist Thought and Practice* No. 23, 1966, p. 107.

49.   Meier, "Yugoslav Communism," p. 70; Fejtö, *A History*, p. 136.

50.   *Socialist Thought and Practice* No. 23, 1966, p. 131.

51. Paul Lendvai, *Eagles in Cobwebs* (New York: Doubleday, 1969), p. 161; Stephen Clissold, "Yugoslavia and the Soviet Union," *Conflict Studies* No. 57, April 1975, p. 19.

52. *Komunist* July 28, 1966.

53. Smailagić, "Socijalistićka revolucija," *Dubrovnik* Vol. 13, No. 4, 1970, p. 125.

54. *Socialist Thought and Practice* No. 23, 1966, p. 119.

55. Krsto Crvenkovski, as cited in Stanko Vujica, *Razmatranja o sadašnjosti Hrvata* (Chicago: Croatia, 1968), p. 59.

56. Latinka Perović, *Savez komunista u novim uslovima* (Belgrade: Sedma sila, 1967), p. 20.

57. George Klein, "Yugoslavia—The Process of Democratization," in Peter A. Toma, ed., *The Changing Face of Communism in Eastern Europe* (Tucson, Arizona: University of Arizona Press, 1970), p. 221.

58. Military precautions were undertaken (Fejtö, *A History*, p. 138) and the police force was doubled in strength at the time (*New York Times* July 3, 1966.)

59. Burks, *The Removal*, p. 18; *Time* July 15, 1966.

60. In VUS of April 5, 12 and 19, 1972 an interview was published with General Ivan Mišković which sheds light on the role of the KOS in the Ranković affair, especially the part published on the 19th.

61. M. George Zaninovich, *The Development of Socialist Yugoslavia* (Baltimore: The Johns Hopkins Press, 1968), p. 150.

62. Stipe Šuvar, *Sociološki presjek jugoslavenskog društva* (Zagreb: Školska knjiga, 1970), p. 158.

63. The opposition of the Serbian Orthodox Church to the independence of the Macedonian Church is a good example. See Lendvai, *Eagles in Cobwebs*, p. 170.

64. *Socialist Thought and Practice* No. 23, 1966, p. 133.

65. Tito announced this decision in December of 1966, recommended by the Federal Executive Council, as "a sign of the humanism and profound moral strength of our society." Hondius, *The Yugoslav Community*, p. 323.

66. Others considered that Tito's decision to pardon Ranković and his group resulted from the need to implement the Reform without "poisoning the atmosphere with a trial." *The Observer* December 11, 1966.

67. Susan Lampland Woodward, "From Revolution to Post-Revolution: How Much Do We Really Know about Yugoslav Politics?" *World Politics* Vol. 30, No. 1, 1977, 147.

68. *Deseta sjednica Centralnog komiteta Saveza komunista Hrvatske* (Zagreb: "Vjesnik," 1970), pp. 49-51.

69. Ivan Supek, *Heretic*, p. 295.

70. *New York Times* July 2, 1966.

71. Ibid., July 3, 1966.

72. Milentije Popović, *Od etatizma ka samoupravljanju* (Beograd: Institut za političke studije FPN, 1970), p. 185.

73. Rusinow, *Yugoslavia: 1966*, p. 9; *Borba* September 15, 1966.

74. *Neue Zürcher Zeitung* July 23, 1983.

75. Dennison I. Rusinow, *The Yugoslav Experiment 1948-1974* (London: C. Hurst, 1977), p. 190.

76. *New York Times* July 3, 1966.

77. Dimitry Pospielovsky, "Dogmas Under Attack: A Traveler's Report," *Problems of Communism* Vol. 17, No. 2, March-April, 1968, p. 47.

78. Ramet, *Nationalism and Federalism*, p. 96.

79. Lendvai, *Eagles in Cobwebs*, p. 158.

80. *Vjesnik* September 4, 1988; *The Times* (London), September 15, 1966; VUS, July 8, 1970.

81. *New York Times* July 2, 1966.

82. Smailagić, "Socijalistička revolucija," *Dubrovnik* Vol. 13, No. 4, 1970, p. 127.

83. *Hrvatski list* No. 2, 1978.

84. *Hrvatski književni list* No. 18, October 1969, reprinted in Bušić, *Jedino Hrvatska*, p. 367.

85. VUS, September 7, 1966.

86. Lendvai, *Eagles in Cobwebs*, p. 162; It was believed that Kardelj was another leading candidate for the succession and as such a threat to Ranković. Allegedly, for that reason Kardelj was shot at, in 1961. *Sunday Telegraph* June 4, 1961; *Nova Hrvatska* No. 8-10, August-October 1961.

87. Vladimir Bakarić, *Socijalistički samoupravni sistem i društvena reprodukcija* (Zagreb: "Informator," 1974), p. 274.

88. Borowiec, *Yugoslavia After Tito*, p. 101.

89. *Hrvatski tjednik* September 3, 1971 and Bušić, *Jedino Hrvatska*, p. 259.

90. *Nedeljne informativne novine* (NIN), May 3, 1970 as cited in David A. Dyker, "Yugoslavia: Unity out of Diversity?" in Archie Brown and Jack Gray, eds. *Political Culture and Political Change in Communist States* (London: Macmillan, 1977), pp. 88, 122.

91. *Hrvatski tjednik* October 1, 1971.

92. Steven Larrabee, "Yugoslavia at the Crossroads," *Orbis* Vol. 16, No. 2, 1972, p. 384.

Notes to Chapter III

1. Šegedin, *Svi smo odgovorni,* p. 142. Interestingly, while the Communists thought that the "factory would solve everything," many in the West also thought that modernization would eradicate the national question in Yugoslavia, as well as in other developing multinational states.

2. See *New York Times* April 16, 1957 and February 18, 1966; *Hrvatski bilten* (London) Vol. 1, No. 4, April 1958; *Nova Hrvatska* (London) No. 11, November 1959 and No. 7-8, November-December 1964; *Vjesnik* March 26, 1966.

3. Bušić, *Jedino Hrvatska,* p. vi.; *New York Times* August 3, 1956.

4. *Nova Hrvatska* No. 6, June 1959, No. 7, July 1959, and No. 6-7, September-October 1963. Report on the death of a female student from an interview with an eyewitness, who lives in Zagreb and wishes not to be identified.

5. Josip Broz Tito, *Tito Omladini* (Belgrade: Mlado pokoljenje, 1961), p. 239 as in Ralph Pervan, *Tito and the Students* (Nedlands W. A.: University of Western Australia Press, 1978), p. 136.

6. The Ustaša movement was organized in 1929 by Ante Pavelić, a lawyer and Croatian representative in the Belgrade Skupština (Parliament). It was organized as a reaction to the assassination of leading political representatives from Croatia, including Stjepan Radić, and to the dictatorship of King Aleksandar. The Ustaša (a rebel) movement advocated revolutionary means against Yugoslavia and stood for the full independence of Croatia. It collaborated with other anti-Yugoslav revolutionary movements especially with IMRO in Macedonia. It also found support in Hungary and Italy. For Italy, where many Croatian political emigrants found refuge at the time, Ustaše were a bargaining chip in its relationship with Belgrade. Hitler's friendly relations with Yugoslavia till March 1941 prevented his

support of the Ustaša movement. But once his pact with Yugoslavia fell through, he decided to support the break-up of Yugoslavia. Pavelić and the Ustaša leaders, with the help of the Axis powers, took power in Croatia in April 1941 and retained it until the end of the war.

7. Šegedin, *Svi smo odgovorni,* p. 163.

8. Samilagić, "Socijalistička revolucija," (II), p. 126.

9. Ibid., p. 126.

10. Peter Klinar, "Izvori pojavnih oblika nacionalizma u Jugoslaviji," in *Federalizam i nacionalno pitanje* (Beograd: Savez udruženja za političke nauke Jugoslavije, 1971), p. 217.

11. NIN March 8, 1964. The interview was also published in *Vjesnik* (Zagreb) March 8, 1964 and reprinted in Bakarić, *Aktuelni problemi,* pp. 113-129.

12. Petar Živković (1879-1953) was a Premier and Minister of Police and the armed forces in the First Yugoslavia. He became a symbol of police terror in Croatia.

13. NIN March 8, 1964. It is interesting to note that Bakarić's stronger criticisms against the central government were omitted from the text of the same interview published in *Vjesnik* (Zagreb), on the same day.

14. *Vjesnik* September 21, 1964.

15. Ibid.

16. Ibid.

17. For example, intellectuals from the Institute for History of the Workers' Movement of Croatia, headed by Dr. Franjo Tudjman, and Većo Holjevac, former mayor of Zagreb, and the head of the Matica iseljenika (Cultural institution for contacts with the Croatian emigrants).

18. *Vjesnik* October 11, 1964.

19. See an interview with Miko Tripalo, VUS October 7 and 14, 1964.

20. See Tripalo, *Bez kompromisa,* pp. 14-16 and 22-27.

21. Muhamed Filipović, "Lenjinovo shvaćanje nacionalnog pitanja," in *Socijalizam i nacionalno pitanje* (Zagreb: Centar za aktuelni politički studij, 1970), p. 43.

22. *Osmi kongres SKJ,* p. 38.

23. Ibid., p. 38.

24. Ibid., p. 39.

25. See Chapter II.

26. *Komunist* July 26, 1962.

27. Tito's speech in Split, as cited in *Nova Hrvatska* No. 1-2, September-October, 1962.

28. Stanko Lasić, *Sukob na književnoj ljevici 1928-1952* (Zagreb: Liber, 1970), p. 279; Miroslav Krleža, *Eseji* Vol. 6 (Zagreb: Zora, 1967). On his later remarks on the speech see *Reporter* No. 5, October 1982.

29. From Tito's speech in Split on May 6, 1962 as cited in *Nova Hrvatska* No. 1-2, September-October, 1962.

30. Meier, "Yugoslav Communism," p. 72.

31. *Borba* December 6 and 14, 1961.

32. The largest single group (87) of Croatian Marxist intellectuals was imprisoned at Kerestinec, near Samobor, at the beginning of World War II. Almost all of them lost their lives as a result of an unsuccessful attempt to escape. There are strong indications that some in the Party wanted the escape to fail. In this way, the Party got rid of the strongest revisionist group in its circles.

The Marxist revisionists in Croatia in the pre-war period were gathered around the literary journal *Pečet,* under Miroslav Krleža's leadership. Their resistance to the bolshevization of the Party resulted in their expulsion from the Party ranks in 1940. Although the Party underwent a major ideological shift after the break with Stalin, the former revisionists were not fully rehabilitated. The major reason for this was the fact that bolshevism and Belgrade centralism were very much intertwined.

33. Šegedin, *Svi smo odgovorni,* p. 145.

34. Ibid., p. 128.

35. Ibid., p. 130.

36. *Croatia Press,* Vol. 20, No. 1-3, 1966; *Politika* March 31, 1966. It is interesting to note that *Politika* is silent about the presence of Cardinal Šeper at the celebration.

37. Miroslav Krleža, "Uvodna riječ," *Forum,* Vol. 10, No. 3-4, March-April, 1966, p. 286.

38. Ibid., pp. 287-288.

39. Krleža wrote this in 1919 as cited in Vujica, *Razmatranja,* p. 19.

40. *Croatia Press,* Vol. 20, No. 1-3, 1966.

41. See Miko Tripalo's speech in *Sedmi plenum CK SK Hrvatske* (Zagreb: Informativna služba CK SKH, 1967), p. 30.

42. Tripalo, *Bez kompromisa,* p. 288.

43. About Mihajlov's case see Nikola Čolak, *Iza bodljikave žice* (Padova: La Ciclografica, 1977), pp. 145-205; "The Dossier of the Mihajlov Case," *Review* (Study Center for Jugoslav Affairs–London) No. 6, 1966, pp. 506-532.

44. It was also published in *Vjesnik* March 19, 1967 with a strong commentary against the signers of the document.

45. *Sedmi Plenum*, p. 38.

46. An English translation of the Declaration is found in *Journal of Croatian Studies* Vol. 7-8, 1966-1967, pp. 6-9 and *Croatia Press* Vol. 21, No. 1-2, 1967.

47. Miko Tripalo, *Sedmi Plenum*, p. 27; *Vjesnik* March 19, 1967; *Telegram* March 31, 1967, April 7 and April 14, 1967; *Times* (London) April 6, 1967.

48. *Sedmi Plenum*, p. 29.

49. *Politika* April 2, 1967.

50. *New York Times* March 25, 1967.

51. *Telegram* April 7, 1967 and *Sedmi Plenum*, p. 38.

52. *Sedmi Plenum*, p. 20. However, his action has not been publicized at all.

53. In his speech in Pristina, Tito stressed that the Declaration had been published without the Party's knowledge. See *Telegram* March 31, 1967. Jure Bilić, a high Party official from Croatia, stated in 1974 that some top Party officials in Croatia, including Miko Tripalo, Secretary of the Party at the time, knew that the Declaration was in the making. See Jure Bilić, *Revolucija i politika* (Zagreb: Narodno sveučilište, 1975), p. 222. Some well known intellectuals from Croatia in conversations with the author also confirmed that some leading republican Party officials knew that the Declaration was in the making. There is, however, some uncertainty if the secret police knew about the move. It seems that the UDBA did know about it.

54. For more on historiography see Chapter V below.

55. Steven L. Burg, "Ethnic Conflict and the Federalization of Socialist Yugoslavia: The Serbo-Croat Conflict," *Publius* Vol. 7, No. 4, 1977, p. 130.

56. Hrvoje Iveković, President of Matica Hrvatska, as reported in *Politika* November 23, 1970.

57. *Kritika* Vol. IV, No. 17, 1971, p. 381.

58. *Hrvatski književni list* (HKL) No. 1, 1968.

59. Ibid.

60. Ibid.

61. Ibid.

62. Ibid.

63. Ibid.

64. Ibid.

65. HKL, No. 8, November 1968, No. 11, February 1969, No. 12, April 1969, No. 15, July 1969 and No. 17, September 1969. "Surplus of labor" in Marxist terminology means a pure profit of one's work. "Etatism" indicates centralized state socialism.

66. The article, however, was published in *Sodobnost* (Slovenia) No. 4, 1970, pp. 408-427 under the title "Nekaj pripomb k mnenjem o rabi jezikov v JLA." Its Croatian translation was published in *Encyclopaedia moderna* No. 12, Spring 1970, pp. 111-119.

67. HKL, No. 3, June 1968.

68. Ibid. and *Croatia Press* Vol. 22, No. 3, 1969.

69. Cited in Stevo Ostojić, *Javni dnevnik* (Zagreb: Globus, 1980), p. 169.

70. Plenum of the Executive Committee of the CC LC of Croatia held May 26, 1969—in *Politika* May 27, 1969.

71. HKL, No. 9, December 1968; *Vjesnik* April 20, 1968, December 14 and 28, 1968 and February 15, 1969; VUS, December 25, 1968, January 25, 1969, January 29, 1969 and August 13, 1969.

72. HKL, No. 15, July 1969.

73. Current indications are that Žanko will be rehabilitated. His name is appearing more and more in Belgrade papers. It has been announced that he is publishing a book about his struggle against the liberal wing in the Party. See *Danas* August 25, 1987.

74. *Borba* July 20, 1969 as cited in Othmar Nikola Haberl, *Parteiorganisation und nationale Frage in Jugoslavien* (Berlin: Ottom Harrassowitz, 1976), p. 116.

75. As cited in Ostojić, *Javni dnevnik,* p. 169.

76. See for example HKL, No. 10, January 1969.

77. Ibid., No. 15, July 1969.

78. *Deseta sjednica,* p. 16.

79. Bilić, *Revolucija*, p. 222.
80. *Deseta sjednica*, p. 16.
81. Ibid., p. 16.
82. *Politika*, May 27, 1969.
83. Ibid.
84. Perić, *Suvremeni*, p. 17.
85. Franjo Tudjman, *Nationalism in Contemporary Europe* (Boulder: East European Monographs, 1981), p. 129; Burg, "Ethnic Conflict," pp. 125-126; Paul Shoup, "The Evolution of a System," *Problems of Communism*, Vol. 18, No. 4-5, July-October 1969, p. 70.
86. A. Ross Johnson, *Yugoslavia: In the Twilight of Tito* (Beverly Hills/London: Sage Publications, 1974), p. 10.
87. *Croatia Press* Vol. 22, No. 1-2, 1969.
88. Popović, *Od etatizma*, p. 291. About the 9th Congress see *Deveti kongres Saveza komunista Jugoslavije* (Zagreb: Narodne novine, 1969).
89. See Haberl, *Parteiorganisation*, p. 58.
90. Dennison I. Rusinow, "Marxism Belgrade Style," *The Antioch Review* Vol. 27, No. 4, 1967-68, p. 485; Supek, *Heretic*, p. 255.
91. See Gerson S. Sher, *Praxis-Marxist Criticism and Dissent in Socialist Yugoslavia* (Bloomington: Indiana University Press, 1977), pp. 205-209 and Fejtö, *A History*, p. 140.
92. Perić, *Suvremeni*, p. 16.
93. *Politika*, July 31, 1969; Shoup, "The National Question," p. 139; Dušan Bilandžić, *Historija socijalističke federativne republike Jugoslavije* (Zagreb: Školska knjiga, 1978), pp. 358-361.
94. HKL, No. 12, April 1969.
95. Tudjman, *Nationalism*, p. 130.
96. See chapter VII below.
97. *Deseta sjednica*, p. 18.
98. Ibid., p. 7.
99. Ibid., p. 6.
100. Ibid., p. 8.
101. Ibid., pp. 49-51.
102. Bilić, *Revolucija*, p. 74.
103. Paul Shoup, "The National Question and the Political Systems of Eastern Europe," in Sylva Sinanian et al., eds. *East Europe in the 1970s* (New York: Praeger, 1972), p. 139.

Notes to Chapter IV

1. Croatians are predominantly Catholic, Serbs Eastern Orthodox. The first developed under the influence of Rome and Vienna, the other under Constantinople and Moscow.

2. Rudolf Bićanić, *Economic Policy in Socialist Yugoslavia* (Cambridge: Cambridge University Press, 1973), pp. 2-3. See also Rudolf Bićanić, "Ekonomske promjene u Hrvatskoj izazvane stvaranjem Jugoslavije 1918," in Ivo Vinski, ed. *Prilozi za ekonomsku povijest Hrvatske* (Zagreb: Institut za Historiju Radničkog pokreta Hrvatske, 1967), pp. 81-111.

3. Rudolf Bićanić, *Ekonomska podloga hrvatskog pitanja* (Zagreb: Second ed., 1938), p. 120; Joseph Rothschild, *East Central Europe Between the Two World Wars* (Seattle and London: University of Washington Press, 1974), p. 278.

4. Ibid., p. 279; Bićanić, *Ekonomska podloga,* p. 63.

5. Šime Djodan, *Ekonomska politika Jugoslavije* (Zagreb: Školska knjiga, 1970), p. 47.

6. Ibid., p. 57.

7. Dimitrije Mišić, *Ekonomika industrije FNRJ* (Belgrade: Naučna knjiga, 1957), p. 270 as in Joseph T. Bombelles, *Economic Development of Communist Yugoslavia 1947-1964* (Stanford, Cal.: Hoover Institute, 1968), p. 4.

8. Most of the economic statistical data for the inter-war period was taken from Bićanić, *Ekonomska podloga.*

9. Ibid., p. 14.

10. Djodan, *Ekonomska politika,* pp. 61-67.

11. See Bićanić, *Ekonomska podloga,* pp. 45, 47-53, 101-125, 221, 126-133, 152-164, 177-201.

12. Djodan, *Ekonomska politika,* p. 64.

13. Rudolf Bićanić, *Ekonomska politika Jugoslavije* (Zagreb, 1962), p. 78 as cited in Branko Horvat, "Yugoslav Economic Policy in the Post-War Period: Problems, Ideas, Institutional Developments," *The American Economic Review* Vol. 61, No. 3 (Supplement), June 1971, p. 73.

14. Rudolf Bićanić, "Economics of Socialism in a Developed Country," *Foreign Affairs* Vol. 44, No. 4, July 1966, p. 647.

15. Šime Djodan, "Različite interpretacije pojma privredne i društvene reforme," *Mogućnosti* Vol. 15, No. 11, 1968, pp. 1346.

16. Bićanić, "Economics of Socialism," p. 649.

17. HKL, No. 11, February-March 1969.

18. Neda Krmpotić in *Vjesnik u srijedu* (VUS), July 22, 1970.

19. Bićanić, *Economic Policy*, p. 41.

20. Djodan, "Različite interpretacije," p. 1346.

21. Šime Djodan, "Prilog razmatranju predloženih izmjena ustava SFRJ," *Kolo* Vol. 6, No. 11, November 1968, p. 472.

22. HKL, No. 13, May 1969; Ibid., No. 17, September 1969; *Hrvatski tjednik*, No. 23, September 23, 1971.

23. HKL, No. 13, May 1969; Šime Djodan, "Hrvatsko gospodarstvo kao osnova kulturnog života hrvatskog naroda," *Dubrovnik* Vol. 14, No. 2, 1971, p. 60.

24. HKL, No. 13, May 1969.

25. There were "nearly 2,000 nonviable 'political factories' in the early Sixties." See Larrabee, "Yugoslavia at the Crossroads," p. 384.

26. On obsoleteness of factories in Croatia and how it compares to other republics see Šime Djodan, "Gdje dr. Stipe Šuvar 'pronalazi' nacionalizam, a gdje ga ne vidi," *Kolo* Vol. 6, No. 4, 1968, p. 702 and Šime Djodan, "Evolucija godpodarskog sustava SFRJ i ekonomski položaj Hrvatske," in *Hrvatski znanstveni zbornik* Vol. 2, 1971, p. 217. An English translation of the article entitled "The Evolution of the Economic System of Yugoslavia and the Economic Position of Croatia," was published in *Journal of Croatian Studies* Vol. 13, 1972. The above reference on p. 79.

27. Šime Djodan, "Aktuelni gospodarski položaj Zagreba," *Kritika* Vol. 3, No. 13, 494.

28. Šime Djodan, "Gospodarska reforma i izbor optimalnog modela rasta," *Kolo* Vol. 6, No. 4, 1968, p. 306.

29. For more on the banking reforms see Marijan Hanžeković, "The economic system since 1965," A postscript in Bićanić, *Economic Policy*, pp. 220-221.

30. For example, a Croatian citizen in a letter to a popular weekly urged the government to look carefully who the people were that "crossed over from certain groups (UDBA) into our economy after the Brioni Plenum (in July 1966)." VUS, August 19, 1970.

31. HKL, No. 13, May 1969.

32. Fred Singleton, *Twentieth-Century Yugoslavia* (London: Macmillan, 1976), p. 156.

33. Djodan, "Gdje," p. 703.

34. *Studentski list* No. 18-19, 1971 as in Bušić, *Jedino Hrvatska,* p. 417; VUS, November 25, 1970.

35. Hrvoje Šošić, "Besprimjerne obmane ili Hrvoje Šošić u 'Generxu'." *Kritika* Vol. 4, No. 18, 1971, p. 451. One Croatian economist concluded that "the centers of financial power have the most important word in Yugoslavia." Dragan Lalić, "Neki gospodarski razlozi suvereniteta republika," HGG, No. 10, September 29, 1971, p. 10. Profits from the country's exporting business were divided in the following way: Serbia 85%, Slovenia 7.5%, Macedonia 2.6%, and Croatia 4.7%. VUS, November 10, 1971.

36. Djodan, "The Evolution," p. 83.

37. *Studenski list,* No. 22, October 26, 1971.

38. Šime Djodan, "Godpodarski položaj Hrvatske," *Kritika* Vol. 4, No. 17, 1971, p. 349. Tito himself acknowledged that "a tremendous amount of capital has been concentrated in a very small number of hands, and it is being invested where they like it the most." Josip Broz Tito, "Jedinstvo federacije pretpostavlja stvaranje jednog autoritativnog tela," (Tito's talk in Zagreb on September 21, 1970.) Reprinted in *Aktuelni problemi daljeg razvoja našej političkog sistema* (Beograd: Komunist, 1970), p. 11.

39. Djodan, "The Evolution," p. 82, About economic development of the eastern and western portions of the country see also *Hrvatsko sveučilište,* No. 11, May 27, 1971; Šime Djodan, "Investicije zapadno od Drine," *Kolo* Vol. 7, No. 7, 1969, pp. 714-717 and Stephen R. Sacks, "Regional Inequality in Yugoslav Industry," *The Journal of Developing Areas* Vol. 11, No. 1, 1976, pp. 66-69.

40. In 1925, 55 percent of the banking business of the country was concentrated in Zagreb alone. In 1971, Croatia's share of banking capital in Yugoslavia was 16 percent. In the early 1970s, Zagreb had less bank capital than Skoplje. Djodan, "Gospoarski položaj Hrvatske," p. 351 and Šime Djodan, "Aktuelni gospodarski položaj Zagreba," p. 497.

41. Hrvoje Šošić, "Hrvatsko gospodarsko čudo—iz razvojnih mogućnosti Hrvatske," *Kolo* Vol. 9, No. 5-6, 1971, p. 544.

42. Ibid., p. 546.

43. Djodan, "The Evolution," p. 87. Retention quota for foreign currency was about 7 percent at the time.

44. *Hrvatski tjednik* No. 28, October 29, 1971.

45. Hrvoje Šošić, *Za čiste račune* (Zagreb: Matica hrvatska, 1970), p. 81-84; Mladen Staničić, "Prava istina o raspodjeli obale," HGG, No. 2, June 7, 1971, pp. 26-29.

46. VUS, March 24, 1971; VUS, August 26, 1970; VUS, December 8, 1971; *Hrvatski tjednik* No. 2, April 23, 1971.

47. George Schöpflin, "The Ideology of Croatian Nationalism," *Survey* Vol. 19, No. 1, 1973, p. 130.

48. Šošić, *Za čiste račune*, p. 78.

49. Pero Krste, as cited in VUS, October 7, 1970.

50. *Zapisnik sjednice iz Karadjordjeva* (Chicago: Hrvatska tiskara, 1975), p. 174.

51. Šime Djodan, "Ustavni amandmani i problem jedinstvenog tržišta," *Kolo* Vol. 9, No. 4, 1971, p. 398.

52. *Komunist*, March 13, 1969 as cited in HKL No. 12, April 1969.

53. Šošić, *Za čiste račune*, p. 18.

54. Djodan, "Prilog razmatranju," pp. 471-472.

55. See for example Stipe Šuvar, *Nacionalno i nacionalističko* (Split: Marksistički centar, 1974).

56. Djodan, "Ustavni amandmani," p. 401.

57. *Zapisnik*, p. 72; Šime Djodan, "Pred kritičnom barijerom," *Dometi* Vol. 2, No. 3, 1969, p. 7; Zoran Jašić, "'Vaskrsenje' izvanbudžetske bilance," HGG No. 14, November 24, 1971, p. 29.

58. N. I. Karlović, "Internal Colonialism in a Marxist Society: the Case of Croatia," *Ethnic and Racial Studies*, Vol. 5, No. 3, July 1982, pp. 276-299.

59. Djodan, "Ustavni amandmani," p. 400; *Hrvatski tjednik* No. 23, September 24, 1971. *Hrvatsko sveučilište* No. 11, May 27, 1971; Šime Djodan, "Jugoslavensko tržište, samoupravnost poduzeća i suverenitet republika," *Kritika* Vol. 4, No. 18, 1971, pp. 484-85.

60. Šime Djodan, "Problemi izgradnje privrednog modela u SFRJ," *Ekonomist* No. 2, 1969 as cited in Djodan, "Gdje," p. 693.

61. Djodan, "Ustavni amandmani," p. 402.

62. Ibid., p. 401. A Croatian student wrote: "We are for the policy of further help to the less developed regions, but at the same time, we are against the fact that Croatia continues to carry the largest burden of that policy." *Studentski list* No. 22, October 26, 1971.

63. Djodan, "Različite interpretacije," p. 1353.

64. *Hrvatsko sveučilište* No. 11, May 27, 1971. It was suggested that there was a need of "political challenge" (konkurencija) to the existing Party monopoly. Marko Veselica, "Hrvatska gospodarska strategija," HGG No. 1, May 24, 1971, p. 21.

65. As cited in Lendavi, *Eagles in Cobwebs,* pp. 140-141.

66. Djodan, "Prilog razmatranju," p. 473.

67. An interview with Dragutin Haramija, "Rijeka u usponu," *Dometi* Vol. 2, No. 2, 1969, p. 2.

68. Bruno Tandara in VUS, August 12, 1970.

69. Djodan, "Prilog razmatranju," p. 472.

70. Djodan, "The Evolution," p. 77; See also Šime Djodan, "Funkcionalizam u službi dominacije," *Kolo* Vol. 9, No. 1-2, 1971, pp. 123-124.

71. *Zapisnik,* p. 74.

72. For more on causes of Croatian immigration see George J. Prpić, *The Croatian Immigrants in America* (New York: Philosophical Library, 1971), pp. 89-100.

73. Ivo Baučić, *The Effects of Emigration from Yugoslavia and the Problem of Returning Emigrant Workers* (The Hague: Martinus Nijhoff, 1972), p. 22; VUS, December 23, 1970; VUS, March 24, 1971.

74. VUS, November 21, 1970.

75. *Hrvatski tjednik* November 26, 1971.

76. Ibid.

77. Fred B. Singleton, "Socialist Federative Republic of Yugoslavia," in Bogdan Szajkowski, *Marxist Governments–A World Survey* (London: Macmillan, 1981), vol. 3, p. 794; VUS, March 24, 1971; Milovan Djilas, "Yugoslavia and the Expansionism of the Soviet State," *Foreign Affairs* Vol. 58, No. 4, Spring 1980, p. 866.

78. *Hrvatsko sveučilište* No. 2, March 25, 1971.

79. Baučić, *The Effects,* p. 12.

80. Ivo Baučić, "SR Hrvatska u vanjskim migracijama radne snage," *Encyclopaedia Moderna* Vol. 5, No. 14, Fall 1970, p. 64. Slightly different statistics in *Hrvatsko sveučilište* No. 2, March 25, 1971; "Neka obilježja suvremenih migracija," *Kritika* Vol. 3, No. 13, 1970, p. 561. According to one source, Croatia had the highest percentage of emigration in the world." See HKL, No. 2, May 1968.

81. VUS, March 24, 1971; Večeslav Holjevac, *Hrvati izvan domovine* (Zagreb: Matica hrvatska, 1967), pp. 337-338.

82. HKL No. 10, January 31, 1969 and *Statistički kalendar Jugoslavije 1982* (Beograd: Savezni zavod za statistiku, 1982), 28:37 as in Ramet, *Nationalism,* p. 21.

83. *Hrvatsko sveučilište* No. 2, March 25, 1971.

84. Franjo Raknić, "Privredni razvitak, privredne mjerei zaposlenost," *Ekonomski pregled,* Vol. 22, No. 7-8, 1971, p. 444.

85. For example, there were 204,000 workers employed in the private sector in 1954. In 1964, there were only 134,000 of such workers. Šime Djodan,"Osvrt na savjetovanje o stanovništvu, emigraciji i zaposlenosti," *Kritika,* Vol. 4, No. 17, 1971, p. 299.

86. "Zaključi Hrvatske pagvaške grupe o stanovništvu, emigraciji i zaposlenosti u SR Hrvatskoj," *Encyclopaedia Moderna* Vol. 6, No. 15, 1971, p. 106.

87. Djodan, "Osvrt na savjetovanje," p. 295.

88. Baučić, *The Effects,* p. 10 and 12.

89. Baučić, "SR Hrvatska," p. 65. For example, in 1962 about 20,000 people from the republic left the country. Holjevac, *Hrvati,* p. 342.

90. VUS, July 26, 1972; Jakov Gelo, "Tradicija ili nešto drugo," HGG No. 5, July 19, 1971, pp. 31-33.

91. *Hrvatsko sveučilište* No. 15, 1971 as in Bušić, *Jedino Hrvatska,* p. 404.

92. Ibid., p. 406.

93. Djodan, "Osvrt na savjetovanje," pp. 292-293.

94. VUS, July 26, 1972; Christopher Bird, "From a Reporter's Notebook," *Problems of Communism* Vol. 18, No. 4-5, July-October 1969, p. 80. A good case study on the subject is found in Mladen Žuvela, "Odlazak radnika iz brodogradilišta 'Split'", *Pogledi* Vol. 2, No. 4-5, 1970, pp. 47-67.

95. For some indications about the social and psychological effects of working abroad on the Croatian workers, see Stjepan Djundja, "Socijalno-psihološki osvrt na hrvatskog radnika tjekom privremene emigracije u zapadnoj Evropi," *Susreti* (Zbornik radova sa susreta hrvatskih studenta u inozemstvu), Vol. 4, No. 4, 1978, pp. 67-87.

96. VUS, December 23, 1970.

97. "Zaključci Hrvatske pagvaške grupe," p. 107.

98. Because of restrictions on private industries, there was a popular saying that most of the country's "guest workers" spent their money on cars, houses, and grave site monuments. For a discussion on private

investments by these workers see Baučić, *The Effect*, pp. 21-44. On the proposals of Croatian intellectuals in this matter see "Zaključci Hrvatske pagvaške grupe," p. 107.

99. *Zapisnik*, p. 174.

100. *Hrvatski tjednik*, No. 25, October 8, 1971.

Notes to Chapter V

1. Ivan Mužić, "Ideje Zapada i Istoka u Hrvata," *Kolo* Vol. 8, No. 9, 1970, p. 1064.

2. Ivo Vidan, "Provicijalizacija–Ali zašto?!?" *Kritika* Vol. 1, No. 2, 1968, pp. 212-215.

3. *Mjesto i položaj hrvatske književnosti–Rasprava* (Rijeka: Biblioteka "Dometi," 1971), pp. 18 and 64; Zlata Derossi, "Položaj hrvatske književnosti u gimnazijama SR Hrvatske," *Kritika* Vol. 3, No. 15, 1970, pp. 887-893.

4. Miroslav Vaupotić in *Hrvatski tjednik* No. 13, July 9, 1971.

5. Vlatko Pavletić in *Hrvatski tjednik* No. 13, July 9, 1971.

6. *Telegram* November 21, 1969; Jozo Ivičević, "Evandjelje po Viktoru Novaku," *Kolo* Vol. 6, No. 8-9, 1968, pp. 227-265; Srećko Lipovčan, "U sjeni ocvale političke arheologije ili šta se krije ispod 'Jugoslavenstva' Viktora Novaka," *Kritika* Vol. 1, No. 3, 1968, pp. 296-319; Ivan Pederin, "Srpski krug kredom doktora Milorada Pavića," *Dubrovnik*, Vol. 14, No. 3, 1971, pp. 58-66; *Hrvatski tjednik*, No. 11, June 25, 1971; Ibid., No. 13, July 9, 1971; Miroslav Vaupotić, "Nekolike opaske uz budući Kongres hrvatske kulture." *Dubrovnik*, Vol. 14, No. 2, 1971, pp. 69-73.

7. Vlatko Pavletić, *Hrvatski tjednik* No. 13, July 9, 1971.

8. For a detailed discussion of this problem see *Mjesto i položaj*, especially pp. 30, 36, 51, and 71; Trpimir Macan, "Kome smeta hrvatsko ime u povijesti Dalmacije?" *Kritika* Vol. 1, No. 1, 1968, pp. 100-105; Ivan Bošković, "Postoji li 'Dubrovačka' književnost?" *Kritika* Vol. 2, No. 8, 1969, pp. 560-582.

9. As cited in Berislav Vodopija, "Prišućivana Hrvatska u izdanjima 'Tehničke knjige," *Kritika* Vol. 4, No. 18, 1971, p. 537.

10. Ivo Frangeš in *Mjesto i položaj*, p. 29.

11. Smiljana Rendić, "Izlazak iz genitiva ili Drugi hrvatski preporod," *Kritika* Vol. 4, No. 18, 1971, p. 417.

12. The Agreement was signed by a small number of Croatian, Serbian and Slovene scholars who happened to be in Vienna at the time. They did not act in any official capacity. Even Ljudevit Gaj, the major figure of the Illyrian movement in Croatia was against the Agreement. See Ljudevit Jonke, *Hrvatski književni jezik danas* (Zagreb: Školska knjiga, 1971), p. 86. For more about Karadžić and his claims see, Ivičević, "Evandjelje."

13. Julije Derossi, "Hrvatski književni jezik u hrvatskim školama," *Kritika* Vol. 4, No. 16, 1971, pp. 54-55. It was declared that the official language of the kingdom was "Serbo-Croatian-Slovene." *Službene novine Kraljevine SHS* No. 142A, June 28, 1921.

14. Dalibor Brozović, "Hrvatski jezik, njegovo mjesto unutar južnoslavenskih i drugih slavenskih jezika, njegove povijesne mijene kao jezika hrvatske književnosti," in Aleksandar Flaker and Krunoslav Pranjić, eds. *Hrvatska književnost u evropskom kontekstu* (Zagreb: Liber, 1978, p. 69).

15. See Jonke, *Hrvatski književni jezik danas,* p. 20. Full text of the document is found in *Hrvatski književni jezik i pitanje varijanata* Special edition of *Kritika* (Zagreb: Matica hrvatska, 1969), p. 2.

16. See Christopher Spalatin, "Language and Politics in Yugoslavia," *Journal of Croatian Studies* Vol. 11-12, 1970-71, p. 85.

17. For detailed analysis of the Novi Sad Agreement see Ljudevit Jonke, *Hrvatski književni jezik 19. i 20. stoljeća* (Zagreb: Matica hrvatska, 1971), pp. 210-221; Stjepan Babić, "Htjenja i ostvarenja Novosadskoga dogovora," *Jezik* Vol. 15, No. 1, 1967-68, pp. 3-13.

18. Šegedin, *Svi smo odgovorni,* p. 150.

19. Jonke, *Hrvatski književni jezik danas,* pp. 111-117.

20. Stjepan Babić, "Za ravnopravnost, ali čega?" *Jezik* Vol. 16, No. 5, 1968/69, pp. 136-138; Radoslav Katičić, "Opseg povijesti hrvatskog jezika," in *Hrvatski znanstveni zbornik* (Matica hrvatska), Vol. 1, 1971, p. 31.

21. Some Beograd scholars continued to talk about "Serbo-Croatian" as a unified language without "variants." Rodoljub Čolaković, for example. See Dalibor Brozović, "O sadasnjem času na kružnici jezičnog sata," *Kritika* Vol. 4, No. 17, 1971, p. 192. "Variants" were considered by some just a "mechanical division" of the same language. *Komunist,* January 21, 1971.

22. A collection of various articles concerning the Dictionary are found in *Hrvatski književni jezik i pitanje varijanata.* Also see an analysis

of the Dictionary by a leading contemporary Croatian linguist, Dalibor Brozović, *Rječnik jezika, ili jezik Rječnika* (Special issue of *Kritika*) (Zagreb: Matica hrvatska, 1969); Božidar Finka, "Rječnik Matica ili glas usnulih i probudjenih savjesti," *Kolo* Vol. 8, No. 2, 1970, pp. 221-230.

23.   See Jonke, *Hrvatski književni jezik danas*, pp. 58, 98-103; *Studentski list* No. 18-19, 1971 as reprinted in Bušić, *Jedino Hrvatska*, pp. 371-379; Avšič, "Nekaj pripomb"; Jakov Gumzej, "Hrvatski zakonodavni sustav-zalog samoupravnog karaktera državnosti," HGG No. 6, August 2, 1971, pp. 6-7; Mate Šimundić, "Suvremeni hrvatski jezik," HGG, No. 5, July 19, 1971, p. 50; Ibid., No. 6, August 2, 1971, p. 66; ibid., No. 7, August 16, 1971, p. 50; Ibid., No. 9, September 15, 1971, pp. 49-50; Ibid., No. 10, September 29, 1971, pp. 49-50; Vladimir Loknar, "Medicina i neki pojmovi iz dodirnih znanosti u "Riječniku Hrvatskosrpskog književnog jezika," *Kritika* Vol. 4, No. 17, 1971, pp. 332-342; Aleksandar Šolc and Juraj Božičević, "Obrada stručnih naziva u rječniku Hrvatskosrpskog književnog jezika," *Kritika* Vol. 2, No. 5, 1969, pp. 208-221.

24.   Petar Šegedin, "Pismo drugu O.," reprinted in Šegedin, *Svi smo odgovorni*, p. 157.

25.   "Matica hrvatska odriče se Novosadskog Dogovora," *Kritika* Vol. 4, No. 17, 1971, p. 381; *Hrvatski tjednik* No. 2, April 23, 1971. It is interesting to note that *Hrvatski tjednik*, the leading voice of the Croatian national revival, concurred on the same day (April 16, 1971). Other Croatian cultural institutions followed Matica hrvatska in renouncing the Novi Sad Agreement. See *Jezik* Vol. 18, No. 5, 1970/71, pp. 138-39 and Vol. 19, No. 1, 1971/72, p. 19; *Marulić* Vol. 4, No. 3, 1971, p. 100.

26.   Mak Dizdar, "Marginalije o jeziku i oko njega," *Život* Vol. 19, No. 11-12, 1970, p. 118. This whole issue of *Život* was dedicated to the problem of language discrimination in Bosnia and Hercegovina.

27.   "Saopćenje Uprave Udruženja književnika Crne Gore o jeziku," *Kritika* Vol. 4, No. 17, 1971, p. 378. On Montenegrin-Serbian language controversy see VUS, November 3, 1971 as well as *Kritika* Nos. 5, 6, 8 and 10.

28.   On number of copies see VUS, September 1, 1971; VUS, January 19, 1972; *Hrvatski pravopis* (Zagreb: Školska knjiga, 1971) reprinted in Great Britain in 1972.

29.   *Hrvatski tjednik* December 3, 1971; VUS, September 1, 1971; Ibid., October 21, 1971; Ibid., November 10, 1971.

30. Alexander Bach, Austrian Minister in the post-1848 period, known for his centralist policies.

31. Croatian Ban (1883-1903) and best remembered for his policies of Magyarization and political oppression.

32. Since 1972 two grammars of the Croatian language were published: Težak-Babić, *Pregled gramatike hrvatskog književnog jezika* Zagreb, 1973 and Barić-Lončarić-Malić-Pavešić-Peti Zečević-Zinka, *Priručna gramatika hrvatskog književnog jezika* Zagreb, 1979. However, both were banned by the regime. A book *Srpski narod i njegov jezik* by Pavle Ivić, a well known Serbian linguist, published by Srpska književna zadruga in 1971, also became controversial, especially his claim that the Serbian language is spoken even by non-Serbs. See *Politika* the June 23, 1972.

33. Julije Derossi, "Hrvatska jezična stvarnost," *Susreti* Zbornik radova sa IX i X Susreta hrvatskih studenata u inozemstvu. Vol. 5, No. 5, 1979, pp. 111-112.

34. Šegedin, *Svi smo odgovorni,* p. 156.

35. VUS, August 25, 1971.

36. Benedikta Zelić-Bučan, "Neprihvatljiv i apsurdan pristup vrednovanju nacionalne povijesti," *Dubrovnik* Vol. 14, No. 1, 1971, p. 100.

37. Josip Jelačić (1801-1859) Croatian Ban, in the post-1848 period. In Croatia he is remembered as the leader of the struggle for Croatian autonomy and abolition of serfdom. Andrija Hebrang (1899-1949) was a leading Communist Party man in Croatia. He spent twelve years in jail in the inter-war period. He died while in jail in Belgrade. There are strong indications that he was killed by Ranković's henchmen as a Croatian nationalist.

38. *Školske novine* February 22, 1971.

39. Šegedin, *Svi smo odgovorni,* p. 154.

40. Zelić-Bučan, "Neprihvatljiv," p. 107.

41. VUS, July 14, 1971.

42. Bruno Bušić in HKL No. 17, September 1969.

43. Franjo Tudjman's concluding speech at his trial on January 19, 1981, as in Boris Katich, ed., *So Speak Croatian Dissidents* (Toronto: ZIRAL, 1983), p. 154.

44. VUS, July 14, 1971.

45. For example in the 19th century Dalmatia and the Military Border were directly under the Habsburg crown; northern parts of Croatia

were under the crown of St. Stephen; Bosnia and Hercegovina after 1878 under shared responsibility of Vienna and Budapest.

46. VUS, July 14, 1971.

47. On this issue see *Hrvatsko sveučilište* No. 7-8, April 29, 1971; VUS, July 1, 1970; Zvane Črnja, "Izmedju regije i nacije," *Dometi* Vol. 4, No. 1-2, 1971, pp. 122-23; Zvonimir Komarica, "O nacionalnoj neopredijeljenosti," *Kritika* Vol. 3, No. 13, 1970, pp. 548-550; "Prosvijed Upravnog odbora DKH protiv načina predstojećeg popisa pučanstva," *Kritika* Vol. 4, No. 16, 1971, pp. 173-74; "Izjava Upravnog odbora Matice hrvatske o pripremama za popis stanovništva SFRJ," Ibid., pp. 174-175.

48. See *Putevi revolucije* Vol. 2, No. 3-4, 1964, pp. 5-416. *Pregled istorije* was supposed to come out in 1959. However, intra-Party historiographical disagreements delayed the project. There were nine co-authors of the book. Six were Serbs, two Macedonians and one Slovene. The main objection to the book's content came from Croatia. About this problem see Bakarić's speech in *Sedmi Plenum CK SK Hrvatske,* pp. 14-16 and 19.

49. *Osmi kongres,* pp. 30-40.

50. Tudjman, *Velike ideje,* p. 162. The chapter in Tudjman's book dealing with causes of the break-up of the First Yugoslavia and the Partisan war in Croatia was delivered as a lecture at a seminar for history teachers in 1964. Because of his conclusions, which did not coincide with the official historiography, he was labeled as a nationalist. The lecture was published for the first time in *Kolo* Vol. 6, No. 8-9, 1968, pp. 201-218 (Part I) and Ibid., No. 10, 1068, pp. 363-378 (Part II).

51. Tudjman, *Velike ideje,* p. 165.

52. Ibid., p. 163.

53. On the importance of statehood for Croatians see Mirjana Gross in *Hrvatsko sveučilište* No. 3, April 1, 1971.

54. Miko Tripalo in *Informativni pregled* CK SKH No. 20, 1971 as cited in Perić, *Ideje,* p. 151. About these accusations see for example Konstantin Fotić, *The War We Lost* (New York: Viking, 1948), and Velimir Terzić, *Jugoslavija u aprilskom ratu 1941* (Titograd: Grafički zavod Crne Gore, 1963). For the Croatian partisan view see Franjo Tudjman, "Uvod u historiju Socijalističke Jugoslavije," (I) *Forum* Vol. 2, No. 2, 1963, pp. 292-352; (II) Ibid., No. 3, pp. 530-564; (III), Ibid., No. 4, pp. 702-741; (IV) Ibid., No. 5, 840-858; (V) Ibid., No. 6, pp. 1087-1122; (VI) Ibid., No. 7-8, pp. 199-233; (VII) Ibid., Vol. 3, No. 1-2, 1964, pp.

139-157, as well as his articles "Uzroci krize," "Zaoštravanje sukoba," "Hrvatska politika" and "Slom."

55.   Tudjman, *Nationalism*, p. 106. On the identification of Ustashism and Croatianism see Šegedin, *Svi smo odgovorni*, p. 163. He himself was suspected of nationalism just because he began an article with the letter "U." Ibid., p. 139.

56.   Franjo Tudjman, "Prosudba povijesne odrednice što oblikuje hrvatsko nacionalno biće," *Dubrovnik* Vol. 14, No. 2, 1971, p. 20. See also Zvonimir Kulundžić, *Tragedija hrvatske historiografije* (Zagreb, 1970), p. 6; VUS, November 10, 1971. For an example of different treatments of Ustasha and Chetniks see Vladimir Dedijer, et al., *History of Yugoslavia* (New York: McGrew-Hill, 1974).

57.   Tudjman, *Nationalism*, p. 163.

58.   Supek, *Heretic*, p. 169.

59.   HKL, No. 15, July 1969 also reprinted in Bušić, *Jedino Hrvatska*, pp. 541-563.

60.   One of the official secrets in Yugoslavia is the fate of the Croatians and others who were handed over by the British to Tito's forces in southern Austria in May 1945. For more on this subject see: Jerome Jareb and Ivo Omrčanin, eds., *The End of the Croatian Army at Bleiburg, Austria in May 1945 According to English Military Documents*. A reprint from *Journal of Croatian Studies* Vol. 28-29, 1977-78, pp. 115-182; John Prcela and Stanko Guldescu, eds. *Operation Slaughterhouse* (Philadelphia: Dorrance, 1970); Nicholas Bethell, *The Last Secret* (London: Andre Deutsch, 1974); Joseph Hećimović, *In Tito's Death Marches and Extermination Camps* (New York: Carlton, 1962); Nikolai Tolstoy, *The Minister and the Massacres* (London: Century Hutchinson, 1986). Ante Beljo, *Yugoslavia–Genocide* (Sudburg: Northern Tribune, 1985).

61.   Vjekoslav Kaleb in *Hrvatski tjednik*, No. 31, November 19, 1971.

62.   *Zpaisnik*, p. 219.

63.   Tudjman, *Nationalism*, p. 164.

64.   See Supek, *Heretic*, p. 170; Tudjman, *Velike ideje*, p. 210.

65.   Supek, *Heretic*, pp. 192-193.

66.   Ibid., p. 191.

67.   Ibid., p. 192.

68.   Ibid., p. 193.

69. Tudjman, *Velike ideje*, p. 198.

70. Ibid., pp. 198-199.

71. Even the name "The Red Republic" indicated their radicalism.

72. Supek, *Heretic*, pp. 170-73. For ideological trends in the Party in Croatia see Tudjman, *Velike ideje*, pp. 263-266.

73. Supek, *Heretic*, p. 171.

74. Ibid., pp. 169-215 and 231; Tudjman, *Nationalism*, pp. 106-107.

75. Supek, *Heretic*, pp. 159-60.

76. On the Hebrang case see Ibid., pp. 213-217; Ivan Supek, *Crown Witness Against Hebrang* (Chicago: Markanton Press, 1983). The official Yugoslav version (versions) are given in Mile Milatović, *Slučaj Andrija Hebrang* (Beograd: Kultura, 1952) and Dragan Kljakić, *Dosije Hebrang* (Beograd: Partizanska knjiga, 1983). These two semi-official versions do not agree on the question of how Hebrang died. Milatović states that he hanged himself (p. 266), while Kljakić says that Hebrang smashed his head on the radiator of his prison cell (p. 310). The Hebrang question is still very much alive in the Party politics and historiography.

Notes to Chapter VI

1. *Deseta sjednica*, pp. 6, 7, 8.

2. M. M. (Marijan Matković), "Polonijada Miloša Žanka," *Forum* Vol. 18, No. 12, 1969, p. 1046.

3. *Deseta sjednica*, p. 8.

4. Ibid., p. 8.

5. Šerif Šehović, "Raskrinkano častohleplje ili zašto je Žanko doživio slom?," *Kritika* Vol. 3, No. 12, 1970, p. 392.

6. See for example "'Slučaj' Podravska Slatina," *Hrvatski tjednik*, No. 6, May 21, 1971 and No. 7, May 28, 1971; *Politik*, May 10, 1971 and May 27, 1971; "Pridraga traži zaštitu," *Hrvatski tjednik*, No. 20, September 3, 1971 and No. 7, May 28, 1971.

7. Bilić, *Revolucija*, p. 50.

8. Ibid., p. 79.

9. *Zapisnik*, p. 178; Bilić, one of Tripalo's opponents, also agreed about the time of the split in the Party leadership. *Revolucija*, p. 129.

10. Tito stated at the meeting: "Here we see today two factions. I

have to tell you that I am bitter (about it). You do not have unity. You are divided." *Zapisnik,* p. 214.

11. Ibid., p. 163.

12. Blažević in ibid., p. 185.

13. Bilić in ibid., p. 131.

14. Ibid., pp. 188-189.

15. *Deseta sjednica,* pp. 49-50.

16. Miko Tripalo, "Medjunacionalni odnosi u Jugoslaviji i promjene u političkom sistemu," *Zbornik Pravnog fakulteta u Zagrebu* 1971, p. 17 and in *Ustavna reforma–Saopćenja sa kolokvija na pravnom fakultetu u Zagrebu.* (Zagreb: Centar za aktuelni politički studij, 1971), p. 11.

17. Ibid., p. 11.

18. Savka Dapčević-Kučar in *Vjesnik,* November 14, 1970.

19. Miko Tripalo, *S poprišta* (Zagreb: Centar za aktuelni politički studij, 1971), p. 353.

20. *Vjesnik,* April 11, 1971.

21. Tripalo, *S poprišta,* p. 351.

22. "Hrvatska na pragu punog prosperiteta," an interview with Miko Tripalo, HGG, No. 3, June 21, 1971, p. 8.

23. Ibid., p. 8.

24. VUS, July 28, 1971.

25. VUS, October 14, 1970; Vladimir Goati, *Perspektive političke avangarde* (Belgrade: Komunist, 1972), p. 142; Bilić, *Revolucija,* p. 182.

26. VUS, October 14, 1970.

27. *Hrvatski tjednik,* No. 16, July 30, 1971.

28. Silvano Bolčić, *O socijalnoj strukturi Jugoslavije* (Belgrade: Centar za društveno-političko obrazovanje, 1967), p. 27. According to another statistic, in 1969 *službenici* made up 43.8 percent of the Party membership, See Bogdan Denić, "Pokretljivost i regrutiranje jugoslavenskog rukovodstva: Uloga SKJ." *Pogledi,* Vol. 2, No. 7, 1971, p. 79.

29. Bolčić, *O socijalnoj strukturi,* p. 29.

30. Tripalo, *Bez kompromisa,* p. 106.

31. Tripalo, as cited in *Izvještaj o stanju u Savezu komunista Hrvatske u odnosu na prodor nacionalizma u njegove redove* (28. Sjednica CK SKH) (Zagreb: SK Hrvatske–CK, 1972), p. 54. It is interesting to note that this quote is not found in Tripalo's interview in HGG No. 3, June 21, 1971 as the report claims. Possibly it is printed elsewhere or perhaps the authors of the *Izvještaj* fabricated it.

32. Supek, *Heretic*, pp. 115 and 117.

33. Slavko Mihalić in VUS, November 17, 1971.

34. Tomislav Ladan in ibid.

35. Danilo Pejović, "Nacionalizam i internacionalizam," *Republika* Vol. 25, No. 8, 1969, p. 386.

36. Petar Šegedin, "Govor na Godišnjoj skupštini Društva književnika Hrvatske," *Kritika* Vol. 3, No. 12, 1970, p. 405.

37. Vaupotić, "Nekolike opaske," p. 70.

38. Nerkez Smailagić, "Hrvatski Ustav—pitanje društveno-političkog odredjenja naše suvremenosti," (III) HGG, No. 13, November 10, 1971, p. 9. See also Vladimir Košćak, "Što je nacija," *Kritika* Vol. 3, No. 15, 1970, pp. 872-879.

39. Vlado Gotovac, "Autsajderski fragmenti," (Svitak treći) *Kritika* Vol. 2, No. 8, 1969, p. 537.

40. Marko Veselica, "Rastakanje hrvatskog nactionalnog bića," HGG, No. 2, June 7, 1971, p. 24.

41. Djodan, "Ustavni amandmani," p. 387. See also Djodan, "Funkcionalizam," pp. 119-128 and an editorial in *Hrvatsko sveučilište*, No. 3, April 1, 1971.

42. Ivan Supek, as cited in *Hrvatsko sveučilište* No. 3, April 1, 1971.

43. Gotovac, "Autsajderski fragmenti" (III), p. 538.

44. Petar Šegedin, "Sudbina," *Forum* Vol. 21, No. 1-2, 1971, p. 33. There were, however, some leading Serbs at the top of the Party's progressive leadership. Srećko Bijelić, for example.

45. Gotovac, "Autsajderski fragmenti" (III), p. 538.

46. Ante Paradžik in *Hrvatsko sveučilište* No. 16, July 1, 1971.

47. Jozo Ivičević in *Hrvatski tjednik* No. 28, October 29, 1971.

48. Sher, *Praxis*, pp. 265-266.

49. Z. Č. "'Praxisov' bijeg od sadašnjosti," *Dometi* Vol. 1, No. 2-3, 1968, p. 82.

50. Danilo Pejović, "Jedno objašnjenje o 'ljevičarstvu' i 'desničarstvu'," *Kolo* Vol. 6, No. 6, 1968, p. 534.

51. Milan Kangrga in *Praxis* No. 3-4, 1971 as cited in *Hrvatsko sveučilište* No. 19, September 22, 1971.

52. Supek, *Heretic*, p. 249.

53. Jure Juras in *Hrvatsko sveučilište* No. 17-18, July 14, 1971.

54. Ivan Babić in *Hrvatsko sveučilište* No. 19, September 22, 1971.

55. Supek, *Heretic*, p. 249.

56. Ramet, *Nationalism*, p. 129.

57. Supek, *Heretic*, pp. 365-366. See also declarations of Miladin Životić as reprinted in *Poruka slobodne Hrvatske* No. 2, 1979.

58. Supek, *Heretic*, p. 297.

59. Vlatko Pavletić, "Uvod u 'Preporod hrvatskih sveučilištaraca'," in *Preporod hrvatskih sveučilištaraca* Special Edition of *Kritika* (Zagreb: Matica hrvatska, 1971), p. I.

60. Ivan Supek, "Rad na reformi Sveučilišta," in *Preporod*, p. 35 and in Zlatko Majstorović, ed. *Za reformu Hrvatskog sveučilišta* (Zagreb: Savez studenata Hrvatske, 1971), p. 73.

61. Ivan Zvonimir Čičak in *Preporod*, pp. 96-97.

62. *Mladost* (Paper of the Youth Alliance of Yugoslavia), March 4, 1971.

63. *Hrvatsko sveučilište* No. 3, April 1, 1971.

64. Dražen Budiša in *Hrvatsko sveučilište* No. 4, April 8, 1971.

65. Ibid., No. 3, April 1, 1971, p. 93.

66. Pavletić, "Uvod," p. III.

67. *Hrvatsko sveučilište*, No. 5, April 15, 1971.

68. Ivan Supek in *Vjesnik* March 16, 1971 cited by Pavletić in "Uvod," p. II.

69. Krunoslav Šuto, "Studentski pokret i aktuelni politički trenutak," HGG, No. 11, October 13, 1971, p. 17.

70. Budiša in VUS, April 21, 1971.

71. Šuto, "Studentski pokret," p. 17.

72. See *Tlo* (Youth paper for the Croatian republic), April 9, 1971 and VUS, June 23, 1971.

73. Mirko Madjor, "Preobrazba Hrvatske—zadatak mladih," HGG, No. 4, July 5, 1971, p. 22.

74. In 1939 peasants made up 77 percent of the total population in Yugoslavia. Their percentage in 1961 was 53.6, in 1969 46, and in 1971 36.4 percent. Bolčić, *O socijalnoj strukturi*, p. 22; Goati, *Perspektive*, p. 13. Different authors give different percentages regarding social segments of the population which indicates that there are a good number of people in "gray" areas. Especially the line between peasants and workers is very unclear. It is claimed that in 1967 there were 1,650,000 peasant-workers in the country. See Stipe Šuvar, "Poljoprivrednici u Savezu komunista i

pitanja dosljednog provodjenja politike u selu," in Franjo Šatović, ed., *Suvremeni društveno-ekonomski problemi razvoja sela* (Zagreb: Savez poljoprivrednih inžinjera i tehničara SR Hrvatske, 1967), p. 156.

75.   Tripalo, interview in HGG, No. 3, June 21, 1971, p. 8.

76.   Pavao Novosel in *Hrvatsko sveučilište* No. 6, April 22, 1971.

77.   April Carter, *Democratic Reform in Yugoslavia* (Princeton: Princeton University Press, 1982), p. 261; Goati, *Perspective,* p. 62.

78.   For example, in 1966 only 5.0 percent of unqualified and 12 percent of semi-qualified workers belonged to the Party. Bolčić, *O socijalnoj strukturi,* p. 29. For statistical details on the young and women in the Party see Šatović, *Suvremeni društveno-ekonomski problemi,* especially pp. 153-160 and *Reforma Saveza komunista Hrvatske* (Zagreb: Centar za aktuelni politički studij, 1970), pp. 42-55.

79.   "Fizionomija jednog štrajka," (Okrugli stol) *Pogledi* (Split), Vol. 2, No. 3, 1970, p. 20.

80.   Ivan Babić, in *Studentski list* No. 22, October 26, 1971.

81.   "Fizionomija jednog štrajka," p. 46.

82.   Official statistics cited in Slobodan Stanković and Zdenko Antić, "Recentralization in Yugoslavia," in Vojtech Mastny, ed., *Soviet/East European Survey, 1983-1984* (Durham: Duke University Press, 1985), p. 267.

83.   There were 55 Matica branches in 1971. Matica was not allowed to organize its branches directly among the workers. Many workers, however, did become members of Matica. This fact became a special concern to the leaders of the Sindicate. See Milutin Baltić, in *Zapisnik,* pp. 84-86.

84.   *Izvjestaj,* pp. 152 and 160.

85.   Baltić in *Zapisnik,* p. 88.

86.   For the circulation figures of different papers in Yugoslavia see *Dometi,* Vol. 1, No. 4-5, 1968, p. 19.

87.   For these and other data about those dismissed from the Party at the beginning of 1972 see *Izvještaj,* pp. 127-130.

88.   Tripalo's interview in HGG, no. 3, June 21, 1971, p. 8.

89.   Tripalo in a speech in Županja, as cited in *Izvještaj,* p. 141. Some foreign observers also agree that the movement was "quite broad indeed" and that progressive leadership had "the support of most segments of Croat society." See Gary K. Bertsch, "The Revival of Nationalism," *Problems of Communism,* Vol. 22, No. 6, 1973, p. 13 and George Klein, "The

Role of Ethnic Politics in the Czechoslovak Crisis of 1968 and the Yugoslav Crisis of 1971," *Studies in Comparative Communism,* Vol. 8, No. 4, 1975, p. 358.

90. Tripalo's interview in HGG, No. 3, June 21, 1971, p. 9.

91. Interview with Bužo Dugeč (January 1986), an active member of the Party and Matica leadership in the late Sixties and early Seventies. Dugeč now lives in West Germany.

92. The best known example of this kind of thinking is Frano Franić, the Archbishop of Split. See *Hrvatski tjednik,* No. 19, August 27, 1971.

Notes to Chapter VII

1. *Vjesnik u srijedu* (VUS) January 20, 1971.

2. The following statistical data indicate Croat underrepresentation in various fields. In 1970, the Federal Ministry of Internal Affairs (Secret Police) had the following national percentages of 'leading officials': Serbs 61%, Croats 16%, Slovenes 9%, Montenegrins 9%, Yugoslavs 1%, others 4%. NIN, May 3, 1970.

TABLE 8
National Composition of 'Functionaries' in
the Federal Institutions in 1969

Serbs	4334	Turks	2	
Croats	504	Jews	14	
Slovenes	187	Slovaks		2
Macedonians	145	Italians		1
Montenegrins	424	Undecided		224
Albanians	11	Others		27
Hungarians	10			

Source: *Ekonomska politika* January 1927, 1969 as in *Hrvatski književni list* No. 13, May 1969.

TABLE 9

Nationality of Yugoslav Officer Corps in 1970
in percentages

General Officers	Officer Corps		Total Population 1971
Serbs	46.7	57.4	39.7
Croats	19.3	14.7	22.1
Muslims	3.2	4.0	5.1
Slovenes	6.3	5.2	8.2
Albanians	0	1.2	6.4
Macedonians	3.9	5.6	5.8
Montenegrins	19.3	10.3	2.5
Others	0.9	1.0	4.6

Source: A. Ross Johnson, *Role of Military in Communist Yugoslavia: An Historical Sketch* (Santa Monica: Rand Paper Series, P-6070 January 1978), p. 19.

Croatians were also under-represented in their own republic. For example, in 1961 80.3 percent of the population in Croatia were Croats but they made up only 65.9 percent of the Party membership. See HKL, No. 13, May 1969. These proportions were similar in 1971.

3.   Savka Dapčević-Kučar as quoted in VUS, July 7, 1971.

4.   Dapčević-Kučar as cited in VUS, February 17, 1971.

5.   Bilić, *Revolucija*, p. 217.

6.   For example, the meeting of the EC of the CC LCC on February 12, 1971.

7.   VUS, February 17, 1971; *Izvještaj*, p. 67.

8.   VUS became especially known for its support of the Party Progressives. Political commentaries of the late Neda Krmpotić were widely read. VUS had a circulation of over 400,000 in the early Seventies; not long after the purges in 1972 it ceased to exist.

9.   Bilić, *Revolucija*, p. 226. It is interesting to note that the leadership of the CPY in the 1930s had made similar demands of the Karadjordjević royal regime: "freedom of work for all Croatian, Slovene, Macedonian, and Albanian cultural, educational, and other national societies and institutions . . . . Lifting the ban on flying Croatian and other national flags emblems and signs." *Odluke Politbiro CK KPJ o zadacima povodom VII kongresa Kominterne* (1935) as cited in Pero

Damjanović, *Tito pred temama istorije* (Belgrade: Institut za savremenu istoriju, 1972), p. 272, n. 18.

10. Antonije Isaković, director of the publishing house *Prosveta* (Belgrade) and a member of the CC LCS, in *Književne novine* October 16, 1971 as cited in VUS October 27, 1971. See also Mihajlo Djurić in *Student* (Belgrade) April 7, 1971.

11. *Hrvatski tjednik* April 16, 1971.

12. VUS, April 21, 1971.

13. About some indications on the confusion in the Party see Tito's speech in Labin May 1, 1971 in *Yugoslav Survey,* Vol. 12, No. 3, 1971, pp. 9-14.

14. *Hrvatsko sveučilište* April 22, 1971. It has been reported that Bakarić, Tito's confidant in Croatia, asked for an "open" session of the CC meeting. But Dapčević-Kučar wanted a "closed" meeting, claiming that an "open" discussion would create confusion among the people and that Tito would not like an open debate on such a subject. It was at this time, supposedly, that Bakarić made the final break with the Progressives. Bušić, *Jedino Hrvatska,* p. 510.

15. Grga Gamulin in *Hrvatsko sveučilište* October 6, 1971.

16. *Hrvatski tjednik,* May 7, 1971.

17. *Borba,* May 9, 1971.

18. *Yugoslav Survey,* Vol. 12, No. 3, p. 18. Mitja Ribičić, President of the Federal Executive Council at the time, stated specifically that the State Security Police was not involved in the plot. *Hrvatski tjednik,* May 7, 1971.

19. As cited in VUS, May 26, 1971.

20. Bušić, *Jedino Hrvatska,* p. 509.

21. See VUS, August 11, 1971. Croatian Party leadership officially accepted the Brioni conclusions at its 20th Session of the CC LCC on May 13-14, 1971. See VUS, May 19, 1971 and *Izvještaj,* p. 74.

22. Twentieth Session of the CC LCC (May 13-14, 1971) as cited in *Izvještaj,* p. 75.

23. NIN, May 16, 1971.

24. As cited in VUS, July 28, 1971. For Party's detailed explanation of Djodan's and Veselica's expulsion from the Party see *Hrvatski tjednik,* August 13, 1971.

25. *Izvještaj,* pp. 97, 98.

26. NIN, October 17, 1971 as cited in Dennison I. Rusinow, *Crisis in Croatia* (III), p. 22.

27. As cited in *Hrvatski tjednik*, July 30, 1971.

28. Ibid.

29. *Zapisnik*, p. 109.

30. Bilić, *Revolucija*, p. 226.

31. Božo Dugeč, "Hrvatsko proljeće," *Republika Hrvatska*, Vol. 35, No. 150, 1985, p. 10.

32. Bilić, *Revolucija*, p. 53.

33. Ibid., p. 52.

34. *Yugoslav Survey*, Vol. 12, No. 3, 1971, p. 11.

35. *Izvještaj*, p. 84. Tito's meeting with the republican leadership took place on July 4, 1971 but his talk was published for the first time in May 1972. See ibid., pp. 82-88. The published text of Tito's speech, however, is "a reconstruction from memory and notes by some who were present" at the meeting. See Rusinov, *Crisis in Croatia* (III), p. 18.

36. *Izvještaj*, p. 86.

37. Some popular songs at the time also indicate there was a popular belief in Croatia that Tito was on the side of the progressives. One of these songs was: "Druže Tito, ti ostavi Jovanku i oženi Dapčevića-Savku." (Comrade Tito, leave your wife Jovanka and marry Dapčević-Savka.) Also Dugeč, "Interview."

38. As cited in *Hrvatski tjednik* September 24, 1971. See also VUS, October 6, 1971.

39. *Izvještaj*, p. 104.

40. As in Rusinov, *Crisis in Croatia* (IV), pp. 7-8.

41. *Izvještaj*, p. 106.

42. *Hrvatski tjednik*, November 12, 1971.

43. Ibid.

44. Ibid.

45. *Izvještaj*, p. 107.

46. *New York Times*, May 25, 1972.

47. Neda Krmpotić in VUS, November 24, 1971.

48. From a conversation with an intellectual from Croatia who wishes to remain anonymous.

49. The 1963 Constitution was amended earlier in 1967 and 1968.

50. *Yugoslav Survey*, Vol. 12, No. 4, 1971, p. 2.

51.   Pero Pirker, Secretary of the EC CC LCC, as cited in VUS, July 7, 1971.

52.   Amendment XX, as cited in ibid.

53.   *Yugoslav Survey*, Vol. 12, No. 4, 1971, p. 2.

54.   Šime Djodan, "Bit hrvatske državnosti po ustavnim promjenama" (II), HGG, No. 13, November 10, 1971, p. 26 and Tripalo, "Medjunacionalni odnosi," p. 16.

55.   Most of the *Praxis* group were unitarists. See Šime Djodan, "Bit hrvatske državnosti," (I) HGG, No. 12, October 27, 1971, p. 25. An American scholar identified them as "centralist-humanist." Ramet, *Nationalism*, p. 127.

56.   As cited in VUS, May 12, 1971.

57.   Djordjević's interview in *Student* (Belgrade), March 30, 1971, as cited in *Hrvatsko sveučilište* April 8, 1971.

58.   *Studentski list*, April 20, 1971; VUS, May 5, 1971.

59.   Djodan, "Bit hrvatske državnosti" (I), p. 26.

60.   Amendment XXV stated: "Every action and every deed which reduces the unity of the Yugoslav united market is anti-constitutional." As cited in Djodan, "Bit hrvatske državnosti" (II), p. 29. On economic aspects of the amendments see also Uroš Dujšin, "Nove ekonomske funkcije federacije i republika kao oligocentrični mehanizam ekonomske politike," in *Ustavna Reforma*, pp. 19-31.

61.   *Hrvatski tjednik*, May 14, 1971.

62.   Mirjana Gross in *Hrvatsko sveučilište*, April 1, 1971.

63.   Neda Krmpotić in VUS, May 5, 1971.

64.   Franjo Tudjman in *Hrvatski tjednik*, September 3, 1971.

65.   Nerkez Smailagić in *Vjesnik*, January 28, 1971.

66.   Ivica Vrkić, as cited in *Izvještaj*, p. 89.

67.   Nerkez Smailagić, "Hrvatski ustav," (III), p. 9.

68.   Djodan, "Bit hrvatske državnosti" (I), p. 29. See also Ivo Petrinović, "Hrvatska kao suverena država i novi smisao republičke državnosti," *Pogledi*, Vol. 2, No. 7, 1971, pp. 5-7.

69.   Jozo Ivičević in *Hrvatski tjednik*, April 23, 1971.

70.   Djodan, "Bit hrvatske državnosti," (I), p. 25.

71.   Ibid.

72.   Ibid. and Djodan, *Hrvatski tjednik*, October 15, 1971. For more on this subject see Perić, *Ideje*, p. 111.

Notes to Chapter VII   249

73. *Hrvatski tjednik,* September 19, 1971; HGG, No. 10, September 29, 1971.

74. See Mirjana Gross, *Hrvatsko sveučilište,* April 1, 1971; *Hrvatski tjednik,* September 10, 1971; Djodan, "Bit hrvatske državnosti," (II), p. 24; *Studentski list* November 23, 1971.

75. Vladimir Veselica, "Hrvatska država," HGG, No. 10, September 29, 1971, p. 7. On the sovereignty debate see also a series of articles entitled "Hrvatski ustav" in *Hrvatski tjednik,* September 10, 1971-December 3, 1971.

76. Djodan, "Bit hrvatske državnosti," (II), p. 27.

77. Amendment IV, point 5.

78. Djodan, "Bit hrvatske državnosti," (II), p. 28.

79. Moša Pijade as cited in Ante Ciliga, "Tito Failed to Solve the National Question in Yugoslavia," in Antun F. Bonifačić and Clement S. Mihanovich, eds., *The Croatian Nation* (Chicago: Croatia, 1955), pp. 262-263.

80. *Studentski list* November 23, 1971; *Izvještaj,* p. 204; *Politika* (Belgrade), November 18, 1971; *Borba,* November 23, 1971; *Hrvatski tjednik,* May 28, 1971.

81. *Izvještaj,* p. 40.

82. *Zapisnik,* p. 119.

83. *Hrvatski tjednik,* September 24, 1971.

84. *Ustav SR Hrvatske* (Zagreb: Narodne novine, 1972), p. 170.

85. *Studentski list* (Izvanredno izdanje), November 26, 1971; *Hrvatski tjednik,* December 3, 1971.

86. For example Ukrainian, Macedonian and Kosovo Clubs.

87. As cited in *Hrvatski tjednik,* November 26, 1971.

88. Ibid.

89. Telegram to Tito as reprinted in *Hrvatski tjednik,* December 3, 1971.

90. Josip Mičija, Secretary of the Students' Association of Croatia, as cited in *Studentski list,* November 26, 1971.

91. Srećko Bijelić in *Zapisnik,* p. 106. See also Dragutin Haramija in ibid., pp. 71-75.

92. Ibid., p. 173.

93. Ibid., p. 7. The next day, however, Tito acknowledged that Croatian economic complaints were justified. See Tito's opening remarks at

the 21st Session in VUS, December 8, 1971 and *Socialist Thought and Practice* No. 45, October-December 1971, p. 66.

94. *Studentski list,* November 26, 1971.

95. Ibid.

96. *Hrvatski tjednik,* December 3, 1971.

97. See Tripalo's speech in Vela Luka on November 29, 1971 as cited in *Izvještaj,* p. 118.

98. Dapčević-Kučar's speech on Zagreb TV November 28, 1971. Excerpts found in *Hrvatsko sveučilište,* December 8, 1971 and VUS, December 8, 1971.

99. VUS, December 8, 1971.

100. *Studentski list,* November 26, 1971.

101. The strike ended on December 3, 1971.

102. *Zapisnik,* p. 18.

103. The leading military personnel had a meeting concerning the situation in Croatia with Tito in May 1971. *Izvještaj,* p. 75. Tito's speech at that meeting was given to the army officers in Croatia for consideration but not to the Party organizations. This indicates a growing gap between the military establishment and the Croatian Party leadership. Another such meeting took place in November 1971. See *New York Times,* May 25, 1972 and *Times* (London), December 17, 1971.

104. Bilić, *Revolucija,* p. 223; *Zapisnik,* p. 16 and 130.

105. Bilić, *Revolucija,* p. 223.

106. *Zapisnik,* p. 208.

107. VUS, December 22, 1971; Tripalo's letter of resignation in Ivo Omrčanin, *Zagreb Croatian Spring* (Philadelphia: Dorrance, 1976), pp. 105-106.

108. *Zapisnik,* pp. 71-75, 60-61, 173-178.

109. For example, see Rusinow, *Yugoslav Experiment,* p. 308.

110. Tito in "Concluding Remarks" at the 21st Session of the Presidium of the LCY, *Socialist Thought and Practice* No. 45, October-December 1971, p. 75.

111. Tito's speech of December 18, as cited by Milorad M. Drachkovitch, "Yugoslavia" in *Yearbook on International Communist Affairs* (Stanford: Hoover Institution, 1972), p. 105.

112. See Tito's interview in *Vijesnik* October 8, 1972. Reprinted also in *Dokumenti SKJ—Nova inicijativa u SKJ* (Belgrade: Komunist, 1972), pp. 14-39. See especially p. 19.

113. Tito's "Concluding Remarks," p. 77.

114. *Socialist Thought and Practice* No. 45, October-December 1971, p. 68; *Izvještaj*, p. 112.

115. Leading Progressives in Croatia were expelled from the Party in May 1972.

116. An interview with Marko Veselica, an intellectual and a leading figure in the movement (1980). Reprinted in Katich, *So Speak,* p. 80.

117. Ibid.

118. *Izvještaj*, p. 127.

119. Most of the jail sentences were from two to seven years.

120. Marko Veselica, Katich, *So Speak,* p. 80. Rusinow, who is known to be sympathetic to the Belgrade regime, also admits that "the number involved have already (June 1972) been larger than in any other settling of accounts experienced by Yugoslav communism since it came to power . . . ." *Crisis in Croatia,* (I), p. 2.

121. See Tudjman's Open Letter to Cvijetin Mijatović and others. Published in *Hrvatski list* (Washington D.C.) No. 6, 1981, p. 13. A number of older Left intellectuals like Petar Šegedin, Grgo Gamulin, Ivan Supek, for example, were silenced but were not put on trial.

122. As cited in Paul Lendvai, "Yugoslavia in Crisis," *Encounter* Vol. 39, No. 2, 1972, p. 68.

123. Text of the letter published in *Hrvatski list* No. 6, 1981, pp. 9-10. It seems that for such reasons a leading American observer of the events in Croatia at the time was "glad that the whistle was blown" on the Croatian national movement. See Rusinow, *Crisis in Croatia,* (I), p. 19.

124. Gotovac, "Open Letter," p. 9.

125. Marko Veselica, Katich, *So Speak,* p. 79.

Notes to Conclusion

1. For example, Bakarić declared: "Our, Croatian nationalism, is growing first of all on the material (economic) basis." in Bakarić, *Aktuelni problemi,* p. 242.

2. The late Franjo Mikulić, a Party official and an active participant in the movement, in an interview published in *Republika Hrvatska,* No. 140, April 1983, p. 53.

3. See Vlado Gotovac, "Planetarna zagonetka," *Kritika*, Vol. 4, No. 16, 1971, pp. 21-23.

4. See for example, Franjo Tudjman, *O povijesti rješavanja hrvatskog pitanja i samoodredjenje naroda u svijetu* (Toronto: Croatian Professional and Businessmen Society, 1987).

5. Franjo Tudjman in "An Open Letter."

6. It seems that the West even encouraged such beliefs. For example, President Richard Nixon during his visit to Yugoslavia went to Zagreb, capital of Croatia, where on October 1, 1970 he declared that the "spirit of Croatia was never crushed and it was never conquered." This was the time when the movement was getting into a high gear and most probably many Croatians interpreted such praises as a sign of support in their struggle for freedom.

Disappointments that no one in the West "lifted a finger" on behalf of Croatians who were persecuted in the post-Karadjordjevo period were clearly expressed by the former student Pro-rector Ivan Zvonimir Čičak. In an interview with a Swedish newsman in 1977, he said: ". . . I became infuriated because I remember how incorrect, dishonest and treacherous the West was towards us. Although we share the same ideals—democratic socialism, the right to work and the right to freedom—the West nonetheless declared us to be fascists and terrorists. These are absurdities which no one here can comprehend." Katich, *So Speak*, p. 42.

7. See Vlado Gotovac, "An Open Letter."

8. According to Hugh Seton-Watson, the purges were not "directed so much at nationalism as at liberalism." *The Imperialist Revolutionaries* (Stanford, Calif.: Hoover Institution Press, 1978), p. 118. However, not a single high ranking Party "liberal" ended up in jail in 1972; only the students, intellectuals and other "nationalists" were persecuted. To be labeled as a "nationalist" is the main offense in Yugoslavia, while "liberalism" has been tolerated and used by the regime as a proof that Yugoslavia is an open society.

9. Nora Beloff, *Tito's Flawed Legacy* (London: Victor Gollancz, 1985), p. 206.

10. Vlado Gotovac, "Trenutak pojedinca," *Hrvatski tjednik*, No. 33, 1971.

Notes to Postscript

1. Diplomatic Correspondent of *The Times* as in Paul Lendvai, "Yugoslavia in Crisis," p. 68.

2.   See *Jedanaesti kongres SKJ. Dokumenti* (Beograd: Komunist, 1978), p. 62.

3.   Edvard Kardelj, "For a Dynamic and Continual Socialism" *Socialist Thought and Practice* Vol. 18, No. 7-8, 1978, p. 14.

4.   *Danas,* November 8, 1988.

5.   See *Memorandum* of the Serbian Academy of Sciences and Art circulated in and outside the country at the end of 1986.

6.   Cited in *Danas,* November 29, 1988.

7.   Ibid., December 12, 1988.

8.   Ibid.

9.   *Dnevnik* (Ljubljana), August 8, 1987 as in *Novu Hrvatska,* No. 16, 1987.

BIBLIOGRAPHY

Primary Sources

Official Documents

Savez komunista Hrvatske. *Deseta sjednica Centralnog komiteta Saveza komunista Hrvatske.* Zagreb: Vjesnik, 1970.

————. *Izvještaj o stanju u Savezu komunista Hrvatske u odnosu na prodor nacionalizma u njegove redove.* Zagreb: SK Hrvatske–CK, 1972.

————. *Reforma Saveza Komunista Hrvatske.* Zagreb: Centar za aktuelni politički studij, 1970.

————. *Sedmi plenum CK SK Hrvatske.* Zagreb: Informativna služba CK SKH, 1967.

Savez komunista Jugoslavije. *Četvrti plenum CK SK Jugoslavije.* Belgrade: Komunist, 1966.

————. "Conclusions of the Seventeenth Meeting of the Presidium of the League of Communists of Yugoslavia." *Yugoslav Survey,* Vol. 12, No. 3, 1971, pp. 15-18.

————. *Deveti kongres SK Jugoslavije.* Zagreb: Narodne novine, 1969.

————. *Dokumenti SKJ–Nova inicijativa u SKJ.* Belgrade: Komunist, 1972.

————. "Fourth Plenum of the Central Committee of the League of Communists of Yugoslavia." *Socialist Thought and Practice,* No. 23, 1966, pp. 103-141. Also in *Croatia Press,* Vol. 20, No. 4-6, 1966, pp. 3-23.

————. *Jedanaesti kongres SKJ, Dokumenti.* Belgrade: Komunist, 1978.

————. *Osmi kongres SK Jugoslavije.* Belgrade: Komunist, 1964.

————. *Peta sednica CK SK Jugoslavije.* Belgrade: Komunist, 1966.

————. "Peta sednica Centralnog komiteta Saveza komunista Jugoslavije." *Jugoslovenski pregled,* Vol. 10, No. 10, 1966, pp. 67-68.

————. *Peti kongres KPJ—Izveštaji i referati.* Belgrade: Kultura, 1948.

————. *Sedmi kongres SK Jugoslavije: Stenografske beleške.* Belgrade: Kultura, 1958.

————. "Third Plenary Session of the Central Committee of the League of Communists of Yugoslavia." *Socialist Thought and Practice,* No. 21, 1966, pp. 85-137.

————. "Twenty-first Session of the Presidency of the League of Communists of Yugoslavia." *Socialist Thought and Practice,* No. 45, 1971, pp. 63-84.

Newspapers and Magazines

Borba
Danas
Hrvatski književni list
Hrvatsko sveučilište
Hrvatski tjednik
Komunist
Mladost
Nedeljne informativne novine
Politika
Školske novine
Studentski list
Telegram
Tlo
Vjesnik
Vjesnik u srijedu

Books

Babić, Stjepan. "Htjenja i ostvarenja Novosadskog dogovora." In *Hrvatski književni jezik i pitanje varijanata.* Zagreb: Matica hrvatska, 1969, reprinted from *Jezik,* Vol. 15, No. 1, 1967-68, pp. 3-13.

Bakarić, Vladimir. *Aktuelni problemi sadašnje etape revolucije.* Zagreb: Stvarnost, 1967.

————. *Socijalistički samoupravni sistem i društvena reprodukcija.* Zagreb: Informator, 1974.

Baučić, Ivo. *The Effects of Emigration from Yugoslavia and the Problem of Returning Emigrant Workers.* The Hague: Martinus Nijhoff, 1972.

Bićanić, Rudolf. *Economic Policy in Socialist Yugoslavia.* Cambridge: Cambridge University Press, 1973.

————. *Ekonomska podloga hrvatskog pitanja.* Zagreb: V. Maček, 1938.

————. "Ekonomske promjene u Hrvatskoj izazvane stvaranjem Jugoslavije 1918." In Vinski, Ivo, ed. *Prilozi za ekonomsku povijest Hrvatske.* Zagreb: Institut za historiju radničkog pokreta, 1967.

Bilić, Jure. *Revolucija koja teče.* Zagreb: Narodno sveučilište, 1975.

Bolčić, Silvano. *O socijalnoj strukturi Jugoslavije.* Belgrade: Centar za društveno-političko obrazovanje, 1967.

Broz, Josip Tito. "Jedinstvo federacije pretpostavlja stvaranje jednog autorativnog tela," in *Aktuelni problemi daljeg razvoja našeg političkog sistema.* Belgrade: Komunist, 1970, pp. 5-12.

Brozović, Dalibor. "Hrvatski jezik, njegovo mjesto unutar južnoslavenskih i drugih slavenskih jezika, njegove povijesne mijene kao jezik hrvatske književnosti." In *Hrvatska Književnost u evropskom kontekstu.* Edited by Aleksandar Flaker and Krunoslav Pranjić. Zagreb: Liber, 1978.

————. *Rječnik jezika ili jezik rječnika.* Zagreb: Matica hrvatska, 1969.

Bušić, Bruno. *Jedino Hrvatska.* (Sabrani spisi.) Toronto: ZIRAL, 1983.

Čolak, Nikola. *Iza bodjikave žice.* Padova: La Ciclografica, 1977.

Djodan, Šime. *Ekonomska politika Jugoslavije.* Zagreb: Školska knjiga, 1970.

————. "Evolucija gospodarskog sustava SFRJ i ekonomski položaj Hrvatske." In *Hrvatski znanstveni zbornik.* Vol. 2. Zagreb: Matica hrvatska, 1971, pp. 165-241. English translation in *Journal of Croatian Studies,* Vol. 13, 1972, pp. 3-102.

Dujšin, Uroš. "Nove ekonomske funkcije federacije i republika kao oligocentrični mehanizam ekonomske politike," in *Ustavna reforma.* Zagreb: Centar za aktuelni politički studij, 1971, pp. 19-31.

Filipović, Muhamed. "Lenjinovo shvaćanje nacionalnog pitanja." In *Social-i nacionalno pitanje.* Zagreb: Centar za aktuelni politički studij, 1970.

Goati, Vladimir. *Perspektive političke avangarde.* Belgrade: Komunist, 1972.

Hanžeković, Marijan. "The economic system since 1965." A postscript in Rudolf Bićanić. *Economic Policy in Socialist Yugoslavia.* Cambridge: Cambridge University Press, 1973.

Hećimović, Joseph. *In Tito's Death Marches and Extermination Camps.* New York: Carlton, 1962.

Hrvatski književni jezik i pitanje varijanata. Zagreb: Matica hrvatska, 1969.

Hrvatski pravopis. Zagreb: Školska knjiga, 1971. Reprinted in London: Nova Hrvatska, 1972.

Ivičević, Jozo. "Odrednice unitarističkog nacionalnog programa I i II kongresa KPJ." In *Hrvatski znanstveni zbornik.* Zagreb: Matica hrvatska, 1971. Vol. 1, pp. 135-179.

Jareb, Jerome and Omrčanin, Ivo., eds. *The End of the Croatian Army at Bleiburg, Austria in May 1945 According to English Military Documents.* Reprinted from *Journal of Croatian Studies.* Vol. 28-29, 1977-78, pp. 115-182.

Jonke, Ljudevit. *Hrvatski književni jezik danas.* Zagreb: Školska knjiga, 1971.

―――. *Hrvatski književni jezik 19. i 20. stoljeća.* Zagreb: Matica hrvatska, 1971.

Kardelj, Edvard. *Razvoj slovenačkog nactionalnog pitanja.* Belgrade: Kultura, 1960.

Katich, Boris., ed. *So Speak Croatian Dissidents.* Norval (Toronto): ZIRAL, 1983.

Katičić, Radoslav. "Opseg povijesti hrvatskog jezika." In *Hrvatski znanstveni zbornik.* Zagreb: Matica hrvatska, 1971. Vol. 1, pp. 27-41.

Klinar, Peter. "Izvori pojavnih oblika nacionalizma u Jugoslaviji." In *Federalizam i nacionalno pitanje.* (Zbornik radova.) Belgrade: Savez udruženja za političke nauke Jogoslavije, 1971.

Krleža, Miroslav. *Eseji.* Zagreb: Zora, 1967.

Kulundžić, Zvonimir. *Tragedija hrvatske historiografije.* Zagreb: by the author, 1970.

Maček, Vladko. *In Struggle for Freedom.* University Park: Pennsylvania State University Press, 1957.

Majstorović, Zlatko., ed. *Za reformu Hrvatskog sveučilišta.* Zagreb: Savez studenata Hrvatske, 1971.

Memorandum Sprske Akademije Nauka i Umetnosti. (Nacrt). Belgrade: Autumn, 1986.

Milatović, Mile. *Slučaj Andrije Hebrang.* Belgrade: Kultura, 1952.

Mjesto i položaj hrvatske književnosti—Rasprava. Rijeka: Biblioteka "Dometi," 1971.

Ostojić, Stevo. *Javni dnevnik.* Zagreb: Globus, 1980.

Perić, Ivan. *Ideje 'Masovnog pokreta' u Hrvatskoj.* Zagreb: Narodno sveučilište, 1974.

————. *Suvremeni hrvatski nacionalizam.* Zagreb: August Cesarec, 1976.

Perović, Latinka. *Savez komunista u novim uslovima.* Belgrade: Sedma sila, 1967.

Petranović, Branko and Zečević, Momčilo. *Jugoslavija 1918-1984—Zbirka dokumenta.* Belgrade: Rad, 1985.

Popović, Milentije. *Od etatizma ka samoupravljanju.* Belgrade: Institut za političke studije FPN, 1970.

Prcela, John and Guldescu, Stanko., eds. *Operation Slaughterhouse.* Philadelphia: Dorrance, 1970.

Preporod hrvatskih sveučilištaraca. (Special Edition of *Kritika.*) Zagreb: Matica hrvatska, 1971.

Radić, Stjepan. *Politički spisi.* Zagreb: Znanje, 1971.

Šatović, Franjo., ed. *Suvremeni društveno-ekonomski problemi razvoja sela.* Zagreb: Savez poljoprivrednih inžinjera i tehničara SR Hrvatske, 1967.

Šegedin, Petar. *Svi smo odgovorni.* Zagreb: Matica hrvatska, 1971.

Šošić, Hrvoje. *Za čiste račune.* Zagreb: Matica hrvatska, 1970.

Starčević, Ante (compiled by Blaž Jurišić). *Misli i pogledi.* Zagreb: Matica hrvatska, 1971.

Supek, Ivan. *Crown Witness Against Hebrang.* Chicago: Markanton Press, 1983.

————. *Heretic on the Left.* An unpublished manuscript. Expanded version of his book *Krivovjernik na ljevici.* Bristol: B.C. Review, 1980.

Šuvar, Stipe. *Nacionalno i nacionalističko.* Split: Marksistički Centar, 1974.

————. *Sociološki presjek jugoslavenskog društva.* Zagreb: Školska knjiga, 1970.

Težak, Stjepko and Babić, Stjepan. *Pregled gramatike hrvatskog književnog jezika.* Zagreb: Školska knjiga, 1973.

Tripalo, Miko. *Bez kompromisa u ostvarenju samoupravnog socijalizma.* Zagreb: Naprijed, 1969.

———. "Medjunacionalni odnosi u Jugoslaviji i promjene u političkom sistemu." In *Ustavna reforma* Zagreb: Centar za aktuelni politički studij, 1971, pp. 11-17.

———. *S poprišta.* Zagreb: Centar za aktuelni politički studij, 1971.

Tudjman, Franjo. *Nationalism in Contemporary Europe.* Boulder: East European Monographs, 1981.

——— -. *O povijesti rješavanja hrvatskog pitanja i samoodredjenje naroda u svijetu.* Toronto: Croatian Professional and Businessmen Society, 1987.

———. *Velike ideje i mali narodi.* Zagreb: Matica hrvatska, 1969.

Veselica, Marko. *The Croatian National Question–Yugoslavia's Achilles' Heel.* London: United Publishers, n.d.

Vlahović, Veljko. "Značaj afirmacije antidogmatskih gledišta i prakse Saveza komunista Jugoslavije." In *Naš put.* Belgrade: Komunist, 1969

Vlajčić, Gordana. "KPJ i nacionalno pitanje 1919-1941." In *Socijalizam i nacionalno pitanje.* Zagreb: Centar za aktuelni politički studij, 1970.

Vukmanović, Svetozar Tempo. *Revolucija koja teče.* Vol. 2. Belgrade: Komunist, 1971.

Zapisnik sjednice iz Karadjordjeva. Chicago: Hrvatska tiskara, 1975.

Articles

Avšić, Jaka. "Nekaj pripomb k mnenjem o rabi jezikov v JLA." *Sodobnost.* No. 4, 1970, pp. 408-427.

Babić, Stjepan. "Za ravnopravnost, ali čega?" *Jezik.* Vol. 16, No. 5, 1968/ 69, pp. 134-147.

Baučić, Ivo. "SR Hrvatska u vanjskim migracijama radne snage." *Encyclopaedia moderna.* Vol. 5, No. 14, 1970, pp. 60-67.

Bićanić, Rudolf. "Economics of Socialism in a Developed Country." *Foreign Affairs.* Vol. 44, No. 4, July 1966, pp. 633-650.

Bošković, Ivan. "Postoji li 'Dubrovačka' književnost?" *Kritika.* Vol. 2, No. 8, 1969, pp. 550-582.

Brozović, Dalibor. "O sadanjem času na kružnici jezičnog sata." *Kritika.* Vol. 4, No. 17, 1971, pp. 190-210.

Č. Z. "'Praxisov' bijeg od sadašnjosti." *Dometi.* Vol. 1, Nos. 2-3, 1968, pp. 82-84.

Črnja, Zvane. "Izmedju regije i nacije." *Dometi.* Vol. 4, Nos. 1-2, 1971, pp. 122-23.

Derossi, Julije. "Hrvatska jezična stvarnost." *Susreti.* Zbornik radova sa IX i X susreta hrvatskih studenata u inozemstvu. Vol. 5, No. 5, 1979, pp. 111-115.

————. "Hrvatski književni jezik u hrvatskim školama." *Kritika.* Vol. 4, No. 16, 1971, pp. 46-64.

Derossi, Zlata. "Položaj hrvatske književnosti u gimnazijama SR Hrvatske." *Kritika.* Vol. 3, No. 15, 1970, pp. 887-893.

Derossi-Bjelajac, Ema. "Karakteristika i dimenzije idejno-političkih devijacija u Savezu komunista Hrvatske." *Naše teme.* Vol. 16, No. 1, 1972, pp. 1-20.

Dizdar, Mak. "Marginalije o jeziku i oko njega." *život,* Vol. 19, Nos. 11-12, 1970, pp. 109-120.

Djilas, Milovan. "Yugoslavia and the Expansionism of the Soviet State." *Foreign Affairs.* Vol. 58, No. 4, Spring 1980, pp. 852-866.

Djodan, Šime. "Aktuelni gospodarski položaj Zagreba." *Kritika.* Vol. 3, No. 13, 1970, pp. 485-500.

————. "Bit hrvatske državnosti po ustavnim promjenama." (I) HGG No. 12, 1971, pp. 23-29; (II) Ibid., No. 13, 1971, pp. 23-30.

————. "Funkcionalizam u službi dominacije." *Kolo.* Vol. 9, Nos. 1-2, 1971, pp. 119-127.

————. "Gdje dr. Stipe Šuvar 'pronalazi' nacionalizam, a gdje ga ne vidi." *Kolo.* Vol. 7, No. 7, 1969, pp. 686-713.

————. "Gospodarska reforma i izbor optimalnog modela rasta." *Kolo.* Vol. 6, No. 4, 1968, pp. 301-308.

————. "Gospodarski položaj Hrvatske." *Kritika.* Vol. 4, No. 17, 1971, pp. 348-352.

————. "Hrvatsko gospodarstvo kao osnova kulturnog života hrvatskog naroda." *Dubrovnik.* Vol. 14, No. 2, 1971, pp. 54-61.

————. "Investicije zapadno od Drine." *Kolo.* Vol. 7, No. 7, 1969, pp. 714-717.

————. "Jugoslavensko tržište samoupravnost poduzeća i suverenitet republika." *Kritika.* Vol. 4, No. 18, 1971, pp. 477-486.

————. "Osvrt na savjetovanje o stanovništvu, emigraciji i zaposlenosti." *Kritika.* Vol. 4, No. 17, 1971, pp. 292-300.

————. "Pred kritičnom barijerom." *Dometi.* Vol. 2, No. 3, 1969, pp. 4-13.

————. "Prilog razmatranju predloženih izmjena ustava SFRJ." *Kolo.*
Vol. 6, No. 11, 1968, pp. 471-473.

————. "Različite interpretacije pojma privredne i društvene reforme."
Mogućnosti. Vol. 15, No. 11, 1968, pp. 1343-1355.

————. "Ustavni amandmani i problem jedinstvenog tržišta." *Kolo.* Vol.
9, No. 4, 1971, pp. 385-404.

Djunđža, Stjepan. "Socijalno-psihološki osvrt na hrvatskog radnika tjekom
privremene emigracije u zapadnoj Evropi." *Susreti.* (Zbornik radova sa
susreta hrvatskih studenata u inozemstvu.) Vol. 4, No. 4, 1978, pp.
67-87

Dugeč, Božo. "Hrvatsko Proljeće.' *Republika Hrvatska.* Vol. 35, No. 150,
1985, pp. 1 12.

Finka, Božidar. "Rječnik Matica ili glas usnulih i probuđjenih savjesti."
Kolo. Vol. 8, No. 2, 1970, pp. 221-230.

"Fizionomija jednog štrajka." (Okrugli stol) *Pogledi.* (Split), Vol. 2, No.
3, 1970, pp. 17-61.

Gelo, Jakov. "Tradicija ili nešto drugo." HGG No. 5, July 19, 1971, pp.
31-33.

Gotovac, Vlado. "Autsajderski fragmenti." (I) *Kritika.* Vol. 2, No 4, 1969,
pp. 69-84; (II) Ibid., Vol. 2, No. 5, 1969, pp. 182-189; (III) Ibid., Vol.
2, No. 8, 1969, pp. 534-559.

————. "Planetarna zagonetka." *Kritika.* Vol. 4, No. 16, 1971, pp. 21-23.

Gumzej, Jakov. "Hrvatski zakonodavni sustav-zalog samoupravnog karaktera državnosti." HGG No. 6, August 2, 1971, pp. 6-7.

Haramija, Dragutin. "Rijeka u usponu." (An interview,) *Dometi.* Vol. 2,
No. 2, 1969, pp. 1-14.

Horvat, Branko. "Yugoslav Economic Policy in the Post-War Period. Problems, Ideas, Institutional Developments." *The American Economic Review.* Vol. 61, No. 3, June 1971, pp. 71-169.

Ivičević, Jozo. "Evandjelje po Viktoru Novaku." *Kolo.* Vol. 6, Nos. 8-9,
1968, pp. 227-265.

"Izjava Upravnog odbora Matice hrvatske o pripremama za popis stanovništva." *Kritika.* Vol. 4, No. 16, 1971, pp. 174-175.

Jasić, Zoran. "'Vaskrsenje' izvanbudžetske bilance." HGG, No. 14, November 24, 1971, p. 29.

Kardelj, Edvard. "For a Dynamic and Continual Socialism." *Socialist
Thought and Practice.* Vol. 18, No. 7-8, 1978, pp. 13-22.

Komarica, Zvonimir. "O nacionalnoj neopredjeljenosti." *Kritika.* Vol. 3, No. 13, 1970, pp. 548-550.

Košćak, Vladimir. "Što je nacija." *Kritika.* Vol. 3, No. 15, 1970, pp. 872-879.

Krivokapić, Boro. "Pitao sam Krležu." (13 Conversations with Krleža, 1973-1981), *Reporter.* No. 5, October 1982, pp. 3-66.

Krleža, Miroslav. "Uvodna riječ na znanstvenom savjetovanju u Zagrebu o 130-godišnjici Hrvatskog narodnog preporoda." *Forum.* Vol. 10, Nos. 3-4, 1966, pp. 281-289.

Kunštek, Edo. "Interpolacija obračuna." *Republika Hrvatska.* Vol. 34, No. 146, 1984, pp. 37-61.

Lalić, Dragan. "Neki gospodarski razlozi suvereniteta republika." HGG No. 10, September 29, 1971, pp. 8-11.

Lalović, Dragan. "O 'pokretu hrvatskih sveučilištarca'." *Ideje.* Vol. 3, No. 1, 9172, pp. 75-98.

Lipovčan, Srećko. "U sjeni ocvale političke arheologije ili šta se krije ispod 'Jugoslavenstva' Viktora Novaka." *Kritika.* Vol. 1, No. 3, 1968, pp. 296-319.

Loknar, Vladimir. "Medicina i neki pojmovi iz dodirnih zananosti u 'Riječniku hrvatskosrpskog književnog jezika'." *Kritika.* Vol. 4, No. 17, 1971, pp. 332-342.

Macan, Trpimir. "Kome smeta hrvatsko ime u povijesti Dalmacije?" *Kritika.* Vol. 1, No. 1, 1968, pp. 100-105.

Madjor, Mirko. "Preobrazba Hrvatske—zadatak mladih." HGG, No. 4, July 5, 1971, pp. 21-24.

"Masovni pokret. Rasprava na temu 'masovni pokret'." *Vidik.* Vol. 19, No. 4-5, 1972, pp. 5-47.

"Matica hrvatska odriče se Novosadskog Dogovora." (Izjava) *Kritika.* Vol. 4, No. 17, 1971, p. 381.

Matković, Marijan. "Polonijada Miloša Žanka." *Forum.* Vol. 18, No. 12, 1969, pp. 1043-1050.

Mikulić, Franjo. "U Domovini i u emigraciji." (An interview.) *Republika Hrvatska.* No. 140. 1983, pp. 47-73.

Mirić, Jovan. "Neke ideje protagonista 'masovnog pokreta' o državi." *Naše teme.* Vol. 16, No. 10, 1972, pp. 1537-1561.

Mužić, Ivan. "Ideje Zapada i Istoka u Hrvata." *Kolo.* Vol. 8, No. 9, 1970, pp. 1061-1067.

"Neka obilježja suvremenih migracija." *Kritika.* Vol. 3, No. 13, 1970, pp. 558-561.

Pederin, Ivan. "Srpski krug kredom doktora Milorada Pavića." *Dubrovnik.* Vol. 14, No. 3, 1971, pp. 58-66.

Pejović, Danilo. "Jedno objašnjenje o 'ljevičarstvu' i 'desničarstvu'" *Kolo.* Vol. 6, No. 6, 1968, pp. 531-534.

————. "Nacionalizam i internacionalizam." *Republika.* Vol. 25, No. 8, 1969, pp. 386-392.

Perić, Ivan. "Ideje 'masovnog pokreta' o odnosima u Savezu komunista i njegovoj komunikaciji s okolinom." *Naše teme.* Vol. 16, No. 6, 1972, pp. 785-807.

Petrinović, Ivo. "Hrvatska kao suverena država i novi smisao republičke državnosti." *Pogledi.* Vol. 2, No. 7, 1971, pp. 5-9.

"Prosvijed Upravnog odbora DKH protiv načina predstojećeg popisa pučanstva." *Kritika.* Vol. 4, No. 16, 1971, pp. 173-74.

Radić, Stephen. "The Story of My Political Life." *Current History.* Vol. 29, October 1928-March 1929, pp. 84-106.

Raknić, Franjo. "Privredni razvitak, privredne mjere i zaposlenost." *Ekonomski pregled.* Vol. 22, Nos. 7-8, 1971, pp. 444-462.

Rendić, Smiljana. "Izlaz iz genitiva ili Drugi hrvatski preporod." *Kritika.* Vol. 4, No. 18, 1971, pp. 417-428.

"Saopćenje Uprave udruženja književnika Crne Gore o jeziku." *Kritika.* Vol. 4, No. 17, 1971, p. 378.

Šegedin, Petar. "Govor na Godišnjoj skupštini Društva književnika Hrvatske." *Kritika.* Vol. 3, No. 12, 1970, pp. 404-405.

————. "Sudbina." *Forum.* Vol. 21, Nos. 1-2, 1971, pp. 26-43.

Šehović, Šerif. "Raskrinkano častohleplje ili zašto je Žanko doživio slom?" *Kritika.* Vol. 3, No. 12, pp. 392-397.

Šimundić, Mate. "Suvremeni hrvatski jezik." (I) HGG No. 5, July 19, 1971, p. 50; (II) Ibid., No. 6, August 2, 1971, p. 66; (III) Ibid., No. 7, August 16, 1971, p. 50; (IV) Ibid., No. 8, August 30, 1971, p. 50; (V) Ibid., No. 9, September 15, 1971, pp. 49-50; (VI) Ibid., No. 10, September 29, 1971, pp. 49-50.

Smailagić, Nerkez. "Hrvatski Ustav—pitanje društveno-političkog obredjenja naše suvremenosti." (I) HGG No. 11, October 13, 1971, pp. 8-12; (II) Ibid., No. 12, October 27, 1971, pp. 7-9; (III) Ibid., No. 13, November 10, 1971, pp. 8-9.

————. "Socijalistička revolucija i nacionalno pitanje." (I) *Dubrovnik.* Vol. 13, No. 3, 1970, pp. 67-92; (II) Ibid., Vol. 13, No. 4, 1970, pp. 112-130.

Šolc, Aleksandar and Božičević, Juraj. "Obrada stručnih naziva u rječniku Hrvatskosrpskog književnog jezika." *Kritika.* Vol. 2, No. 5, 1969, pp. 208-221.

Šošić, Hrvoje. "Besprimjerne obmane ili Hrvoje Šošić u 'Genexu'." *Kritika.* Vol. 4, No. 18, 1971, pp. 439-452.

————. "Hrvatsko gospodarsko čudo–iz razvojnih mogućnosti Hrvatske." *Kolo.* Vol. 9, Nos. 5-6, 1971, pp. 540-552.

Staničić, Mladen. "Prava istina o raspodjeli obale." HGG, No. 2, June 7, 1971, pp. 26-29.

Supek, Ivan. "Rad na reformi Sveučilišta." In *Preporod Hrvatskog sveučilišta*. Zagreb: Matica hrvatska, 1971, pp. 35-39.

Šuto, Krunoslav. "Studentski pokret i aktuelni politički trenutak." HGG No. 11, October 13, 1971, pp. 16-17.

"The Dossier of the Mihajlov Case." *Review.* (Study Center for Jugoslav Affairs–London) No. 6, 1967, pp. 506-532.

Tripalo, Miko. "Hrvatska na pragu punog prosperiteta." (Interview) HGG No. 3, June 21, 1971, pp. 4-9.

Tudjman, Franjo. "Hrvatska politika u prvim godinama borbe protiv Vidovdanskog centralističko-hegemonističkog poretka." *Kritika* Vol. 3, No. 14, 1970, pp. 570-617.

————. "Prosudba povijesne odrednice što oblikuje hrvatsko nacionalno biće." *Dubrovnik.* Vol. 14, No. 2, 1971, pp. 14-21.

————. "Raspre o uzrocima sloma monarhističke Jugoslavije i o pretpostavkama razvitka narodnooslobodilačke borbe u Hrvatskoj." (Pt. I) *Kolo.* Vol. 6, No. 8-9, 1968, pp. 201-218; (Pt. II) Ibid., Vol. 6, No. 10, 1968, pp. 363-378.

————. "Slom vidovdanskog parlamentarnog centralizma i državnopolitička kriza Kraljevine SHS." *Hrvatski znanstveni zbornik.* Vol. 1, 1971, pp. 51-114.

————. "Stjepan Radić i hrvatska državnost." *Riječi* Vol. 3, No. 2, 1971, pp. 9-34. Also in *Kritika.* Vol. 4, No. 18, 1971, pp. 386-401.

————. "Uvod u historiju Socialističke Jugoslavije." *Forum.* Vol. 2, No. 2, 1963, pp. 292-352, Ibid., No. 3, pp. 530-564, Ibid., No. 4, pp. 702-741, Ibid., No. 5, pp. 840-858; Ibid., No. 6, pp. 1087-1122, Ibid., No. 7-8, pp. 199-233, Ibid., No. 1-2, 1964, pp. 139-157.

————. "Uzroci krize monarhističke Jugoslavije od ujedinjenja 1918. do sloma 1941." *Forum.* Vol. 6, No. 1-2, 1967, pp. 73-111.

————. "Zaoštravanje sukoba i pokušaj nagodbe izmedju pobornika centralizma i federalizma u Kraljevini SHS (1924-1927). *Forum.* Vol. 10, No. 6, 1971, pp. 920-955.

Vaupotić, Miroslav. "Nekolike opaske uz budući Kongres hrvatske kulture." *Dubrovnik.* Vol. 14, No. 2, 1971, pp. 69-73.

Veselica, Marko. "Hrvatska gospodarska strategija." HGG No. 1, May 24, 1971, pp. 20-22.

————. "Rastakanje hrvatskog nacionalnog bića." HGG No. 2, June 7, 1971, pp. 23-25.

Veselica, Vladimir. "Hrvatska država." HGG No. 10, September 29, 1971, pp. 4-7.

Vidan, Ivo. "Provincijalizacija–Ali zašto!?" *Kritika.* Vol. 1, No. 2, 1968, pp. 212-215.

Vlajčić, Gordana. "Kominterna i KPJ o državopravnom aspektu rješavanja jugoslavenskog nacionalnog pitanja 1919-1929." *Naše teme.* Vol. 15, No. 10, 1971, pp. 1692-1722.

Vodopija, Berislav. "Prešućena Hrvatska u izdanjima 'Tehničke knjige'." *Kritika.* Vol. 4, No. 18, 1971, pp. 536-37.

"Zaključci Hrvatske pagvaške grupe o stanovništvu, emigraciji i zaposlenosti u SR Hrvatskoj." *Encyclopaedia Moderna.* Vol. 6, No. 15, 1971, pp. 105-107.

Zelić-Bućan, Benedikta. "Neprihvatljiv i apsurdan pristup vrednovanja nacionalne povijesti." *Dubrovnik.* Vol. 14, No. 1, 1971, pp. 99-115.

Žuvela, Mladen. "Odlazak radnika iz brodogradilišta 'Split'." *Pogledi.* Vol. 2, Nos. 4-5, 1970, pp. 47-67.

Secondary Sources

Books

Auty, Phyllis. *Yugoslavia.* New York: Walker, 1965.

Banac, Ivo. "The Communist Party of Yugoslavia during the Period of Legality, 1919-1921." in Banac, Ivo, ed. *The Effects of World War I: The Class War after the Great War.* New York: Brooklyn College Studies on Society in Change, 1983, pp. 188-230.

Beljo, Ante. *Yugoslavia-Genocide.* Sudbury: Northern Tribune, 1985.

Beloff, Nora. *Tito's Flawed Legacy.* London: Victor Gollancz, 1985.

Bethel, Nicholas. *The Last Secret.* London: Andre Deutsch, 1974.

Bilandžić, Dušan. *Historija socijalističke federativne republike Jugoslavije.* Zagreb: Školska knjiga, 1978.

————. *Ideje i praksa društvenog razvoja Jugoslavije, 1945-1973.* Belgrade: Komunist, 1973.

Bombelles, Joseph T. *Economic Development of Communist Yugoslavia 1947-1964.* Stanford, Cal.: Hoover Institute, 1968.

Bonifačić, Antun and Mihanovich, Clement, eds. *The Croatian Nation.* Chicago: Croatia, 1955.

Borowiec, Andrew. *Yugoslavia After Tito.* New York: 1977.

Burks, R. V. *The Removal of Ranković: An Early Interpretation of the July Yugoslav Party Plenum.* Santa Monica, California: The Rand Corporation, RM-5132-pr, August 1966.

Carter, April. *Democratic Reform in Yugoslavia.* Princeton, New Jersey: Princeton University Press, 1982.

Čolaković, Rodoljub, et al. *Pregled istorije Saveza komunista Jugoslavije.* Belgrade: Institut za izučavanje Radničkog pokreta, 1963.

Damjanović, Pero. *Tito pred temama istorije.* Belgrade: Institut za savremnu istoriju, 1972.

Dedijer, Vladimir, et al. *History of Yugoslavia.* New York: McGrew-Hill, 1974.

Despalatovich-Murray, Elinor. *Ljudevit Gaj and the Illyrian Movement.* Boulder: East European Quarterly, 1975.

Drachkovitch, Milorad M. "Yugoslavia" in *Yearbook on International Communist Affairs.* Stanford: Hoover Institution, 1972, pp. 101-114.

Dyker, David A. "Yugoslavia: Unity out of Diversity?" In Brown, Archie and Gray, Jack, eds. *Political Culture and Political Change in Communist States.* London: Macmillan, 1977.

Fejtö, Francois. *A History of the People's Democracies—Eastern Europe Since Stalin.* New York: Praeger, 1971.

Fisher, Jack C. *Yugoslavia: A Multi-National State.* San Francisco: Chandler, 1966.

Franičević, Marin. "Razdoblje Renesansne književnosti." in *Povijest hrvatske književnosti.* Vol. 3. Zagreb: Liber-Mladost, 1974.

Gross, Mirjana. *Povijest pravaške ideologije.* Zagreb: Sveučilište u Zagrebu, Institut za hrvatsku povijest, 1973.

Haberl, Othmar Nikola. *Parteiorganisation und nationale Frage in Jugoslavien.* Berlin: Otto Harrassowitz, 1976.

Hoffman, George W. and Neal, Fred W. *Yugoslavia and the New Communism.* New York: The Twentieth Century Fund, 1962.

Holjevac, Većeslav. *Hrvati izvan domovine.* Zagreb: Matica hrvatska, 1967.

Hondius, Frits W. *The Yugoslav Community of Nations.* The Hague: Mouton, 1968.

Johnson, Ross A. *Role of Military in Communist Yugoslavia: An Historical Sketch.* Santa Monica: Rand Paper Series, P.6070, January 1978.

————. *The Transformation of Communist Ideology: The Yugoslav Case, 1945-1953.* Cambridge, Mass.: The M.I.T. Press, 1972.

————. *Yugoslavia: In the Twilight of Tito.* Beverly Hills and London: Sage Publications, 1974.

Klein, George. "Yugoslavia—The Process of Democratization." In Toma, Peter A., ed. *The Changing Face of Communism in Eastern Europe.* Tucson, Arizona: University of Arizona Press, 1970.

Kljakić, Dragan. *Dosije Hebrang.* Belgrade: Partizanska knjiga, 1983.

Lasić, Stanko. *Sukob na književnoj ljevici 1928-1952.* Zagreb: Liber, 1970.

Lendvai, Paul. *Eagles in Cobwebs.* New York: Doubleday, 1969.

Meier, Viktor. "Yugoslav Communism." In Griffith, William E., ed., *Communism in Europe.* Vol. 1. Cambridge, Mass.: The M.I.T. Press, 1964.

Mužić, Ivan. *Hrvatska politika i jugoslavenska ideja.* Split: 1969.

————. *Stjepan Radić.* Zagreb: HKD sv. Ćirila i Metoda, 1987.

Omrčanin, Ivo. *Zagreb Croatian Spring.* Philadelphia: Dorrance, 1976.

Pervan, Ralph. *Tito and the Students.* Nedlands, W. A.: University of Western Australia Press, 1978.

Prpić, George J. *The Croatian Immigrants in America.* New York: Philosophical Library, 1971.

Ramet, Pedro. *Nationalism and Federalism in Yugoslavia, 1963-1983.* Bloomington: Indiana University Press, 1984.

Rothschild, Joseph. *East Central Europe between the Two World Wars.* Seatle and London: University of Washington Press, 1974.

Rusinow, Dennison I. *Crisis in Croatia.* American University Field Staff Reports. *Southeast Europe Series.* Vol. 19, Nos. 4-7 (June-September) 1972.

————. *The Yugoslav Experiment 1948-1974.* London: C. Hurst, 1977.

————. *Yugoslavia: 1966.* American University Field Staff Report. *Southeast Europe Series.* Vol. 13, No. 6, 1966.

Seton-Watson, Hugh. *The Imperialist Revolutionaries*. Stanford: Hoover Institution Press, 1978.

Sher, Gerson S. *Praxis–Marxist Criticism and Dissent in Socialist Yugoslavia*. Bloomington: Indiana University Press, 1977.

Shoup, Paul. *Communism and the Yugoslav National Question*. New York: Columbia University Press, 1968.

——. "The National Question and the Political Systems of Eastern Europe." In Sinanian, Sylva et al., eds. *East Europe in the 1970s*. New York: Praeger, 1972.

Šidak, Jaroslav. *Studije iz hrvatske povijesti XIX stoljeća*. Zagreb: Sveučilište u Zagrebu-Institut za hrvatsku povijest, 1973.

Singleton, Fred B. "Socialist Federative Republic of Yugoslavia." In Szajkowski, Bogdan. *Marxist Governments–A World Survey*. London: Macmillan, 1981.

——. *Twentieth-Century Yugoslavia*. London: Macmillan, 1976.

Stanković, Slobodan and Antić, Zdenko. "Recentralization in Yugoslavia." in Mastny, Vojtech, ed. *Soviet/East European Survey, 1983-1984*. Durham: Duke University Press, 1985.

Taylor, A. J. P. *The Habsburg Monarchy 1809-1918*. Chicago: University of Chicago Press, 1976.

Terzuolo, Eric R. "Soviet-Yugoslav Conflict and the Origins of Yugoslavia's Self-Management System." In Vucinich, Wayne S., ed. *War and Society in East Central Europe*. New York: Columbia University Press, 1982.

Tolstoy, Nikolay. *The Minister and the Massacres*. London: Century Hutchinson, 1986.

Tomasevich, Jozo. "Immediate Effects of the Cominform Resolution on the Yugoslav Economy." In Vucinich, Wayne S., ed. *War and Society in East Central Europe*. New York: Columbia University Press, 1982.

Vujica, Stanko. *Razmatranja o sadašnjosti Hrvata*. Chicago: Croatia, 1968.

Zaninovich, George M. *The Development of Socialist Yugoslavia*. Baltimore: The Johns Hopkins Press, 1968.

Articles

"A Chronology of the Croatian Language." *Journal of Croatian Studies*. Vol. 25-26, 1984-1985, pp. 247-252.

Bertsch, Gary K. "The Revival of Nationalism." *Problems of Communism.* Vol. 22, No. 6, 1973, pp. 1-15.

Bird, Christofer. "From a Reporter's Notebook." *Problems of Communism.* Vol. 18, No. 4-5, 1969, pp. 78-88.

Bigelow, Bruce. "Centralization Versus Decentralization in Interwar Yugoslavia." *Southeastern Europe* Vol. 1, Pt. 2, 1974, pp. 157-172.

Boban, Branka. "Shvaćanje Antuna i Stjepana Radića o mjestu i ulozi seljaštva u gospodarskom, društvenom i političkom životu." *Radovi* Institut za hrvatsku povijest, Vol. 12, 1979, pp. 265-304.

Bukowski, James. "Yugoslavism and the Croatian National Party in 1867." *Canadian Review of Studies in Nationalism.* Vol. 3, No. 1, 1975, pp. 70-87.

Burg, Steven L. "Ethnic Conflict and the Federalization of Socialist Yugoslavia: The Serbo-Croatian Conflict." *Publius.* Vol. 7, No. 4, 1977, pp. 119-143.

Clissold, Stephen. "Yugoslavia and the Soviet Union." *Conflict Studies.* No. 57, April 1975, pp. 4-19.

Denić, Bogdan. "Pokretljivost i regrutiranje jugoslavenskog rukovodstva: Uloga SKJ." *Pogledi* Vol. 2, No. 7, 1971, pp. 67-81.

Frey, Cynthia W. "Yugoslav Nationalism and the Doctrine of Limited Sovereignty." *East European Quarterly.* (I) Vol. 10, No. 4, 1976, pp. 427-457; (II) Ibid., Vol. 11, No. 1, 1977, pp. 79-108.

Gaži, Stjepan. "Stjepan Radić: His Life and Political Activities." *Journal of Croatian Studies.* Vol. 14-15, 1973, pp. 13-73.

Gross, Mirjana. "Croatian National-Integrational Ideologies from the End of Illyrism to the Creation of Yugoslavia." *Austrian History Yearbook* Vol. 15-16, 1979-1980, pp. 3-33.

Karlović, N. I. "Internal Colonialism in a Marxist Society: the Case of Croatia." *Ethnic and Racial Studies.* Vol. 5, No. 3, 1982, pp. 276-299.

Klein, George. "The Role of Ethnic Politics in the Czechoslovak Crisis of 1968 and the Yugoslav Crisis of 1971." *Studies in Comparative Communism.* Vol. 8, No. 4, 1975, pp. 339-369.

————. "Workers' Self-Management and the Politics of Ethnic Nationalism in Yugoslavia." *Nationality Papers.* Vol. 5, No. 1, 1976, pp. 1-21.

Krešić, Stephen. "The Principal Characteristics of Croatian Literary Culture in the Middle Ages." *Journal of Croatian Studies.* Vol. 25-26, 1984-1985, pp. 13-87.

Larrabee, Steven. "Yugoslavia at the Crossroads." *Orbis*. Vol. 16, No. 2, 1972, pp. 377-395.

Lendvai, Paul. "National Tensions in Yugoslavia." *Conflict Studies*. No. 25, 1972, pp. 4-17.

————. "Yugoslavia in Crisis." *Encounter*. Vol. 39, No. 2, 1972, pp. 68-75.

Pospielovsky, Dimitry. "Dogmas Under Attack: A Traveler's Report." *Problems of Communism*. Vol. 17, No. 2, 1968, pp. 41-47.

Raditsa, Bogdan. "The Disunity of the Slavs." *Orbis*. Vol. 10, No. 4, 1967, pp. 1082-1090.

Rubinstein, Alvin Z. "Whither Yugoslavia." *Current History*. Vol. 64, No. 381, May 1973, pp. 202-206.

Rusinow, Dennison. "Marxism Belgrade Style." *The Antioch Review*. Vol. 27, No. 4, 1967-68, pp. 477-490.

Sacks, Stephen R. "Regional Inequality in Yugoslav Industry." *The Journal of Developing Areas*. Vol. 11, No. 1, 1976, pp. 66-75.

Schöpflin, George. "The Ideology of Croatian Nationalism." *Survey*. Vol. 19, No. 1, 1973, pp. 123-146.

Shoup, Paul, "The Evolution of a System." *Problems of Communism*. Vol. 18, No. 4-5, 1969, pp. 67-77.

Šidak, Jaroslav. "Počeci političke misli u Hrvata—J. Križanić i P. Ritter Vitezović."*Naše teme*. Vol. 16, No. 7-8, 1972, pp. 1118-1135.

————. "Prilog razvoju jugoslavenske ideje do g. 1914." *Naše teme*. Vol. 9, No. 8-9, 1965, pp. 1290-1317.

Spalatin, Christopher. "Language and Politics in Yugoslavia." *Journal of Croatian Studies*. Vol. 11-12, 1970-71, pp. 83-104.

Stokes, Gale. "Yugoslavism in the 1860's." *Southeastern Europe*. Vol. 1, Pt. 2, 1974, pp. 126-135.

Woodward, Susan Lampland. "From Revolution to Post-Revolution: How Much Do We Really Know about Yugoslav Politics?" *World Politics*. Vol. 30, No. 1, 1977, pp. 141-166.

Živančić, Milorad. "Slavenska ideja od humanizma do Ilirizma." *Zbornik Zagrebačke slavističke škole*. Vol. 1, 1973, pp. 137-146.

Newspapers and Magazines

Croatia Press
Daily Telegraph
Foreign Broadcasting Information Service (FBIS)

Hrvatski bilten
Hrvatski list
Neue Zürcher Zeitung
Nova Hrvatska
Poruka slobodne Hrvatske
Sunday Telegraph
Svijet
The New York Times
The Guardian
The Observer
The Times
Time

INDEX

Administrative socialism, 31, 33
Avšič, Jaka, 66

Bach, Alexander, 115
Bakarić, Vladimir, 44, 50, 51, 52, 53, 72, 125, 132, 180, 246
Baltić, Milutin, 38, 102
Bela I–King of Hungary, 6
Bićanić, Rudolf, 78, 80, 82
Bilić, Jure, 130, 131, 166, 185, 224
Bjelić, Srećko, 136, 183
Blažević, Jakov, 132, 165, 185
Bloch, Ernst, 145
Bogdanov, Vaso, 70
Branimir–ruler of Croatia, 5
Brezhnev, Leonid, 38, 193
Broz, Josip (Tito), 3, 22, 27, 31, 34, 36-40, 44, 52-55, 73, 76, 81, 92, 97, 98, 104, 119, 122-125, 131, 133, 162, 163, 165-167, 169, 170, 175, 177-184, 189, 193, 196, 198, 201, 204, 207, 217, 247
Budiša, Dražen, 148, 179
Bušić, Bruno, 81, 121

Catholic Church, 155-157
Chetniks, 121, 125, 168

Čičak, Ivan Zvonimir, 147, 149
Comintern, 26, 27, 28
Constitutional amendments (1971), 169-171
Ćosić, Dobrica, 55, 204
CPY and national question, 25-30
Croatian emigration and demography, 97-103
Croatian Literary Gazette (HKL), 64-72
Croatian national ideologies, 12-21
Croatian national revival, 19th century, 7, 9-12
Croatian Peasant Party, 2, 18-21, 79, 120
Cvetković-Maček Agreement, 2

Dapčević-Kučar, dr. Savka, 69, 75, 128, 134, 135, 137, 138, 159, 160, 163, 168, 178-180, 183, 246, 247
Declaration on the Croatian Language, 59-64, 224
Dizdar, Mehmedalija Mak, 113
Djilas, Milovan, 33, 123
Djodan, Šime, 81, 91, 93, 96, 99, 164, 171, 184
Djordjević, Jovan, 170

Dolenc, Stane, 206
Dragosavac, Dušan, 168, 169, 180

Economic crisis (1980s), 199-200
Economic grievances in Croatia 83-91
Economy in the inter-war period, 78-80
Eighth Congress LCY, 22, 25, 34, 35, 47, 52, 53, 70, 119

Factionalism in the LC in Croatia, 127-139, 162-169
Fifth Congress CPY 27
Fourth Plenum LCY (1966), 25, 35, 36, 37, 38, 39, 59, 72, 73
Francis Joseph, 16
Frangeš, Ivo, 70

Gaj, Ljudevit, 10, 234
Garašanin, Ilija, 2, 3, 106
Gorkić, Milan, 26, 27
Gošnjak, Ivan, 39
Gotovac, Jakov, 66
Gotovac, Vlado, 142, 185, 195
Gundulić, Ivan, 212

Haramija, Dragutin, 96, 169, 181
Hasanbeg, 212
Hebrang, Andrija, 116, 124, 125, 155, 239
Helen, Queen of Croatia, 6
Historiography, 115-125
Holjevac, Većeslav, 62, 222
Humanism in Croatia, 7-8

Illyrian Provinces, 8, 211
Illyrism, 8, 9, 10, 11, 16, 108
Intelligentsia in Croatia, 55-57, 139-144

Intra-national relations (1980s), 201-209
Ivić, Stjepan, 165
Ivičević, Jozo, 29, 143

Jelačić, Josip (ban), 116, 117, 236
Joseph II—Habsburg ruler, 11
Jovanović, Djoko, 184

Kačić-Miošić, Andrija, 213
Kangrga, Milan, 145
Karadjordjevics, 80, 104, 107
Karadjordjevo putsch, 179-182
Karadžić, Vuk, 108, 115
Kardelj, Edvard, 23, 24, 33, 44, 123, 198, 199, 201, 206
Kerestinec escape, 223
Kermauner, Taras, 205
Khuen-Hedervary, Dragutin, 115, 117
Kidrić, Boris, 33
Koloman—King of Hungary, 6
KOS, 39
Kosovo battle, 2
Kovoso conflict, 195, 201-203
Kozičić Benja, Šimun, 212
Križanić, Juraj, 213
Krleža, Miroslav, 1, 54, 55, 58, 59, 62, 70, 184, 223
Kunštek, Edo, 216

Ladislaus—King of Hungary, 6
Language issues, 107-115
Lukić, Radomir, 42

Maček, Vladko, 51
Marković, Sima, 26, 28
Martinac the priest, 212
Marulić, Marko, 212

Marxist revisionism in Croatia, 54, 223

Matica hrvatska, 57, 62, 67, 70, 71, 132, 141, 148, 151, 154, 155, 160, 162, 166, 167, 173, 175, 178, 184, 188-190

Matica iseljenika, 62, 222

Matković, Marjan, 70

Meštrović, Ivan, 2, 210

Mihajlov, Mihajlo, 60, 224

Mikulić, Branko, 207

Military Border, 212

Milošević, Slobodan, 203, 208

Mišković, Ivan, 39, 219

Mohacs battle, 6

Moskovljević, Miloš, 112

Muslim nationality, 214

Napoleon, 8, 211

Ninth Congress LCY, 72, 73

Novi Sad Agreement, 110, 111, 113, 114, 115

Orbini, Mavro, 213

Pacta conventa, 6

Pan-Slavism, 9, 12

Paradžik, Ante, 148

Party of Right, 15-18

Party purges (1972), 182-186

Pavelić, Ante, 211, 222

Pavlović, Teodor, 213

Peasantry, 151-155

Pijada, Moše, 175

Pirjevac, Dušan, 55

Planinc, Milka, 180

Popović, Milentije, 42

Praxis group, 144-146

Pribićević, Svetozar, 2

Pribojević, Vinko, 212, 213

Radić, Antun, 18

Radić, brothers, 13, 156

Radić, Stjepan, 2, 18-21, 116, 154, 190, 210, 214

Radovan, King Zvonimir's son, 211

Ranković, Aleksandar, 25, 34, 35-46, 52, 53, 59, 62, 63, 73, 82, 90, 111, 112, 187, 203, 204, 208, 218, 219

Ritter-Vitezović, Pavao, 213

Rusinow, Dennison, 4

Šarić, Jure, 164

Second Congress CPY, 29

Šegedin, Petar, 46, 70

Self-management in practice, 92-96

Šeper, Franjo Cardinal, 223

Seventh Congress LCY, 23, 24

Šibl, Ivan, 164, 181

Šižgorić, Juraj, 213

Skerlić, Jovan, 109

Smailagić, Nerkez, 43

Socialist realism, 54

Šošić, Hrvoje, 89, 90

Špiljak, Mika, 44

Stalin, Joseph, 26, 30, 31, 49

Starčević, Ante, 15, 16, 17, 18, 116, 156, 190, 213, 214

Stefanović-Karadžić, Vuk, 213

Stepinac, Alojzije Cardinal, 156, 185

Stjepan Trpimir—king of Croatia, 5, 6, 211

Strossmayer, Josip Juraj, 13, 14, 16, 17, 190

Student demonstrations (1959), 48

Student leadership elections of (1971), 147-149

Student protests (1968), 146

Student strike (1971), 176-179

Student trials in Croatia (1950s and 1960s), 47

Student role in the national movement, 146-151
Supek, Ivan, 41, 125, 139, 147, 149
Supilo, Frano, 2, 116, 210
Šuvar, Stipe, 207
Svačić, Petar—king of Croatia, 6

Tenth Plenum of the CC LCC, 68, 69, 72-76, 133, 148, 158-160, 162, 186, 188
Tomislav—king of Croatia, 5
Tripalo, Miko, 35, 60, 64, 81, 91, 95, 131, 134-139, 155, 163, 164, 178, 179, 183
Trumbić, Ante, 2, 210
Tudjman, Franjo, 62, 70, 74, 119, 121, 184, 222, 237
Twenty-first Session of Presidium LCY, 158, 181, 182

UDBA (SUP), 39, 43f, 48
Ujević, Tin, 64

Ustaše and Ustašism, 20, 49, 51, 120, 121, 122, 124, 125, 130, 162, 165, 168, 221, 222

Veselica, Marko, 234
Vienna Agreement, 234
Vrančić, Antun, 212

Workers, 151-155
Writers Association of Croatia, 58, 62, 70, 71

Yugoslav Committee, 2
Yugoslav socialism, 30-35
Yugoslavism, 1, 9, 13, 14, 15, 16, 23, 24, 33, 44, 104, 126, 143, 154, 155

Žanko, Miloš, 68, 74, 76, 128, 129, 130, 225
Živković, Petar, 50, 222
Zoranić, Petar, 212
Zvonimir—king of Croatia, 6, 211